Game, Set, Match

The University of North Carolina Press Chapel Hill

Game, Set, Match

Billie Jean King AND THE REVOLUTION IN WOMEN'S SPORTS

SUSAN WARE

This volume was published with the assistance of the Greensboro Women's Fund of the University of North Carolina Press. Founding contributors: Linda Arnold Carlisle, Sally Schindel Cone, Anne Faircloth, Bonnie McElveen Hunter, Linda Bullard Jennings, Janice J. Kerley (in honor of Margaret Supplee Smith), Nancy Rouzer May, and Betty Hughes Nichols.

Library of Congress Cataloging-in-Publication Data
Ware, Susan, 1950–
Game, set, match : Billie Jean King and the revolution in women's sports /Susan Ware.
p. cm.
Includes bibliographical references and index.
ISBN 978-0-8078-3454-1 (cloth : alk. paper)
1. King, Billie Jean. 2. Women tennis players—United States—Biography.
3. Sex discrimination in sports—United States. 4. Women athletes—United States—Social conditions. I. Title.
GV994.K56W37 2011
796.342092—dc22
[B]   2010032662

15 14 13 12 11   5 4 3 2 1

TO IMOGENE FISH, Trailblazer

Contents

Illustrations

A section of photographs begins on page 105.

Game, Set, Match

I know that when I die, nobody at my funeral will be talking about me. They'll all just be standing around telling each other where they were the night I beat Bobby Riggs.
—BILLIE JEAN KING

On the evening of September 20, 1973, an estimated 48 million Americans tuned their televisions sets to an unlikely event: a tennis match at the Houston Astrodome between a twenty-nine-year-old, five-time Wimbledon champion at the top of her game and a fifty-five-year-old former tennis great long past his prime. Many people at the time sensed that all the hoopla surrounding this $100,000, winner-take-all "Battle of the Sexes" between Billie Jean King and Bobby Riggs was about more than just a tennis match, although nobody could really say why. Was it because the country was sick of Watergate, inflation, and the energy crisis and wanted a diversion? Was the match a referendum on the new—and to many, troubling— social movement called women's liberation? Was the circus atmosphere an example of media hype gone awry? In fact, the contemporary and historical significance of the match derived from the congruence of all three—a "perfect storm," as it were, in the history of sports, entertainment, and modern feminism.[1]

In 1973 Billie Jean King was the right feminist in the right sport at the right moment in American history. What she proved that night in a courageous performance of physical prowess and nerves of steel was that women did not choke, women were not frail and weak, women could face pressure and take it—live, on national television, with no second takes. In just under two hours, she forced a reexamination of what it meant to be female and an athlete, or as a *New York Times* editorial later put it, "In a single tennis match, Billie Jean King was able to do more for the cause of women than most feminists can achieve in a lifetime." Donna Lopiano of the Women's Sports Foundation suggests comparing it to a woman winning the presidency: "That was the magnitude of the sports barrier in those days. For a woman to be accepted on an equal playing field was so far beyond one's comprehension. That's what Billie Jean represented. If it doesn't seem like such a big thing today, it's because the measuring sticks of old no longer apply, and today's have no relevance to what happened then." As soccer coach April Heinrichs said in 1999, "When we look back in 20 years, I really think we are going to say that the Billie Jean King–Bobby Riggs tennis match, Title IX and the 1999 Women's World Cup are the three largest pillars supporting women's sports in this country."[2]

Whenever Billie Jean King was asked whether the Riggs match was the biggest of her career, she always distinguished between its athletic significance (no) and its social significance (definitely yes). "I wanted to help the women's movement and it did. I wanted to make the Virginia Slims tour flourish, and it did. I wanted to help men and women understand each other better. And they did." To this day, strangers, especially women, still approach her to tell her that the match changed their lives: giving them the courage to go back to school, take up a new sport, or leave an unsatisfactory personal relationship. For all its feminist flourishes, however, King seemed most proud to have brought tennis to a far greater national audience than traditionally followed the game: "On that night, I think, the game of tennis finally got kicked out of the country clubs forever and into the world of real sports, where everybody could see it." Or as she put it after the match, "This is a culmination of a lifetime in sport. Tennis has always been reserved for the rich, the white, the males—and I've always pledged to change all that. There's still a lot to be done, but this is certainly a great high point."[3]

The debut of Open Tennis in 1968, which toppled the old "shamateur" system by allowing professional and amateur tennis players to compete for prize money in tournaments such as Wimbledon and the U.S. Open, was a major step in taking tennis into the modern era. Billie Jean King actively lobbied for this change, but then found she had a second battle to fight: winning parity for women professionals from tennis association leaders and tournament directors who believed nobody cared about women's tennis, certainly not enough to pay women prize money anywhere near equal to men. In 1970 a group of nine women led by King broke off and formed their own professional tour, which soon came to be known as Virginia Slims. Billie Jean King always claimed her activism was driven by much more than just prize money: "The money's fine, but everyone's talked about the money so much they forget what the purpose was, for me anyway. The purpose is to enable women to play and to make people pay attention." The press quickly dubbed them "women's lob."[4]

For her activism Billie Jean King earned a reputation as the "clenched fist of women's tennis," but the Battle of the Sexes wasn't just about her. She needed a foil, a coconspirator, perhaps an enabler, and Bobby Riggs was more than happy to play all those roles. As her doubles partner Rosie Casals once said, only half in jest, "Bobby Riggs did more for women's tennis than anybody."[5]

Robert Larimore Riggs had been one of the top-ranked American players in the 1930s, "a tennis natural" in Pancho Segura's opinion and a true tennis legend who swept all three Wimbledon titles (men's singles, doubles, and mixed doubles) in 1939. Showing an early affinity for gambling, he placed a bet on that unlikely trifecta with London bookies and won a tidy sum. With no opportunities left as an amateur, he turned professional, but that just meant endless exhibition matches in out-of-the-way places for not much money. After a stint in the armed services during World War II, followed by marriage and an undemanding career, he found his calling as a hustler, always ready to take on a challenge in tennis, golf, or whatever, as long as there was a wager involved. "If I can't play for big money, I play for a little money. And if I can't play for a little money, I stay in bed that day." He almost always won, even if he played carrying an umbrella, with a dog on a leash, or with a suitcase in one hand. On the rare occasions when he lost, he always paid his bets. He was a showman, but an honest one. "All my life everything has been a contest. . . . I love the competition—and that's the thing I crave, like some guys crave alcohol and other guys crave women. I crave the game."[6]

Wondering how to get a piece of the action—and the money—gravitating toward tennis in the new open era, Riggs came up with the idea of challenging a top woman player. Billie Jean King was his first choice, but she turned him down repeatedly, feeling she had nothing to gain—and a lot to lose—from such a match. Undeterred, Riggs went after Margaret Court, the Australian player then ranked number one in the world. Thinking it would be just a Sunday afternoon exhibition match with a tidy pay off, she accepted. Like so many opponents before and after her, Court underestimated Bobby Riggs, whose 6-2, 6-1 demolition of her on May 13, 1973, became known as the Mother's Day Massacre. When the leading woman tennis player in the world loses to an over-the-hill male player who, in Rosie Casals's memorable words, "is an old man, he walks like a duck, he can't see, he can't hear and, besides he's an idiot," it does not say much for the depth of the women's professional tennis tour then struggling to establish its legitimacy. As soon as Billie Jean King heard the results, she knew that she had to play Riggs to uphold the honor of the women's game she was fighting so hard to promote.[7]

As the hype began to build in late August and early September of 1973, practically every major magazine and newspaper devoted significant coverage to this "story," which straddled the line between sports, news, and entertainment.[8] Bobby Riggs supplied about 90 percent of the copy, having realized that outrageous statements against women's lib got him more attention than sticking to tennis. Three examples: "I plan to bomb Billie Jean King in the match and set back the Women's Lib movement about another 20 years"; "The best way to handle women is to keep them pregnant and barefoot"; and, "Women play about twenty-five percent as good as men, so they should get about twenty-five percent of the money men get." Most of this sexist posturing was for show. When journalist Nora Ephron asked Riggs what he really knew about women's liberation, he replied, "You're not going to believe this. Nothing."[9]

One of the things that made this match so irresistible was that it promised to crown a winner—and a loser—in what was both a tennis match and a national debate about women's changing roles. Everybody had an opinion, everybody could pick a side, and by the end of the night, somebody would win—what a perfect incentive to bet on the outcome. Of course betting on sports events (legal or otherwise) was very much part of male sports culture, but tennis matches did not usually draw this attention. Jimmy the Greek gave odds at 5-2 Riggs, and a lot of wagers were laid. Not all of them involved cash. As Bobby Riggs said, "Men can bet against their wives, bosses can bet against their secretaries. The outcome may determine who does the dishes or pays for the movies in millions of homes. Everybody cares."[10]

While the media coverage made it sound like all men backed Riggs and all women backed King, she had plenty of male supporters, as writer Dan Wakefield realized in an admittedly unscientific survey: "Billie Jean's staunch male supporters included my local druggist, my neighborhood banker, the building manager of the Atlantic Monthly Company (he had recently bought his own tennis racket) and my retired father in Indianapolis." But King forged a special bond with women, who embraced the tennis star the way the African American community had celebrated boxer Joe Louis in the 1930s. To King's chagrin, however, many female tennis pros, including a teenaged Chris Evert on ABC's pregame warm-up show, predicted that Riggs would prevail. Reflected a mature Evert many years later with a laugh, "I was such an idiot. I've changed since."[11]

Billie Jean King relished her underdog role: "Up until now, I've always been the heavy. You know, I'm the leader. I'm responsible for women's tennis. For once, I'm the underdog. I love it." Riggs's seemingly effortless win over Court gave a lot of credibility to the idea that even a middle-aged man could beat a woman at the top of her game, which in turn played on long-standing beliefs about women's physical and emotional inferiority compared to men. As Michael Murray observed in *Commonweal*, "By some magic of timing and circumstances, this confrontation between an aging playboy hustler and a tennis-obsessed woman came to symbolize many of the resentments and excitements that constitute the mixed-up American male-female relationship at the moment." Among the major news vehicles, only the *Wall Street Journal* picked her to win.[12]

In retrospect, an interesting undercurrent in the media coverage was the prominent role of Marilyn Barnett, the hairdresser-turned-personal-secretary-turned-lover who would sue Billie Jean King in a "palimony" suit in 1981. Barnett is everywhere in the coverage, even fleetingly visible in the ABC telecast. *Newsweek* called her "the equivalent of a second" in King's corner, "who sits worshipfully at courtside during her workouts, oversees her diet and weight program, and attempts to shield her from most journalists." On the night of the match, the *New York Times* described the "25-year-old pale, willowy blonde" as "perhaps the calmest person in the house." Although King did not consider herself a lesbian at the time (she was still married to her husband, Larry), the strain of concealing the relationship must have added to the stress of the match. Today the press probably would be all over it, but in 1973 the line still held—tenuously—between what was considered news and what was considered off-limits in speculating about a celebrity's private life.[13]

Without the national television coverage for which ABC paid an estimated $750,000, complete with Howard Cosell in a hairpiece and tux and tennis players Rosie Casals and Gene Scott as combative color commentators, the event would never have had the impact on the national psyche that it did. One media commentator observed, "TV has demonstrated again its capacity to focus the entire country on a single event, unifying millions of people, for the space of those moments, as they have rarely been before." Less charitably, the New York Times called the televised production "an unholy alliance between Miss America and the Rose Bowl Parade." The event's most immediate predecessor was the much-hyped boxing match between Muhammad Ali and Joe Frazier in 1971, staged, not coincidentally, by Jerry Perenchio, the same promoter who had Bobby Riggs come into the Astrodome surrounded by scantily clad women and Billie Jean King enter on a throne carried by equally scantily clad men. If one of the main trends of the second half of the twentieth century was the coming together of sports and entertainment, then this Battle of the Sexes represented a key milestone.[14]

The match itself could have seemed anticlimactic, that is, if the stakes hadn't been so high for Billie Jean King, who was carrying, it seemed, the expectations of half the population on her shoulders. "So much was going on to make women feel things were changing in the world," she recalled. "But in their own lives, not much had changed. There was a disconnect there. That's what made this match huge. Huge!" Her task was clear: "I just had to win." She later admitted that for years afterward she would wake in the middle of the night still thinking she had to play Riggs, only to gratefully fall back to sleep realizing that she already had.[15]

Billie Jean King arrived in Houston "feeling fit and that there was not one more thing I could do to prepare. That's the greatest feeling as an athlete." Rather than being thrown off by the hype and the pressure ("Pressure is a privilege" is a favorite King mantra),[16] the tennis star embraced the chance to publicize her sport and the cause of women's tennis before a huge national audience: "I can remember winning a championship and there were only three reporters there," she told the assembled press corps. "I remember. I'm glad you're all here tonight." Bobby Riggs spent his time schmoozing with his supporters, guzzling vitamins (reportedly 415 a day), and basking in the limelight. All this off-court activity did him in. Lornie

Kuhle said of his close buddy, who looked exhausted and drained from the moment he stepped on the court, "It was like Bobby finally realized that the final exam was here and he hadn't studied for it."[17]

Billie Jean King built her tennis career around an aggressive serve-and-volley game and that was how she originally planned to play Riggs. But when she walked onto the court she did what champions do—adjust—and switched to what she later called "Plan B." Sensing that Riggs might not be strong enough to go the distance in a five-set match, she decided to prolong points by running him around the court and hit balls softly so that he would have to generate all the pace. Sure enough, Riggs began to tire visibly in the first set, although not before breaking her serve at 2-all to take the lead. King broke right back and won the first set 6-4 on a Riggs double fault. Even though Riggs continued to have trouble with his serve in the second set, they remained on serve until King broke him in the eighth game and then served out the set 6-3. Continuing to play steady if unspectacular tennis against her ill-prepared and outclassed opponent, Billie Jean King methodically controlled the tempo of the match throughout the third set—that is, until she was up 5-3 with Riggs serving, and the two played the second-longest game of the match. King just couldn't seem to finish him off (is she choking, fans wondered?) as the game went repeatedly to deuce. On match point number three Riggs feebly netted a backhand, and it was finally game, set, match, Billie Jean. Riggs seemed so tired that King marveled he had the energy to jump over the net to congratulate her.[18]

Time to celebrate—or eat crow. *Sports Illustrated*, which the week before had predicted Riggs would win, called King's performance "a classic example of a skilled athlete performing at peak efficiency in the most important moment of her life." So many people had been seduced by the media hype to think about this match only in gender terms that they forgot that it was also a match pitting the young versus the old, which was painfully on display as the match unfolded. To his credit, Riggs was gracious in defeat, admitting to his opponent at courtside, "You were too good." Rumors that Riggs deliberately lost the match have been consistently—and convincingly—denied by all parties over the years.[19]

Billie Jean King's decision to play Bobby Riggs was a conscious political act. She always realized that the match was much bigger than just tennis, and she was willing to put her hard-won credibility on the line to prove the point that women deserved just as much respect as men. Even though the outcome now seems preordained, at the time people really felt it could go either way. Would a loss by King have irrevocably damaged the history of women's sports or derailed second-wave feminism? Probably not, but it would have been an embarrassing, indeed humbling affirmation of many of the old stereotypes that women at the time were trying to upend. But victory—how satisfying. Olympic swimmer Donna de Varona relished the result: "The guy was older and was this and that, but the truth is, it was a worldwide movement that needed a finishing statement. And Billie Jean King gave it to us." Future sportswriter Christine Brennan captured the sweet vindication as only a fifteen-year-old aspiring athlete could: "We won. The girls won."[20]

LOOKING BACK FROM today's perspective, when so much has changed for women in sports and society, it is hard to recapture how high the stakes were in 1973 and how closely aligned this tennis match was to the fundamental political and social controversies of the day. Americans at the time did not realize it, but the Battle of the Sexes was one of the first public manifestations of a revolution in women's sports that has been reshaping American society ever since. One of the main catalysts was the passage of Title IX in 1972. Another was the revival of the broad-based social movement called second-wave feminism in the 1960s and 1970s. And the third was the charismatic figure of Billie Jean King to bring the two together.

The controversy surrounding Title IX foreshadowed the politicization of women's sports in the 1970s. The law was originally passed in 1972 to address widespread discrimination against women in all aspects of higher education; only gradually did it dawn on supporters and then opponents that the law would have its most wide-ranging impact on athletics. The battles over equitable distribution of sports resources quickly brought to light some of the most egregious examples of sex discrimination, such as female athletes getting 1 percent (if that) of sports budgets, having to hold bake sales to pay for their own uniforms and travel expenses, or being forced to practice at 6:00 in the morning or 10:30 at night because those were the only times the gym was available. Once Title IX began to raise the nation's consciousness about sports, parents and students alike began challenging discrimination in athletics wherever they found it, and the women's sports revolution took off. So profound has been this sea change that many female athletes today have no idea how recent, or how hard fought, the opportunities they take for granted are.[21]

Title IX was not conceived in a vacuum. The revival of second-wave feminism in the 1960s and 1970s provided a key backdrop for the tremendous energy gravitating toward women's sports.[22] The momentum began to build with such initiatives as the President's Commission on the Status of Women from 1961 to 1963, the passage of Title VII of the Civil Rights Act of 1964 banning sex discrimination in employment, and the founding of the National Organization for Women (NOW) in 1966. The movement reached new constituencies when consciousness-raising groups sprang up on campuses and radical feminists staged a protest against the Miss America pageant in Atlantic City in 1968. On August 26, 1970, the fiftieth anniversary of the passage of the Nineteenth Amendment giving women the vote, NOW orchestrated marches and protests in cities across the country that suggested the mass potential of this new movement. That year Robin Morgan published the groundbreaking anthology *Sisterhood Is Powerful*.[23]

While popular memory credits the decade of the 1960s as an era of social protest and change, the greatest breakthroughs for the women's movement occurred in the 1970s, especially early in the decade. Suddenly so many things seemed possible, so many formerly settled ideas up for grabs. In fact, one can speak of the period from 1970 to 1975 as something of a "feminist moment," when the proponents of women's liberation forced their way onto the national agenda and won significant victories before a backlash set in. In March 1972, after languishing for almost fifty years, the Equal Rights Amendment cleared both the Senate and the House and was sent to the states for what looked like speedy ratification. In June 1972 Congress passed the Education Amendments Act containing Title IX. That year *Ms.* magazine was launched, and Congresswoman Shirley Chisholm ran for president. In January 1973 the Supreme Court upheld a woman's right to abortion in *Roe v. Wade*. These breakthroughs were not uncontested, and there was a real edginess to relations between the sexes in the early 1970s. (The term gender did not come into widespread use until the 1980s and 1990s.) Debates over such issues as sex discrimination, pay equity, and equal opportunity raged not only in the halls of Congress and chambers of the Supreme Court, but in offices, restaurants, and living rooms across the country.

Billie Jean King's epic match with Bobby Riggs occurred right in the middle of these "superheated" times.[24] King came to feminism through sports, not vice versa, and tennis always remained her top priority. As journalist Grace Lichtenstein aptly observed, "Billie Jean liked seeing her face on the cover of *Ms.*, but she loved seeing it on the cover of *Sports Illustrated* even more." King's outspoken advocacy of better treatment for women in professional tennis propelled her into the feminist limelight, where she became one of the prominent faces, along with women such as Gloria Steinem, Betty Friedan, and Bella Abzug, that the public associated with the powerful, if often controversial, new movement. Then, as now, there was disagreement about its priorities, and sport was never all that high on its agenda. And yet popular athletes like King brought welcome publicity and accessibility to the feminist cause. As journalist Selena Roberts noted, Billie Jean King gave "a polarized women's movement exactly what it needed: a mainstream face."[25]

Billie Jean King was very aware of her power to shape public opinion, which was one reason that she embraced her tennis celebrity with such enthusiasm. "It's easier to change attitudes through sports," she always asserted. "Sports are a visual example of what the world could be." Here the role of popular culture was crucial. The widely disseminated images of path breakers such as Billie Jean King encouraged ordinary women (and probably a few men) to think that maybe they could do new things too—not necessarily win Wimbledon, compete in the Indianapolis 500, or be elected to Congress, but do something more than what their society had told them they could do. As *womenSports* magazine said of race car driver Janet Guthrie in 1976, "Now, instead of saying, 'Oh, I can't do that,' women are beginning to say, 'Yes, I can.'" And the more women who successfully met these new challenges, the harder it became to hold onto old stereotypes and shibboleths about women as the second or weaker sex.[26]

It is too strong to say that without feminism Billie Jean King would have been just another athlete, but she certainly would have been of much less interest historically. Because of her relationship to second-wave feminism, she came to embody the aspirations and dreams of the modern women's movement in her role as a popular heroine from the world of sports. Too often the histories of sports and feminism have operated on separate, not always parallel tracks, to the detriment of both. Billie Jean King was the rare athlete who made the connection and affirmatively tried to bring the two closer together.

In the 1970s, the predominant thrust of feminist sports activism was a focus on equal rights, especially increasing participation opportunities and winning equal access for girls and women to the existing sports structure. As Billie Jean King later recalled, "In the '70s we had to make it acceptable for people to accept girls and women as athletes. We had to make it okay for them to be active. Those were much scarier times for females in sports—we had to create the opportunity." This call for equal opportunity was behind Billie Jean King's challenge to the tennis establishment, and equal rights was the motivating idea behind the Battle of the Sexes. The focus on winning access was also at the core of Title IX's emphasis on creating participation opportunities and making sure that girls and women received equal resources to boys and men in educational settings. To use a sports metaphor, it was about getting girls into the game.[27]

The height of Billie Jean King's advocacy intersected with the launching of the women's sports revolution in the 1970s that made women's access to sport a right rather than a privilege in just over a generation. Inspired in large part by Title IX, girls and women found many new chances to participate in recreational sports and competitive athletics, which in turn helped to erode the stigma attached to being a female athlete. High school participation rates jumped from one out of twenty-seven in 1971 to one out of three by the end of the decade. With tennis blazing the trail as a model, women also found the glimmerings of new professional opportunities to compete in sports outside of educational settings. Most important, Title IX, despite constant attacks, served as a legislative and political force in favor of better treatment for women.

None of this would have happened so quickly without the symbiotic relationship between the women's sports revolution and modern feminism, with Billie Jean King serving as the bridge between the two. Most women athletes were not closely aligned with the women's movement, nor was equality in sports a high priority for second-wave feminism compared to other "body" issues such as abortion, rape, self-defense, and sexuality; but that does not mean that sports and feminism were not influencing each other in subtle and often profound ways. Once questions of feminism and equal rights entered the national dialogue in the 1970s, these powerful new ways of thinking about women's social roles and physical capabilities challenged the monolith that was men's sports, pried open the small, insular world of women's sports, and caused fundamental change in both. In turn, women athletes provided a strong, visual example of "women's liberation in action."[28] No one personified these twin thrusts better than Billie Jean King.

TO TELL THIS STORY calls for a combination of biography and history. Chapters that focus primarily on Billie Jean King are interspersed with thematic chapters on the early days of Title IX, the history of women's sports, and the relationship between sports and second-wave feminism. Providing the thread that ties the narrative together, Billie Jean King appears in every chapter, but sometimes only in a supporting role. Although this is not a conventional biography, it provides a full analysis of her life and its significance for twentieth-century U.S. history, especially where matters of sport and feminism are concerned. In fact, I would argue that only by setting King's life in this larger context does her true historical significance come through, something that would be lost in a more traditional sports biography.

Chronologically the story is grounded primarily in the period from the late 1960s through the early 1980s. There are several reasons for this timeframe. Most obviously, those years coincide with the height of Billie Jean King's playing career and her widest influence as a popular heroine from the world of sports. The 1970s, especially the early part of the decade, also represent the highpoint of second-wave feminist activism. The decade was also crucial for the fate of Title IX. The narrative ventures into the early 1980s to finish off an important story—the battle between the National Collegiate Athletic Association and the Association for Intercollegiate Athletics for Women over control of women's intercollegiate sports. And it introduces a new story—the outing of Billie Jean King in 1981 by a woman who was her former lover—in order to connect King's life to the wider issues of homophobia and lesbianism in women's sports, as well as the history of gay rights. It does not, however, provide a detailed history of Title IX from the 1980s to the present because that topic has been well told in other recent books.[29]

The thematic core of the book is an exploration of the benefits and limits of liberal feminism. With its emphasis on individual achievement, equal opportunity, and striving for political and legal equality within the mainstream of the dominant culture, liberal feminism is best understood as one strand—the lowest common denominator, as it were—of the broader, multifaceted social movement referred to as second-wave feminism. Billie Jean King is a classic liberal feminist, challenging any archaic notions of female inferiority by insisting that men and women be treated as equals and pragmatically working within the system to bring about social change. Her philosophy put a premium on opening doors for women and allowing them to demonstrate that they could compete on an equal plain with men, leading by example and serving as an opening wedge toward more equal gender roles. She would have agreed wholeheartedly with Eleanor Roosevelt's straightforward definition: "Fundamentally, the purpose of

Feminism is that a woman should have an equal opportunity and Equal Rights with any other citizen of the country."[30]

Billie Jean King's individualistic stance toward women's advancement was part of a long philosophical tradition that stretched back to the classic liberalism that developed in the seventeenth and eighteenth centuries in Europe alongside the emergence of modern capitalism. This brand of liberalism, which emphasized tenets such as rationality, individualism, equality, citizenship, and especially liberty, was most closely associated with the philosophers John Locke and Jean-Jacques Rousseau. Starting in the late eighteenth and early nineteenth centuries, philosophers such as Mary Wollstonecraft, Harriet Taylor, and John Stuart Mill called for the extension of liberal freedom and responsibility to women, who had previously been relegated entirely to dependence on men in the private realm. Women too should be seen as autonomous and rational individuals with commensurate rights and responsibilities to men's, they argued. With its commitment to individualism and self-reliance, alongside a critique of accepted notions of women's inferiority, liberal feminism offered a vision of women as truly equal partners of men in the public realm.[31]

This liberal feminist approach was also the main thrust behind Title IX in the 1970s. Title IX's focus on getting women more participation opportunities and access to the dominant athletic system—or to put it another way, a larger piece of the athletic pie—fit the model of working for change within the existing political and legal system. This liberal feminist stance produced enormous breakthroughs for women in sports in the 1970s but also had some less-than-salutary consequences, such as the decline in opportunities for women coaches and administrators and the absorption of women's sports into a corporate, market-driven model based primarily on competition and winning at all costs. In addition, by focusing so single-mindedly on issues of access, sports activists often failed to challenge the core principles of a system that had denied women athletes their rights and opportunities in the first place. As a result, the sports world was free to continue to treat women as second-class citizens, even as their participation opportunities increased dramatically; prejudices such as racism and homophobia remained deeply rooted and hard to ferret out. In hindsight, therefore, this commitment to working within the system hinted that the women's sports revolution might not be very revolutionary after all.

At the same time there are aspects of liberal feminism that do have the potential to force a truly revolutionary rethinking of how the sports world is structured and maintained. If we think of athletes as individuals first, exhibiting a wide range of overlapping talents and skills, and then only secondarily as male or female, why is it necessary to keep the two sexes so rigidly separated in most aspects of athletic participation and competition? This conundrum was raised by the National Organization for Women in the 1970s in the context of how to implement Title IX, but the idea of men and women competing together was just too radical then to have any realistic chance of acceptance. After four decades of explosive growth in women's athletics and female athletic capabilities, it is time to revisit the provocative question of why sports remain caught in a separate-but-equal framework while the rest of the world has gone coed. The tenets of liberal feminism offer an intriguing way to jumpstart that conversation.

On the tennis court and off, Billie Jean King put a human face on the abstract ideals of liberal feminism. Throughout her career she worked strenuously to increase access and open opportunities for women athletes—getting them a piece of that pie, a place at that table. She also pushed to make women's tennis an attractive and exciting option on par with the men's game, accepting that women needed their own professional tour to shine and succeed as athletes. At the same time she was willing to take Bobby Riggs's dare in 1973 for a "Battle of the Sexes" that challenged the separatist paradigm of sports that kept men and women from competing against each other. Her founding of World Team Tennis, with its coed roster comprised equally—and purposely—of men and women, also constituted an assault on the rigidly gendered sports status quo. Work within the system, but also embrace the ability to step outside the box and think about sports in new ways; keep women's athletics separate from men's when necessary, but also encourage all athletes, male and female, to participate and compete as individuals. To Billie Jean King, these were all logical and necessary choices to advance the broader cause of fostering equity and fairness for women in sports.

If informed that her career encapsulated the open-ended but sometimes-contradictory possibilities of liberal feminism as applied to sports, Billie Jean King would probably roll her eyes and say, "Please, no labels. Let's just get on with it."[32] And yet the promise and limitations of liberal feminism as they played out in her life provide essential keys to understanding the broad revolution in women's sports that has occurred since the 1970s—its undeniable accomplishments and its still-unfinished agenda. Decades after her playing days ended, Billie Jean King's legacy continues to shape the women's sports revolution she helped to spark.

Chapter One   The Making of a Sports Icon

In her 1982 autobiography, Billie Jean King reflected on the changes that she had seen in the first forty years of her life, a time of enormous transitions for women, tennis, and America in general. "Any woman born around 1943 has had to endure so many changes—in her educational experience, in her working life, in sex, in her roles, her expectations. But with me, it always seemed like I was also on the cutting edge of that change." She continued, "I was brought up in a very structured universe—in my family, in school, in tennis, in every part of my world. Then, all of a sudden, the rules all started to change, and it seemed there weren't any rules left. I tried to go with the flow, but always seemed to find myself out in front and on the line." This sense of being ahead of her times, a trailblazer on a variety of personal and professional fronts, characterizes many aspects of Billie Jean King's life. She remains positive about the future: "I have to be. I'm always 20 years ahead of the times."[1]

Practically as soon as the American public began to take notice of a brash young Californian named Billie Jean Moffitt King, fans and detractors alike realized that there was more to her than just her tennis. "Billie Jean is not just a tennis player," noted a fan in the *Reader's Digest* in 1974. "She's a cause." Like other sports stars such as Muhammad Ali, Jackie Robinson, and Joe Louis, who grabbed national attention to become icons of their individual sports and ambassadors of sport in general, Billie Jean King won a following for her role in transforming amateur tennis into a successful professional sport with broad national appeal. Soon after, she emerged as one of the nation's most prominent and outspoken champions for the female sex—"Mother Courage with a backhand." In 1990 *Life* magazine named her one of the hundred most influential people of the twentieth century.[2]

And yet, as with any idol or icon, it is important not to conflate Billie Jean King the symbol with Billie Jean King the person. "Even my own autobiography sitting up there on my shelf gives me the willies," she told *womenSports* in 1977. "It's like two different people. There's me, and then there's that tennis player. I feel like I'm not what I am." Fearless and bold in public but more conventional in private, she struggled to reconcile her transgressive (for the time) sexual feelings with her desire to be universally liked and respected. America at the time was not ready for a gay tennis superstar, so her sexual orientation was kept firmly closeted. To her the rationalizations were compelling: she didn't want to hurt women's tennis, and she didn't want to embarrass her parents, who would have found such a choice incomprehensible. This deceit meant that for most of her career—even after she was outed in 1981—she was living a lie. As we will see in chapter 6, King's search for acceptance, from her public and especially from herself, turned into a lifetime journey.[3]

BILLIE JEAN MOFFITT was a war baby. When she was born on November 22, 1943, her twenty-five-year-old father, Bill, was in the navy, stationed in Norfolk, Virginia, as a physical education leader for stateside troops; her mother, Betty, had stayed home in Long Beach, California, for the duration of his active duty. Like many children conceived during wartime, Billie Jean was named after her absent father instead of her mother's original choice of Michelle Louise. King later couldn't resist imagining the headlines: "Michelle Louise Whips Bobby Riggs in Straight Sets."[4]

Both her parents had grown up in broken homes during the Depression, and memories of those hard times were not easily dispelled. Her mother remembered a succession of stepfathers and times when all the family could afford to eat was potatoes. Her father's mother deserted the family when

Bill was thirteen, leaving him with adult-sized responsibilities for a younger brother after an older sister died of cancer. Born and raised in Montana, at some point in the 1930s Bill, like so many other depression-era migrants, made his way to California, where he enrolled at Long Beach City College and played on the basketball team. He met and married Betty in 1941 and soon after entered the service. When he was released from active duty, Bill Moffitt got a job as a firefighter in Long Beach, and he and Betty bought a compact (1,000 square feet) three-bedroom tract house in a nice but hardly fancy neighborhood. There they lived the American dream of home owner-ship and nuclear family life that was the epitome of the immediate postwar period. In 1948 their second child, Randall James (Randy), was born.[5]

Like much of California, Long Beach experienced dramatic growth dur-ing the 1940s as part of wartime mobilization, playing an especially criti-cal role as a major seaport just twenty miles south of the terminus of Los Angeles. In the postwar period, government spending for what came to be known as the military-industrial complex continued to fuel exponen-tial economic development and population growth in Long Beach and surrounding areas. Media writer John Leonard (who also grew up there) once described the city's suburban sprawl architecture as a place "where churches looked like airports, the high schools looked like filling stations, [and] Midwestern geriatrics trolled housing tracts in go-carts."[6] Long Beach and nearby Orange County were also noted for their preponderance of fun-damentalist and Pentecostal churches, and the strong conservative politi-cal views of their residents, especially on the subject of anticommunism. It was no accident that Orange County in the 1960s was the seedbed for the modern Republican conservative revolution known as the New Right. With only slight hyperbole, a sociologist once referred to "the orange cur-tain" that "metaphorically surrounds Orange County, California and keeps it seemingly free of liberal thinking."[7]

Bill Moffitt fit the profile of a strongly conservative, hyperpatriotic, an-ticommunist citizen, often intolerant of those who didn't share his views, including, at times, his only daughter. "I guess my parents were prejudiced, not so much against individuals as against groups," she later recalled. "I remember one discussion with my father about homosexuals when I was about ten. It wasn't much of a discussion, actually: he made it clear he had very little tolerance for them. . . . It was all a strange contradiction, because they brought Randy and me up to always treat each person as an individual, as a human being, but when it came down to the broader issues, I guess they were really pretty narrow." Her future husband put it in a less flattering framework, calling the Moffitts "straight out of Archie Bunker."[8]

Complementing their conservative political views, the Moffitts had a very traditional marriage: "Dad was the boss, the breadwinner, the one who made all the final decisions. Even though mom wasn't afraid to speak up, she wasn't nearly as opinionated as dad." It was obvious to everyone that Billie Jean got much of her competitive drive—and temper—from him. The most important family rule was dinner every night at 5:30 sharp, "or dad would go into a tirade." Her mother, always the peacekeeper in the family, painted the mealtime ritual in warmer tones: "Family dinner has always been an important event in our home. It was discussion time, warm, pleasant, and an opportunity to exchange ideas. It made us a very close family." Feeling so well grounded in this secure family environment as a child was an important precondition for Billie Jean King's success, athletic and otherwise. And yet just as noticeable was her early desire not to grow up to be a typical South California housewife like her mother, struggling to get by on a firefighter's salary. Class as much as gender fueled the future tennis star's ambition. "I like being different," she once said. "I also like being successful. I somehow always knew that I would succeed."[9]

In later years Billie Jean King felt a real bond of kinship with fellow tennis player Chris Evert, who though a decade younger, also came from a very traditional family background in Florida. (Note also the shared advantage of growing up in climates where you can play tennis outdoors all year.) Their suburban houses even looked alike, but the similarities went deeper than postwar décor: "In both houses you could feel the discipline in the air." Even though the Everts were Catholic and the Moffitts Protestant, "there was a lot of black-and-white thinking in both. Her father was a real disciplinarian. We both learned to be perfectionists."[10]

As an active girl fond of pick-up football, speedball, baseball, or whatever else was being played on the street ("Small but quick, I was the scourge of 36th street"), Billie Jean earned the unavoidable label of tomboy, a term she disliked, as did her parents.[11] As a child, however, Billie Jean showed little interest in any traditional female accomplishments, despite her mother's attempts to introduce her to sewing and embroidery. Even if she didn't know then that Babe Didrikson Zaharias was probably the best all-around athlete, male or female, of the twentieth century, Billie Jean certainly would have agreed with her when she was asked if there was any sport she didn't play. Babe's pithy reply: "Dolls."[12]

An avid recreational athlete himself, Bill Moffitt was ahead of his times in encouraging his daughter to play sports, but her athletic dreams were abruptly shaken when she approached adolescence. In a story told by countless women athletes across the generations, Billie Jean had her epiphany at a baseball game: "But what struck me like a thunderbolt as I watched the game on the diamond that day was that there were no women on the field. My life-long ambition to become a professional baseball player was shattered." Years later a sportswriter for the *Los Angeles Times* substituted football for baseball, divining King's later activism from a similar (imagined) gender epiphany: "King has never forgiven nature for the dirty trick it played on her in preventing her from being a safety for the Green Bay Packers."[13]

Not only would there be no professional baseball career such as the one her brother Randy later pursued as a relief pitcher for the San Francisco Giants, but Billie Jean got the strong message that if she insisted on continuing to play sports, she must choose one that was more ladylike, or at least more acceptable for women. Swimming and golf were options, but tennis was an even better choice for a girl who loved to run and hit a ball. When a fifth-grade classmate named Susan Williams introduced her to tennis, she immediately fell in love with the sport. As she later put it succinctly, "The thing I like about tennis is that you're using your mind and body as one."[14]

Soon after she first stepped onto a tennis court, Billie Jean Moffitt set her sights high. In an oft-recounted story (actually, most of her stories are oft-recounted), when Betty Moffitt picked her daughter up after her first group lesson on a Long Beach public court, eleven-year-old Billie Jean told her, "I'm going to be the Number One tennis player in the whole world." "That's fine, dear," her mother replied, and just kept on driving.[15] When later asked if she was surprised at this announcement, Betty Moffitt said matter-of-factly, "Bill and I took her at her word. She was and is the kind of girl who means what she says." As her daughter later explained to a journalist, "I'd had a sense of urgency since I was born. When you can see things so clearly, it's hard on you. You see this vision and everyone looks at you like you've got three heads when it's a no-brainer." For Billie Jean King, her vision was to be the best tennis player in the world.[16]

Tennis changed Betty Moffitt's life almost as much as her daughter's, as she chauffeured and chaperoned Billie Jean on the daily after-school trips to public courts around Long Beach for her lessons and then later to tournaments in the greater Los Angeles area. "I never thought of any of the thousands of hours I spent watching Billie Jean play tennis as a sacrifice," she recalled. To friends who raised that point, "I told them that if they had a child who was as interested as Sis [Billie Jean's childhood nickname] and who put so much effort into a project, they would be willing to go along with her, too." In contrast to today's over-controlling sports parents, her mother always made sure that Billie Jean had a well-balanced childhood, with piano lessons and school getting equal time with sports.[17]

One of the striking things about the Moffitt family is that their traditional postwar nuclear family, with one girl and one boy, ended up producing two professional athletes—Billie Jean in tennis and Randy in baseball. Reflecting their somewhat modest family circumstances, journalist Selena Roberts later said of the Moffitts, "Somehow Bill and Betty helped create a tennis superstar and a major league pitcher on a coupon-clipper's budget." Still, having two athletic children to equip and transport put a strain on a firefighter's salary, and Betty Moffitt sometimes worked as an Avon Lady or sold Tupperware to bring in some extra cash. Billie Jean and Randy always remained grateful for their parents' combination of support without strings or pressure: "I think the reason we are here today is that our parents did not live through us; they stood behind us," their daughter said proudly. "There is a big difference."[18]

Billie Jean Moffitt took to tennis, but tennis took a little time getting used to her. She never forgot her early run-ins with the tennis establishment, including one painful slight when she was not allowed to be in a group photograph at a tournament because she was wearing tennis shorts (which her mother had specially sewn for her) rather than the requisite tennis dress. From the start she had an outsider's sense that made her want to shake up the game from its country-club tonyness and make it more of a people's sport. Part of this came from her public court exposure and her lower-middle-class family background. Yet she cautioned against exaggerating her family's financial straits: "We weren't nearly as poor as it was fashionable to make us out to be. It was just that anybody in tennis who wasn't in the country club was always stereotyped as indigent." Still, her parents always felt much more comfortable in a baseball crowd cheering Randy than at a tennis match watching Billie Jean.[19]

Having only been introduced to the sport at age eleven, Billie Jean quickly began climbing the tennis ladder. Even if she deplored the haughtiness of tennis culture, she loved the game too much to just walk away from it. In the 1950s and early 1960s, tennis really wasn't all that changed from the genteel, country-club sport it had been in the 1920s and 1930s. For example, it would have been heretical to show up to play in anything but "tennis whites." Balls were white too, racquets were wooden, and many clubs featured immaculately groomed grass courts. With the exception of a few ranked players such as Helen Jacobs and Alice Marble who played in shorts, women competed in demure tennis dresses or skirts that almost reached their knees. When designer Ted Tinling added lace to the panties that Gussy Moran wore under her dress for her Wimbledon debut in 1949, it created an international sensation.[20]

This tennis world was extremely insular and hierarchical, tightly controlled by the United States Lawn Tennis Association (USLTA) and local groups such as the Southern California Tennis Association, which Perry Jones ("a fussy old bachelor who hated girls," in Billie's words) ran like a dictatorship.[21] Tournaments, local and national, were organized by age divisions and all were amateur. Opportunities to play in these tournaments, receive reimbursement for travel expenses, or access to other advantages such as coaching and sponsorship were under the thumb of tennis association leaders who had a vested interest in the status quo. If players were lucky, they received token per diem and travel expenses, and they often stretched their budgets by staying in the private homes of tennis supporters at tournaments; obviously such a set-up privileged tennis players whose families were affluent enough to subsidize their participation in the sport. Top tennis players received cash under the table—appearance money or prize money—for playing; professional tennis players, who mainly played exhibition matches, were barred from all the prestigious tournaments. Newspaper coverage was limited, and television coverage virtually nonexistent.[22]

This world of tennis was also rigidly segregated well into the 1950s. The black counterpart to the USLTA was the American Tennis Association (ATA), which ran its own tennis program as well as championship tournaments for youth and adults. The ATA had nurtured the athletic careers of such outstanding black female athletes as Isadore Channels in the 1920s, Ora Washington in the 1930s, and a young Althea Gibson in the 1940s, but like baseball players in the segregated Negro Leagues, these women had no opportunities to demonstrate their skill or compete against white players. It took determined public advocacy by Alice Marble in 1950 for Althea Gibson to be invited to play in a grass-courts tournament on the East Coast.

This invitation in turn paved the way for Gibson and a small number of other African American players to compete in tournaments such as the U.S. Open and Wimbledon.[23]

Billie Jean Moffitt, who felt like an outsider in this clubby world because of both class and gender (although not race), often bumped up against its rules and traditions and then nursed grievances, sometimes for the rest of her life, for the treatment she received. Case in point: the inadequate financial support she was given to attend the national girls' fifteen-and-under championship in Ohio in 1958. Her parents could not afford to underwrite her travel costs to the tournament, and at fourteen she was deemed too young to travel without a chaperone. When her nemesis Perry Jones turned down her request for funding, a group of local boosters came up with some cash, but the sum was too small to stretch for airfare for her and her mother, so they had to sit up on the train all the way from California. Seeded fourth, she lost in the quarterfinals; it was the first time she had ever played on clay. After the championship, other team members went on to play in tournaments on the East Coast and then on the European circuit, but a tearful Billie Jean and her mother had to turn around and return to California for lack of funds. Such slights just increased her determination to succeed.[24]

Billie Jean's first coach was Clyde Walker of the Long Beach Recreation Department, who quickly realized that she had enormous promise. Soon she was showing up after school for free lessons at whatever Long Beach neighborhood park he was scheduled to coach at that day. She never forgot that she got her start on public courts rather than at a fancy country club. When the United States Tennis Association renamed its facility in Flushing Meadows the Billie Jean King National Tennis Center in 2006, a delighted and grateful King repeatedly drew attention to the fact that these courts were public courts too, just like the ones she learned to play on.[25]

In the fall of 1959, a Wilson Sporting Goods representative arranged for the sixteen-year-old rising star to have private lessons with former Wimbledon great Alice Marble, who lived up the coast in the Tarzana district of Los Angeles. Alice Marble was part of the first generation of women to play power tennis—an attacking, serve-and-volley game that she had honed under the legendary teacher Eleanor ("Teach") Tennant, who also coached Bobby Riggs.[26] Each Saturday Betty or Bill Moffitt would drive their daughter up to Los Angeles for her weekend sessions and then pick her up on Sunday. Besides the technical help Billie Jean received, the young player began to see herself as part of the larger history of the game through her association with Marble: "For the first time in my life, I sensed some kind of legacy that I was part of." Largely as a result of Alice Marble's tutelage, her national ranking rose from number nineteen in 1959 to number four in 1960.[27]

Yet this relationship with Marble came to an abrupt end, perhaps, Billie Jean speculated, because Marble was not comfortable with the young player's determination to succeed Marble and become the best player of all time. (Marble remembered it differently: when she came down with pleurisy and pneumonia, she thought her young charge cared more about her missed lesson than her coach's well-being, and Marble terminated the relationship.) The rising tennis star also had a fraught encounter around this time with top-ranked Maureen (Mo) Connolly, who bluntly told her she would never make a champion because she was too self-centered and egotistical. Not surprisingly, many of the traits that made Billie Jean so good at tennis, such as her fierce ambition and large ego, often rubbed people the wrong way. Still, as she later recalled, "to have two ex-champions as great as Alice and Maureen blast you when you're still in your teens is pretty tough. Those two incidents left a mark on me, and I still remember them vividly."[28]

In June 1961 Billie Jean Moffitt graduated from the Long Beach Polytechnical High School. She certainly was an acceptable student, but not a brain. "Not everyone is meant to be an A student," she told *Seventeen* in 1974. "Everyone can't be a great athlete, either." Billie Jean never apologized for her single-minded devotion to tennis and never questioned the sacrifices she made to reach her goals: "Sure tennis is demanding and it creates some tunnel vision. But I'm not really a believer in the well-rounded individual; it often means that a person has no particular distinction."[29]

She proved where her distinction lay several weeks after graduation when she and partner Karen Hantze teamed up at Wimbledon to win the women's doubles title, the youngest—and the first unseeded—pair to do so. She was seventeen years old. The doubles partners were too broke to go to the traditional Wimbledon ball, but were delighted when a young Boston sportswriter named Bud Collins offered to take them out for a celebratory spaghetti dinner. After her return to the states, *Sports Illustrated* selected Billie Jean Moffitt for its Faces in the Crowd feature, a tantalizing taste of the public celebrity that she craved for herself and her sport. In retrospect Billie Jean regretted that she had never set definite targets to shoot for, other than wanting to be "the best." "I never planned it very well—not in a long-term, overall way. I never sat down and said, I want to do this, I want to aim for that, I'll set that goal. I'm sure I could have won more than twenty Wimbledon titles if I'd plotted things better."[30]

With no clear career path before her, Billie Jean entered Los Angeles State College (later California State University, Los Angeles) in the fall of 1961 as a commuter student; the following fall she took an apartment near campus. As a nationally ranked tennis player (number three in 1961), one would have thought she would qualify for an athletic scholarship, but in pre–Title IX days such scholarships for women were nonexistent. Because of tight finances, she took odd jobs to pay for school, got by on $90 a month, and basically limited her competitive tennis playing to the summer, which, she quickly realized, was no way to get closer to her ambition to be the top player in the world. And yet she was getting noticed. In her return to Wimbledon in 1962, she beat reigning champion Margaret Smith (later Court) in the first round, an enormous upset, and then made it as far as the quarterfinals; she and Karen Hantze repeated their doubles victory. In 1963, she made it to the Wimbledon singles final, where she met top-seeded Smith again. This time, Smith handily dispatched her unseeded challenger 6-3, 6-4.[31]

The press didn't quite know what to make of the player they couldn't resist calling "Little Miss Moffitt." Except she wasn't exactly little, the result of her life-long struggle with her weight. Here is how *Sports Illustrated* described her in 1963: "Billie Jean, the daughter of a fireman in Long Beach, Calif., stands 5 feet 6 inches tall, has brown hair, light blue eyes, a small impertinent nose and a weight problem." The year before *Time* had called her "the chunky, bespectacled little Californian," drawing attention to how unusual it was, then or now, to have a tennis champion who wore glasses. (Her career offers a fashion Rorschach for eyewear from the 1950s to the present. She changed her glasses more often than she did her hairstyle.) The press was just as interested in her spunky personality as her appearance. The *New York Times* noted after her 1963 Wimbledon run, "The bespectacled tomboy from Southern California is the liveliest personality to hit the international circuit in years. She has courage and she has color, a combination rarely found in tennis today."[32]

Driven, focused, and single-minded in her determination to get to the top, even from a young age Billie Jean Moffitt fit the personality type likely to succeed at tennis. "I expect to win every time I step on a tennis court and I'm truly surprised when I don't.... On my very best days I have this fantastic, utterly unselfconscious feeling of invincibility." She claimed she could always tell when she was going to play a great match "because I woke up in the morning feeling everything. I was so alert. I could feel the water in my hair in the shower." Tennis mentor Frank Brennan, who first got to know the tennis player in the early 1960s when she stayed in his New Jersey home during a tournament, enumerated further traits King possessed that were key to her success: "Singlemindedness. A pride that drove her to succeed at all costs, and a stubborn will not to be humiliated, especially in front of a crowd." He added tellingly, "She's a ham. The more people watching, the better Billie Jean becomes."[33]

Billie Jean Moffitt was an indifferent student at Cal State and growing increasingly frustrated about her prospects in tennis. In the fall of 1964 she made the dramatic decision to drop out of school and head for Australia to work with noted coach Mervyn Rose, her expenses paid by an Australian benefactor. This was a real commitment to her career; no more dilettantism. Even though at times she felt like she was starting over from scratch, the improvements from Rose's tutelage were soon evident. She worked hard on her forehand, always the weakest part of her game, and retooled her serve. She also focused more on playing percentage tennis—that is, choosing the best shot to use in a given situation, like hitting approach shots down the line, but going crosscourt to put shots away. Determined to master full-court play so she would not be limited to a single style, she nevertheless gravitated toward the aggressive serve-and-volley game that suited her personality so well. When she returned from Australia, the fundamentals of her trademark game were firmly in place.[34]

The decision to take off for Australia was made much harder because it separated her from Larry King, the man she would marry the following year. They met in the fall of 1962 at Los Angeles State, introduced by a mutual friend who thought they would hit it off. Larry, too, was a tennis player, on scholarship, but he had no aspirations of a professional career. Their first date wasn't for another six months, but pretty soon they realized they were getting serious. His initial introduction to her parents had not been auspicious (a biochemistry major, he had asked her dad about the pH of the soil in their backyard lawn, which Bill Moffitt found pretentious), but the Moffitts soon came around. In retrospect, they could not have asked for a more loyal—perhaps too loyal—son-in-law.[35]

Larry and Billie Jean got engaged in October 1964 just before she left for Australia and were married the following year on September 17, 1965. The wedding photos show a beaming Billie Jean (without her glasses) and a handsome Larry in a white dinner jacket, both looking very young, which they were: her twenty-one to his twenty. Explaining the problems that were evident in the marriage from the very start, King often pointed to their youth when they got married, publicly wondering whether they should have married at all. But living together was not an option in those conservative times, especially with parents like Bill and Betty Moffitt. "I married him so I could be an honest woman," she joked, "and then he was the one person who gave me the courage to go back to being a [tennis] bum."[36]

Larry King's background was similar to that of both of Billie Jean's parents. He was born in Dayton, Ohio, in 1944, but his family, which was originally from Finland, moved to Los Angeles just after the war. After losing his mother at an early age, he grew up in a blended family of two siblings, two stepsiblings, and a half-brother after his father remarried. He had been working since he was twelve and was always happiest when he had a job to do or a problem to solve; he coupled a lifelong tendency to keep his feelings bottled up inside him with a fierce determination to make something of his life. Larry was also blond and cute in a California kind of way, and quite a catch. Although they didn't know it at first, both their careers would be totally tied up in Billie Jean's success in the world of tennis.[37]

Larry King played a critical role in the development of his wife's career. In the 1960s he helped to plant the seeds of her feminism by pointing out how unfair it was that a second-rate player like him, the seventh player on a six-person team, had a tennis scholarship while she did not, even though she was a far superior competitor.[38] He also supported and nurtured her tennis aspirations: "Billie Jean, I just don't see how you can give up something where you have the potential to be best in the world—the best of all." In 1964 he prodded her to give up her listless pursuit of a college degree to go to Australia to work on her game; after their marriage he continued to press her to keep on with tennis. "We felt Billie Jean's potential was as a tennis player. There was no point in her becoming just another housewife. She was immensely talented. I didn't feel her talent should be wasted." Already the promoter, Larry recognized Billie Jean as his star product. As he once quipped with perhaps more truth than he intended, "I'm more of a business agent than a husband."[39]

From the very beginning the marriage was haunted by Billie Jean's uncertainty about her sexuality, or as Larry later called it, her "identity problems." Long before Marilyn Barnett came on the scene in 1972–73, Billie

Jean had been exploring her sexual feelings for other women, yet in those pre-Stonewall times she lacked the political or social context to come to grips with herself as lesbian or bisexual, words she never remembered hearing when she was growing up. Mainly, she recalled, "We didn't talk about that stuff then."[40]

When people did start talking about "that stuff" in the 1970s, she always held back because she feared that any revelations about her sexuality would irrevocably damage the fledging women's tour. In addition, she was deeply afraid, rightly so, of the impact any kind of declaration about her sexual identity would have on her conservative parents.[41] Even though her relationships with women were something of an open secret on the tour, in those days sports coverage still respected a strict line in not reporting about athletes' private lives, so the rumors never made it into print. And other tennis players, concerned about public fears of rampant lesbianism within women's sports, certainly had plenty of incentives to keep mum. So Billie Jean King managed to avoid publicly dealing with the issue when it first surfaced and, it turned out, for years afterward.[42]

The early years of Billie Jean and Larry's marriage found two very young and very ambitious people trying to muddle through a minefield of challenges: the wife's confusion about her sexuality; the husband's attempts to build the kind of successful business career he had always wanted, which depended on his wife's public visibility and popularity; her fears of upsetting and alienating her parents and potential sponsors if word of her bisexuality leaked out; the monumental changes that were about to reconfigure the sport of tennis. Even without the uncertainty about her sexual orientation, both of them sensed that a conventional marriage would never have worked for them. Larry called it a conscious trade-off in an article cloyingly titled "My wife, Billie Jean by her husband" in the *Ladies' Home Journal* in 1974: "If a couple wants to achieve a great deal, and if they want independent careers, they can't live a typical life. If they'd rather be typical they have to settle for achieving less. Billie Jean and I both like to achieve." They proudly presented themselves as a team—"the all-American boy-girl couple," in Grace Lichtenstein's somewhat catty phrase—and basically said that the exact dimensions of their marriage were nobody's business but their own.[43]

In retrospect Billie Jean and Larry King were bound together in ways so deep and conflicted that they defy conventional understandings. As Larry put it in the early 1970s, "We've loved each other for a long time even though we're not really husband and wife." Billie Jean welcomed the respectability of being married, in effect, using Larry as her beard; Larry watched his career ambitions flourish as the public partner of his superstar wife. In their own version of an open marriage, he looked the other way when she had relationships with women, and she did the same when he had affairs. A divorce would have meant severing myriad business relationships—what Billie Jean called the "two big intersecting circles" of their lives—as well as the complicated personal ones. In the end both concluded that on balance there were benefits to their public charade, even as their personal lives diverged.[44]

And they remained committed to their own idiosyncratic definition of what love and marriage should entail. As Larry later told journalist Selena Roberts, "I was young and naïve, but I was her husband, good, bad, or indifferent, you know, I'd help her with her problems. The bottom line was, I didn't see any reason to get divorced because Billie Jean had identity problems. I felt that even when it all got sorted out, if Billie Jean was going to grow old and gray, she would be much better off growing old and gray with me than with any other person on the planet." Larry clung to that view, and Billie Jean went along, all through the tennis boom of the 1970s, through the public glare of Marilyn Barnett's palimony suit in the early 1980s, until the couple finally divorced in 1987.[45]

WHEN LARRY AND BILLIE JEAN got married in 1965, he still had one more year of school. His senior year he worked nights in an ice cream factory to support his new wife and pay for their expenses, proving to a doubting Bill Moffitt that he was capable of taking care of his daughter. Not having much money seemed perfectly normal to both of them: "When Larry and I were in college and didn't have a dime between us, we used to just sit and talk about our dreams for tennis." Determined to be a good wife, Billie Jean stayed home that fall and winter, but instead of just putting her tennis racket away during the school year, as she had been doing in high school and college, she played tennis every day, thanks to the hospitable southern California climate. While Larry made plans to enroll in law school at Berkeley after his graduation ("Mrs. King will swap racket for recipes," predicted the *Washington Post*), she set her sights on Wimbledon.[46]

Wimbledon always held a special place in the heart of Billie Jean King. As she joked in 1982 when she got to the semifinals at age thirty-eight before losing to Chris Evert, "I'll think about winning Wimbledon when I'm 100."

She loved the traditions, the setting, the knowledgeable patrons, the respect and care for the players, but especially she loved the history: "Every time I walk onto the Centre Court at Wimbledon, I think of all those people who came before me—Suzanne Lenglen, Alice Marble, Helen Wills Moody, Althea Gibson, Maureen Connolly—all those players left me something. I wouldn't play the way I play without them." Continuing the legacy she began in 1961 with her doubles victory, in 1966 Mrs. L. W. King (as she was known at stodgy Wimbledon) beat Brazilian Maria Bueno in three sets to win the singles crown, her first Grand Slam singles title. Finally the coveted number one ranking was hers. The next year she swept all three titles—singles, doubles, and mixed doubles. Larry accompanied her to Wimbledon in 1966 but was miserable, "hanging around like a puppy dog." From then on, he rarely traveled with her to tournaments.[47]

Yet the thrill of those Wimbledon victories was tempered by a lingering sense that it could have been bigger, much bigger. "I played some of my greatest matches in 1966, 1967," King recalled ruefully. "Maybe 1,000 people saw them." Or as she said in 1975, "When I really wanted attention, it wasn't there. When I came back after winning Wimbledon in '66, nobody cared. To be appreciated in my own country was all I wanted, and I got nothing."[48]

It is not totally accurate to say that she got no press coverage: sports reporters continued to file stories about her with the bemused, often belittling stereotypes so prevalent when describing women athletes at the time. For example, in 1966 *Sports Illustrated* called the twenty-three-year-old player who had just won Wimbledon "a bouncy little girl." Especially galling to King were reporters' questions about when she planned to retire, which started when she was in her early twenties. "I finally had won Wimbledon a couple of times, and I'm looking at them like, jeez!" A subtext of the retirement questions was when the "bouncy, 23-year-old Long Beach, Calif. housewife" would settle down and have kids. "Why don't you go ask Rod Laver why he isn't at home?" she would huff in reply, even as she would offer the obligatory statement that of course she and Larry wanted children, but just not now.[49]

At this point in her career, Billie Jean King was all dressed up with nowhere to go. She was ranked number one in her sport, but she wanted more—more recognition, more opportunities, and more money, especially the chance to make a living at what she did best. To do that tennis had to leave its insular, country-club atmosphere and venture out into the mainstream of American sports. As she said in 1967 when she sat for an interview for the women's pages of a newspaper, "That's the trouble with this sport. We've got to get it off the society page and onto the sports pages."[50]

What Billie Jean King was really up against was the vestiges of tennis as a purely amateur sport, a façade (and a lie) that would be challenged and then collapse in 1968, in part because of her advocacy. Arthur Ashe, then the second-ranked American male player, said it best in 1967: "We all deserve Oscars for impersonating amateurs." For years tournament directors and tennis officials had made under-the-table payments to top players to guarantee their participation, which in turn drew the spectators who made the events profitable. While no tennis players were going to get rich under this system, they could more than cover their expenses and have some left over. King herself estimated that in 1967, her last full year as an amateur, she grossed just under $20,000 ("I haggled pretty good and got almost as much as the men"), which sounds like a tidy sum until you remember she had to cover most of her travel and lodging expenses. She was less successful with her long-term nemesis, the USLTA. As she recalled caustically, "The USLTA paid me $196 a week in expenses—half that if I stayed in private houses—so I could help draw crowds that put money into its pot, and where that money went, your guess is as good as mine." No wonder *Life* in 1967 described the "myopic housewife of Berkeley, California," as "the most colorful and outspoken critic of tennis today."[51]

This striving for professional status for tennis, accompanied by a desire to wrest its control from the elite, country-club set, was what initially drove Billie Jean King as a rebel in her sport; the attention to women's issues came later. "It was the hypocrisy of the thing that bugged me the most. I wanted the chance to make money, honest money, doing what I did best. It was that simple." As she said on more than one occasion, "I can't even get a credit card. How can I tell them I've got a job."[52]

Two sportswriters later called the arrival of Open Tennis "the first giant step towards today's all-embracing, big money professionalism." For Billie Jean King the onset of Open Tennis meant signing a contract with the National Tennis League that went into effect on April 1, 1968. She was guaranteed $40,000 a year for two years, and she joined Ann Jones, Françoise Durr, and Rosie Casals as "the only women tennis professionals in the world who actually earned our money by playing." The tour, which also included Ken Rosewall, Roy Emerson, Pancho Gonzales, and Rod Laver, started in Europe and was nothing but a string of one-night stands; King remembered never being so tired in her life. The tour actually folded before her contract ended, and she went back on the regular tennis circuit. Professional tennis wasn't quite ready for prime time yet.[53]

The 1968 Wimbledon was the first major tournament played under the new rules, and both the men's and women's titles were won by professionals. Rod Laver received $4,800 for his victory, while Billie Jean King only got $1,800, about par for the gender gap in prize money at the time. For King, it was her third straight title, which ironically soured her relationship with the British press and public, who loved underdogs but did not warm to repeat winners, especially brash American ones.[54]

And yet all was not well with her tennis career, as King later recalled: "The years from 1968 to 1970 should have been the best tennis years of my career, but because of a lot of things, they turned out to be the worst." She was plagued by knee problems, which kept her in almost constant pain and necessitated surgery and extensive rehabilitation in 1968 and 1970. An added distraction was that when Larry finished his law degree at Berkeley in 1969 they moved to Hawaii, where he hoped to set up his practice. Not that she spent much time there, but she felt totally out of place in the social scene, plus the added travel time to tournaments on the mainland was a real burden. Rumors of a possible divorce circulated widely.[55]

Lurking underneath this personal and professional uncertainty was the nagging realization that in the transition to Open Tennis, the women were—in Larry King's apt description—getting "squeezed out." Having won round one to take the sport professional, women now found out that they had to fight a second battle: to get gender equity for women professionals. This struggle consumed Billie Jean King for the next three years.[56]

The story of the founding of the women's professional tour revolves around the actions of three individuals: the charismatic advocacy of Billie Jean King, the astute professional savvy and contacts of tennis promoter Gladys Heldman, and the financial and marketing support of Joseph P. Cullman, the chief executive officer of Philip Morris. After several years of watching the purses for men's tournaments grow while women's shrank, plus a decline in the number of women's tournaments overall because tennis promoters claimed that nobody would pay to watch women play, the final straw was the Pacific Southwest Open run by Jack Kramer. The tournament, scheduled for September 1970, offered top prize for men of $12,500 and $1,500 for women—a ratio of eight to one. Even more galling, women players were guaranteed no money, not even expenses, unless they made the quarterfinals. Kramer was never known as a friend of women's tennis

(King later threatened to withdraw from the Riggs match if he served as one of the color commentators for the ABC broadcast), and he refused to meet the women's demands for at least one-quarter of the purse. In fact, he probably would have been quite happy to cancel the women's draw and turn all the prize money back to the men.[57]

Tired of being marginalized and treated like second-class citizens, the women players turned to Gladys Heldman, the founder and publisher of *World Tennis* magazine, who quickly put together a women-only tournament in Houston the same week; Joseph Cullman kicked in $2,500 (one third of the $7,500 purse) on behalf of Philip Morris for what was to be called the Houston Virginia Slims Invitational. With great ceremony and more than a little faith, Billie Jean King and eight other women (henceforth known as the "Original Nine"), including Rosemary Casals, Nancy Richey, and Gladys Heldman's daughter Julie, risked expulsion from the USLTA when they signed $1-a-year contracts, a moment immortalized by a photo of them holding dollar bills in the air. Rosie Casals won that first tournament, but the real winner was the cause of women's tennis, which received more media coverage that week than it had the entire previous year.[58]

After the Houston tournament, Larry King and his business partner Dennis Van der Meer proposed that their company, TennisAmerica, be hired to run the women's tour, seemingly oblivious to the potential conflicts of interest since his wife was its main draw. Instead the players stuck with Heldman.[59] By early 1971, Heldman had already arranged fourteen tournaments with combined prize money of $189,000. Because the women's movement was taking off at the same time, the public automatically linked what Gladys Heldman dubbed "women's lob" with women's lib, but feminist ideology was not the driving force behind the women's tour. "It was actually more a matter of survival than ideology," King recalled.[60]

The early years of what came to be known as the Virginia Slims tour suffered from the absence of three of the big names in women's tennis — Margaret Smith Court, Evonne Goolagong, and Chris Evert — who stayed loyal to the USLTA, which had set up its own competing women's tour. (The USLTA acted not out of any sympathy or commitment to the future of women's tennis but rather from fear that they might lose control of the women's side of the game entirely. The National Collegiate Athletic Association took a similar stance toward women's sports in the first decade of Title IX's existence.) Chris Evert was the prize that everyone wanted, because it was clear practically from the start that this talented and photogenic Florida teenager was going to be central to the future of the sport. Billie Jean flew to Florida to meet with the Evert family, but Jimmy Evert, Chris's conservative dad, made the decision that she would not join the Slims tour. As Chris recalled several decades later, "in my defense, at just 16 years old, I wasn't a feminist," adding, "I wasn't burning my bra because I wasn't even wearing one yet."[61]

While many of the women tennis players resented or snubbed this rising star with her two-fisted backhand and icy composure, Billie Jean King went out of her way to befriend her. Having such an attractive and appealing star, especially when television was beginning to discover that tennis could be a profitable addition to its sports menu, was going to help them all, she reasoned. That, however, didn't keep King from wanting to beat the young aspirant. At the U.S. Open in 1971, where the sixteen-year-old had a phenomenal run of victories, Evert and King met in the semifinals. Billie Jean feared that the women's tour would have no credibility if she, its leading moneymaker, couldn't beat this kid, no matter how talented and poised she was. Age and experience triumphed, and King won handily, dispatching Evert back to start her junior year at St. Thomas Aquinas High School in Fort Lauderdale. King went on to beat her doubles partner Rosie Casals in the final and repeated as the U.S. Open champion in 1972.[62]

In the early years of professional tennis, there really wasn't enough money or fan interest to support two competing tours, and in 1973 they agreed to merge into a single organization. One casualty of the merger was the outspoken Gladys Heldman, with whom the USLTA establishment refused to work; having been the facilitator for the revolt, she was forced out just as her vision was paying off. "I was out, but the war was over and that was the most important thing," she recalled graciously as she stepped aside and returned to *World Tennis*. When the tour began in 1971, the minimum purse was set at $10,000; by 1973, the figure was $35,000. The following year after the tours combined, it was $50,000. No one doubted anymore that fans would pay money to see women play. According to King, women tennis players made more gains between 1970 and 1973 than in the entire thirty years before.[63]

Even with Gladys Heldman gone, Virginia Slims stayed, proving a critical, and controversial, ally to the new women's tour. The Virginia Slims slogan—"You've come a long way, baby"—copied and, many believed, demeaned the ideas of modern feminism. In 1975 the *New York Times* noted that at base the rationale behind the women's tour was to promote cigarettes and the slogan "served the purpose perfectly as it identified a commercial product and a woman's sport with women's liberation, a triple-pronged assault that must have seemed irresistible." This didn't bother Billie Jean King one bit, who enthused about the slogan, "I love it. I think it's true. I'm in this (Women's Lib and Lob) whether I like it or not. I just want to play tennis."[64]

This partnership was forged at a moment fraught with uncertainty for the tobacco industry as a whole: the Surgeon General's report linking smoking with cancer had appeared in 1966, and cigarette advertising was banned from television as of January 2, 1971. Nevertheless the tobacco company reaped enormous benefits from this decades-long association, as the Philip Morris marketing manager admitted as early as 1976: "When we started out, we had no idea where we were going. We were doing the women a favor. Our name was carrying tennis. But within a year and a half that all began to change. The sport began to carry the product. We had been instrumental in developing a popular sport and we were benefiting from our association with it." A spokesperson for Virginia Slims put it in even stronger terms in 1983: "We [Virginia Slims] wouldn't be here if it weren't for Billie Jean King."[65]

While King always admitted that it was a "real moral conflict" about whether to accept money from a company whose product was associated with lung cancer, she argued that women's tennis needed the money or "we'd be at the mercy of male officials as we always have been." King justified the support because the company never asked women tennis players to smoke and because cigarettes, however unhealthy, were legal. Weighing the costs and benefits, "I came to realize that Slims was doing us and the sport so much good that I'd have to live with my misgivings. You give a little to accomplish something big." Or as she was quoted in *Sports Illustrated* in 1972: "If I hadn't played—I'll be truthful—there wouldn't have been a circuit. I wasn't about to deprive 80 girls of a living, and I do know people who drink and smoke a lot and also play great tennis." She never wavered in her belief that the tour had made the right choice, even though this association meant that women's tennis—and her name—was forever linked in the public mind with cigarettes. Others have not been as charitable, and lingering criticisms about Virginia Slims' sponsorship dogged the tennis star—rightly—for the rest of her career.[66]

As her pragmatic approach to sponsorship suggested, for Billie Jean King professional tennis was always made up of equal parts business and entertainment. As she told *Sports Illustrated* in 1972, "We're in big business, and until people face reality we'll be dabbling in nonsense forever. . . . If we can get the money, we deserve it." She asked rhetorically, "Do female entertainers get paid less than male entertainers? No. Their pay depends on whether they draw at the box office. Entertainment value, getting people through the turnstiles, that's the name of the game." When critics pointed out that men played three out of five sets while women played two out of three, King would reply, "People don't want to see stamina; they want to see *skill*." (Bud Collins put it another way: "Sometimes a shorter opera is much better than a long one.") Nor did she shy away from exploiting the sex appeal of both male and female players. "I think tennis is a very sexy sport," she said, "and that is good. The players are young, with excellent bodies, clothed in relatively little. It offers the healthiest, most appealing presentation of sex I can imagine, and we in sport must acknowledge that and use it to our advantage."[67]

This emphasis on professionalism runs through Billie Jean King's public statements in the early 1970s much more than feminism. To her mind, a sport was not taken seriously in America if it wasn't professional; if women's tennis—and by extension, women's sports—was going to win the recognition it desired and deserved, it needed a professional basis. Jerry Diamond, an early tennis executive associated with the women's tour, summed up Billie Jean King's vision: "She made it possible for women to earn a living playing tennis. . . . It's as though she invented the NBA or pro football, OK?" When she testified before Congress in 1973 in support of the Women's Educational Equity Act, she noted, "As an amateur, I was saying the same things I am saying to you today, and nobody could care less." She was right.[68]

Billie Jean King was never shy about the importance she placed on money, even though her open pursuit of that goal often dismayed tennis purists. As she told *Life* in 1971, "Money is everything in sports. It made me a star." That was the year that King made $100,000 in earnings, the first woman in sports to reach that pinnacle. (By way of comparison, the average income in 1971 was $10,600, and the average price of a new home was $25,200.) Her feat earned her a somewhat stilted congratulatory phone call from President Richard Nixon, and also, she hoped, the respect of the average sports fan: "'Big money' is the common denominator. The guy in the factory can relate to me. He says, 'If she makes all that much, she *must* be good.'" Some players on the tour, however, resented the money King received, and wondered if her activism wasn't just a way to grab more attention—and cash—for herself. As one player told Grace Lichtenstein,

"Whatever Billie Jean says she's doing for *us*, she's really doing it for herself." Jealousies and resentments aside, without Billie Jean King there probably would not have been a women's tour, and everyone knew it.[69]

Of her nonstop activism on behalf of women's tennis in the 1970s, King later observed, "People thought I was angry. I wasn't. I was determined." In joint pursuit of maintaining her number one ranking and establishing women's tennis on a sound footing, her life became "an endless succession of not only tennis but also public appearances, airport lobbies, interviews, motels, meetings, and dirty laundry." Before every tournament, she would fly into the city, rent a car, and then visit local media outlets to try to drum up publicity for the tournament and for women's tennis in general. Chris Evert remembered playing Billie Jean King in a "sluggish" night game in the early 1970s. "Later I found out she had spent all day in New York for meetings regarding tour sponsorship. She was always one to put the group ahead of her own tennis." Evert added respectfully, "Every sport needs a Billie Jean King."[70]

All this activism took its toll. In her 1974 autobiography, written to capitalize on the Riggs match, King put it this way: "But being Number One was a twenty-four-hour job, and my personality just didn't allow me the luxury of letting up at all, even for a minute." She sounded more tired, and more damaged, when she revisited that period in her 1982 memoir: "I have never been the same since 1972. Those couple years were so intense. I just gave, gave, gave, and afterward there was something that just wasn't there for me to draw on anymore. . . . Making women's sports acceptable, and making women's tennis, particularly, into a legitimate big-league game was a crusade for me and I threw my whole self into it in ways that exhausted me emotionally as much as they did physically."[71]

This headline from the *Washington Post* on February 22, 1972, didn't help: "Abortion Made Possible Mrs. King's Top Year." A year earlier she had gone off birth control pills because of complications; she thought her period was regular enough to be safe, but she miscalculated. (Actually she and Larry spent so little time together that many friends were surprised that he managed to get her pregnant in the first place.) A strong believer in a woman's right to choose and still committed to the possibility of having children in the future, she made the decision to have an abortion in California, with Larry's strong support. In 1967 California had been one of the first states to liberalize its abortion laws by allowing hospital committees to approve so-called therapeutic abortions when pregnancy would affect the physical or mental health of the woman, or in cases of rape or incest, as long as the procedure was performed by a doctor in an accredited hospital. Calling it "the simplest operation I've ever had," King did have two main gripes: the cost ($580, which she thought was outrageous for such a quick procedure) and the fact that her husband, not she, had to give consent for it.[72]

What for her had been a totally private decision that she had shared with only a few friends became a matter of public controversy a year later when she signed a petition that stated, "I have had an abortion. I publicly join millions of other women in demanding a repeal of all laws that restrict our reproductive freedom." Inspired by a public manifesto by 343 prominent French women stating that they had had abortions, a New York feminist named Barbaralee D. Diamonstein enlisted the support of fifty-three prominent women including Gloria Steinem, Judy Collins, Susan Sontag, Nora Ephron, and Billie Jean King to kick off a comparable American campaign. This was an exceptionally courageous act then: women, especially well-known public figures, simply did not talk about abortion, which remained illegal in most states. (*Roe v. Wade* was not decided until January 1973.) The petition appeared in the inaugural issue of *Ms.* magazine, which came out in January 1972. A month later sportswriter Mark Asher asked King about the petition for an article in the *Washington Post* and she hedged, saying she strongly supported the right to abortion and that "whoever has to have the baby is the one who should make the decision." When the article flatly stated that she had had an abortion, it was not quoting her directly, but the damage was done, especially when it was picked up by the wire services. King had never told her parents about the abortion, and they were mortified to learn about it from an article in the *Los Angeles Times*.[73]

And yet what began as a moment of personal courage soon became surrounded by obfuscation. When the story was picked up in *Time* a month later the article repeated King's general support for abortion reform but stated that, despite signing the ad, she had not had an abortion, quoting her as saying, "I wish I'd known more about the ad before I agreed to sign it." Her 1974 autobiography discussed the abortion unapologetically and said Larry had seen the petition in the mail and told her she would probably want to sign it, which she did. "I was almost sure the petition said that we signees were only in favor of legalized abortion, *not* that we'd had abortions ourselves," she asserted then. Her 1982 autobiography did not mention the petition, only the criticism she received for having an abortion. But in an HBO documentary in 2006 and a recent book by Selena Roberts, Billie

Jean King claimed she never saw the letter and that Larry signed her name without telling her, which certainly puts a very different spin on it. There is enough evidence from the time to dispute that retrospective assertion, but the shifting story—and blame—is yet another example of Billie Jean King's tendency to put expediency ahead of principle when it came to her public image.[74]

Not all the publicity she received in 1972 was so painful. That September she won her third U.S. Open title. In December she and UCLA coach John Wooden were named Sportsman and Sportswoman of the Year by *Sports Illustrated*, the first time a woman had been honored. Showing her tendency to assume that what was good for Billie Jean King was good for everyone else, she saw it as "a three-way triumph: for me, for women's tennis, and for women everywhere."[75] Soon after the division between the Virginia Slims tour and the USLTA-backed tour was healed, and all the top women players were competing in the same tournaments. And in 1973, a truly stunning turn of events: the U.S. Open became the first major tournament to award equal prize money to men and women. The fact that Wimbledon did not meet that standard until 2007 confirms what a far-sighted breakthrough for equality it was.[76]

There was one final item on Billie Jean King's activist agenda: the establishment of a players' union. As far back as 1964 King had tried to organize an informal "strike" by women players over the unequal under-the-table payments they received, but no one else wanted to rock the boat. The need for an organization to stand up for women's interests and speak in a unified voice seemed like a no-brainer to King, even if her fellow athletes didn't yet see it that way: "So often, athletes look everywhere else for the answer to their problems but to themselves. Yet they're the people who are unhappy with the status quo! Athletes have to be convinced that it's in their self-interest to set up and control their own organizations." King made her final push at Wimbledon in June of 1973, when she invited all the women professionals to the Hotel Gloucester and then had one player lock the door until they agreed to form the Women's Tennis Association (WTA). In addition to her success as a labor organizer that June, King also won a coveted Wimbledon triple—singles, doubles, and mixed doubles championships.[77]

This frenzied, twenty-four-hours-a-day lifestyle provides the context for the Battle of the Sexes match with Bobby Riggs: it was yet another commitment on an already overcrowded athletic and professional agenda. The match was officially announced to the press in July, with the requisite media event in New York City to start the publicity juggernaut in motion. For the rest of the summer, King kept up her commitments on the women's professional tour, knowing that if she bailed from any of the tournaments, she would leave the organizers in the lurch. She was also struggling with injuries and medical problems, including a bout of hypoglycemia. At the U.S. Open in early September, she defaulted to Julie Heldman, raising concerns about her physical condition. But when the night of the Riggs match finally arrived three weeks later, she was as ready as she ever would be, and her preparation showed. After her victory, journalist Grace Lichtenstein proclaimed her a "national folk heroine — an athletic Eleanor Roosevelt."[78]

THE BATTLE OF THE SEXES cemented Billie Jean King's stature as America's first female sports superstar. King loved her role as the self-described "mother of modern sports" because it gave her the platform to "make social change" at the same time it provided the basis for her successful professional career as a tennis star and women's sports advocate. She also craved the public adulation that celebrity brings. She often paraphrased Bill Bradley's description of playing basketball before an adoring crowd, "I just want to go out there and eat up all those love vibes." Using her celebrity and fame as a bully pulpit to bring her feminist-tinged brand of tennis to a wide national audience, she became one of the most well-known athletes of her time.[79]

American history is full of iconic sports heroes, but until Billie Jean King they were almost exclusively men. Sportswriters and pundits have long debated what elevates a journeyman athlete into an icon, and there seem to be no general rules, except that in each case the athlete comes to stand for something more than just himself and his individual sport. Legendary sports heroes such as Babe Ruth, Knute Rockne, Jack Dempsey, Mickey Mantle, and Jackie Robinson were very much of their times yet also somehow transcended them. These heroes loomed large in the nation's consciousness, embodying American ideals of hard work and fair play, upward mobility through sports, and the physical grace and perfection of athletic performance. Of course the unsullied public reputations of some of these heroes, so "Godded up" by adoring sportswriters that they seemed almost superhuman, rarely matched their often tawdry off-field lives, but the public showed no thirst for such details. In earlier and less intrusive times, such inconvenient facts were considered strictly off limits.[80]

For most of the twentieth century there was no way for a woman to win the kind of celebrity status that male sports heroes held. Sport was like a boys' tree house with a "No Girls Allowed" sign posted outside: women athletes were shut out from the popular professional and amateur sports that built the careers of sports legends in the first place. To be sure, some female athletes enjoyed a certain notoriety, even fame, at the height of their careers: Gertrude Ederle was lionized in 1926 after she swam the English Channel; Helen Wills Moody and Suzanne Lenglen won renown in tennis in the 1920s and 1930s. Babe Didrikson Zaharias, one of the best all-around athletes of all time, won three track and field medals at the 1932 Olympics and later dominated the women's professional golf tour until her premature death in 1956. But Americans at midcentury weren't ready to embrace a talented female athlete, even one named Babe, with the same degree of idolatry accorded to the legends of baseball, football, and boxing.[81]

Starting in the 1930s and 1940s, black athletes provided a new kind of sports idol more connected to the social and political issues of the day. Like women's sports, black athleticism had a long and rich history, but it mainly played out in segregated venues out of sight of mainstream America. When an African American athlete entered the white realm of organized sport, that moment was necessarily packed with meaning. For example, Joe Louis's victory over German Max Schmeling in 1938 was widely interpreted as a blow to Hitler's theories of racial superiority.[82]

Without Joe Louis there probably would have been no Jackie Robinson, and no integration of Major League Baseball in 1947. Seven years before the Supreme Court outlawed segregation in Brown v. Board of Education, Robinson entered the vanguard of the civil rights revolution when he broke the color line with the Brooklyn Dodgers. Showing how sport can indirectly influence politics and society, sportswriter Roger Kahn observed, "By applauding Robinson a man did not feel that he was taking a stand on school integration or on open housing. But for an instant he had accepted Robinson simply as a hometown ball player. To disregard color, even for an instant, is to step away from old prejudices, the old hatred. That is not a path on which many double back."[83]

Both Joe Louis and Jackie Robinson were referred to, somewhat patronizingly, as "credits to their race." By the 1970s conditions were finally ripe for a female athletic superstar such as Billie Jean King to emerge as a "credit to her sex." Unlike Babe Didrikson Zaharias just fifteen years earlier, or Althea Gibson, who broke the color line in tennis when she won back-to-back Wimbledon and U.S. Open titles in 1957 and 1958, Billie Jean King was the beneficiary of a fortuitous set of circumstances, starting with the fact that tennis was ready to burst into a new level of popular acceptance and thus provide a professional vehicle to sustain her career and build celebrity recognition. Simultaneously the women's movement and the passage of Title IX put questions of feminism and women's sports squarely on the national agenda, which in turn maximized interest in women's sports and created a mass base ready to embrace a female superstar.

Once again timing is everything, and Billie Jean King was never shy about seizing the moment. In 1978 sportswriter Robert Lipsyte put the tennis star in a category with Joe Namath and Muhammad Ali as celebrity athletes "whose impact on the nation's psyche was as deep and significant as their effect on the games they played." In addition to their prowess in their chosen sports, all three had something more: "Call it magnetism or sex appeal or charisma, it allowed people to use them as extensions of their hopes and daydreams as living symbols of the ultimate."[84] Nowhere was this more in evidence than the Battle of the Sexes.

As a popular sports superstar, Billie Jean King quickly moved beyond just tennis to become a symbol for something even bigger: women's rights and women's changing roles in society. Sportswriter Frank Deford, who wrote some of the most probing early profiles of her and later collaborated on her autobiography, predicted in 1975 that she would be the most significant athlete of the twentieth century, more so even than Muhammad Ali. Unlike civil rights "firsts," "hers is a deeper and wider legacy: she has prominently affected the way 50% of society thinks and feels about itself in the vast area of physical exercise." He then put his finger on why individuals like King were so important to the larger process of social change: "Still, the fact remains that in the modern United States, in the modern world, the promulgation and acceptance of sharp new attitudes—what are called *movements* or *trends*—utterly depend on the emergence of a personality to embody the philosophy. . . . When was the last time you saw two minutes of an *idea* on the six o'clock news?" Like her friend Gloria Steinem, a media superstar who personified the goals of second-wave feminism for the country as a whole, Billie Jean King personified the women's sports revolution in popular culture. In turn, her talent for keeping herself in the public eye allowed her to weather the critical transition for any athlete when playing days are over and retirement looms.[85]

In 1975 Billie Jean King won her sixth (and final) Wimbledon singles title, crushing Evonne Goolagong Cawley 6-0, 6-1, and promptly announced her retirement, calling herself "the most fortunate woman athlete who ever lived up to this time." Thirty-one years old, she was just plain tired—tired of keeping the tour going, tired of the travel, tired of the politics. Plus she needed another round of surgery on one of her knees. "Now I can have beer and ice cream," she gleefully told the press.[86]

Not surprisingly, the retirement did not stick. The next year she was back on the tour. "Retiring was the best thing I ever did," she said, "because I learned that I didn't want to be retired. I drank my beer and I ate my ice cream, and I saw myself getting soft and fat and said, 'Hey, that's not me.'" After considering other career options and opportunities, she realized that what she really loved best was playing tennis. And she felt she could still be competitive even as she aged: "I still had the ability. And I missed the game. As you get older, you acquire a different perspective. You realize the joy and love of what you do. It's like a Horowitz playing the piano, or a Nureyev dancing. You keep remembering how much you like it." To naysayers who questioned why she was still playing at the then-ancient age of thirty-six, she replied: "People forget that I didn't have these opportunities until I was past 25. I know what I've got. I know it's a privilege to be here. Tennis is what made me. Why should I leave it if I can play at a level that makes me happy?" Validation of that outlook came at Wimbledon in 1979 when she eclipsed the record previously held by the venerable English player Elizabeth Ryan and won her twentieth title paired with Martina Navratilova in women's doubles. She finished her career with thirty-nine Grand Slam titles overall.[87]

Billie Jean King used to joke that she could get high just by hitting a backhand. She took physical as well as emotional pleasure from the game: "Sometimes I go up for an aggressive volley and really smash it, and I find myself thinking, 'How unladylike—but how great it feels.' Any kind of experience that is so close to perfection can't be bad, can it?" For her, tennis was "a medium of self-expression": "I love that the ball doesn't come over the net twice in the same way in a lifetime and that I'm always in the process of finding new solutions." As her active playing days on the women's tournament were drawing to a close, Billie Jean King could draw satisfaction from what she had accomplished in the 1960s and 1970s for women's tennis and for women in general. Luckily after 1972 it was not up to her alone to fight the good fight where women in sports were concerned, thanks to "two funky little Roman numerals" called Title IX.[88]

Thirty years after the Bobby Riggs match, Billie Jean King dramatically recalled her feelings about its larger historical significance for reporter Selena Roberts. "My job in the match, and I remember this being very clear, was to change the hearts and minds of people to match the legislation of Title IX and what we were trying to do with the women's movement. It was to validate it, to celebrate it, and to get going toward changing a world where we had equality for both genders." King had voiced similar sentiments on the twenty-fifth anniversary of the match in 1998: "Title IX had just passed, and I would see people [looking] for an excuse to backtrack. I wanted to change the hearts and minds of people to match the legislation we had just gotten in place." Recently she upped the ante by claiming that she had helped get Title IX passed in the first place.[1]

Billie Jean King's memory is playing tricks on her. Without challenging the larger significance of the match for either the emerging feminist movement or the struggle for gender equity in sports, a more historically grounded look at the early days of Title IX suggests that public awareness of the law in general and its impact on women's sports in particular was not necessarily as widespread in the fall of 1973 as her retrospective memories claimed. Passed without fanfare a little more than a year earlier, Title IX was never mentioned by name in all the voluminous coverage the match received. When Billie beat Bobby, she wasn't carrying the banner for Title IX precisely because the law was not yet associated with women's sports in the popular mind. That changed soon after, in part because of her role in raising the nation's consciousness where women's sports were concerned. Just as important an influence on the early days of Title IX were the actions of a small band of Washington insiders—bureaucrats, activists, and lobbyists—who gradually realized that this little-noticed general education law would have its most profound impact on an area no one had anticipated: sports.

Even if Billie Jean King exaggerated her role in the passage of Title IX, she always grasped its larger significance: "Oh, my God, it's the third most important piece of legislation in the 20th century. There was the vote, civil rights in the '60s, and Title IX in the '70s." The events leading up to Title IX's passage in 1972, and the struggle ever since to figure out how to implement the law fairly, demonstrate how athletics became part of the broader political and cultural struggles of contemporary American life. Title IX also provides a textbook case of the difficulties—and the rewards—of putting abstract principles of liberal feminism such as equal opportunity and gender equity into concrete, everyday practice. From the start the law sparked high expectations as well as conflict and ambiguity, which continue to this day. So too does the revolution in women's sports that Title IX helped to set in motion.[2]

THE LEGISLATION THAT Congresswoman Edith Green correctly predicted would be "the most revolutionary thing in higher education in the 1970s" had its roots in the civil rights legislation of the 1960s. Title IX was modeled directly on Title VI of the Civil Rights Act of 1964, which prohibited discrimination against the beneficiaries of programs receiving federal money on the basis of race, color, and national origin, but not sex. The better known Title VII outlawed discrimination in employment on the basis of race, color, national origin, and sex. As the story is often told, the sex provision had been added by Howard Smith, a conservative Southern representative, who hoped to undercut support for federal civil rights legislation with what he saw as a frivolous amendment. Women members of Congress such as Representative Martha Griffiths of Michigan did not see the issue of sex discrimination as frivolous at all and had been planning to introduce their own amendment to make sure it was covered in the law. For both the right and wrong reasons, it passed, giving women an important legal tool to fight sex discrimination in employment.[3]

Unfortunately neither Title VI nor Title VII covered sex discrimination in educational institutions, a gap Title IX would be designed to plug. In the meantime, a budding feminist activist named Bernice Resnick Sandler found a creative way to extend federal oversight into higher education. In 1965 President Lyndon Johnson had signed Executive Order 11246, which forbid discrimination on the basis of race in employment practices by federal contractors and mandated affirmative action plans to address past discrimination; in 1967 this executive order was amended to include sex discrimination. While researching federal antidiscrimination laws in 1969, Sandler noticed a footnote about this amendment and the proverbial light bulb went off in her head. "Even though I was alone," she recalled, "I shrieked aloud with my discovery: I had made the connection that since most universities and colleges had federal contracts they were forbidden from discriminating in employment on the basis of sex." When she contacted the director of the Office of Federal Contract Compliance in the Department of Labor, he confirmed her interpretation.[4]

It is impossible to tell the story of the passage of Title IX without giving Bunny (as she is universally known) Sandler a starring role as the "godmother of Title IX." Sandler's personal introduction to sex discrimination came in 1969 when, having finished her doctorate at the University of Maryland, she was not considered for a full-time position in the department where she was already teaching because, as a colleague told her, "Let's face it. You come on too strong for a woman." To her surprise and chagrin, no laws prohibited sex discrimination in education, that is, until she made the connection between Johnson's executive order and university contracts. Based on her discovery, the Women's Equity Action League (WEAL) filed a class action complaint in January 1970 against all the colleges and universities in the country, and the University of Maryland in particular, charging "an industry-wide pattern" of discrimination against women, especially in admissions, hiring, promotions, and salary discrepancies. The material she collected in support of the suit, especially the documentation of employment discrimination on campus, circulated widely, thanks to a Xerox machine made available by an ally at the Ford Foundation. (At the time most information circulated in mimeographed form; a fancy Xerox machine was a real luxury for most organizations.) Meanwhile activists pressed the Departments of Labor and Health, Education and Welfare to enforce the regulation.[5]

It is useful to pause to remember how new the topic of sex discrimination was in 1970, especially in education. The words had just entered the lexicon with the Civil Rights Act of 1964; phrases like sexism and sexual harassment were not even in common usage. Many of the things we would today call sex discrimination, such as women needing higher grades and test scores for admittance to colleges or professional schools arbitrarily capping the percentage of women, were simply accepted as the way things were. In fact, Bunny Sandler observed, "The issue of sex discrimination in education was so new that I received many letters from women and men asking me if it was true that such discrimination existed, and if so, could I send them proof."[6]

Representative Edith Green, a Republican member of Congress from Oregon, was one who took note. A leading education specialist and, not coincidentally, a member of WEAL, Green was planning to hold Congressional hearings on this topic; Sandler helped her compile a list of witnesses for the legislation Green planned to introduce. In June and July of 1970 Green held seven days of hearings on the barriers that women faced in higher education and then hired Sandler to edit the written record of the hearings. The resulting two-volume, 1,300-page document, which included both testimony and supporting material, provided convincing refutation of the view commonly held, especially by leaders in higher education, that there was no discrimination in education, or that if there was, it wasn't really a problem. Showing the political savvy of the emerging feminist network in Washington, D.C., Edith Green received permission to reprint 6,000 copies of the report, and Sandler helped her distribute them to educational leaders and the press, as well as each member of Congress. As Sandler concluded, "The hearings probably did more than anything else to make sex discrimination in education a legitimate issue."[7]

The 1970 hearings set in motion a chain of legislative events that culminated two years later in the passage of Title IX. While Green's original plan had been to amend the Civil Rights Act of 1964 to cover education, she realized such a strategy might expose the still-new law to other, potentially crippling amendments, so she concentrated instead on developing separate legislation to accomplish her purpose. In the spring and summer of 1971, she held another round of Congressional hearings. Green's draft legislation was one of several bills introduced in the House. Around the same time, Senator Birch Bayh of Indiana, a good friend of the emerging women's movement and a strong supporter of the Equal Rights Amendment then under consideration, drafted similar legislation in the Senate. As the bills worked their way through the legislative process, private colleges and universities lobbied successfully to exempt undergraduate admissions from coverage. Another exemption covered military schools and the service academies; a third allowed private men's and women's colleges to remain single-sex if they chose.[8]

As the final bill neared passage in the spring of 1972, Sandler and other representatives of women's groups in Washington offered to lobby on its behalf, but Representative Green warned them off, reminding them that "the less that people knew about the bill, the better its chances were for passage." But it is wrong to imply that the provision on sex discrimination only slipped through because no one knew it was there. The *Chronicle of Higher Education* had taken note of the topic as early as July 1970,[9] and in August of 1971 the *New York Times* weighed in editorially against the inclusion of the sex discrimination provision, calling its potential impact, especially on admissions policies, "educationally unsound."[10] Still, in 1972 Title IX was seen as a fairly minor bill, one of Edith Green's pet projects, certainly lacking the historical gravitas of the civil rights legislation of the 1960s. That view would soon change, thanks to athletics.

The National Collegiate Athletic Association (NCAA) later tried to claim that Congress had not intended to include athletics under Title IX's coverage, but the record lacks any sustained discussion of the subject.[11] Senator Bayh provided one of the few references during floor debate on August 6, 1971, when he said: "I do not read this as requiring integration of dormitories between the sexes, nor do I feel it mandates the desegregation of football fields. What we are trying to do is provide equal access for women and men students to the educational process and the extracurricular activities in a school, where there is not a unique facet such as football involved. We are not requiring that intercollegiate football be desegregated, nor that the men's locker room be desegregated." On the occasion of the thirtieth anniversary of the passage of the law, Representative Patsy Mink, who considered Title IX to be "one of my most significant efforts as a member of Congress," reminded readers of the *Congressional Record* that athletics was not part of the original discussion. "Our primary goal was to open up educational opportunities for girls and women in academics," adding that the most controversial issue at the time was the application of Title IX to admission policies.[12]

After the final differences were ironed out in a Senate-House conference committee, the Education Amendments Act containing Title IX was approved by the Congress on June 8, 1972, and signed by President Nixon on June 23. In addition to the sex discrimination provision, the $19 billion bill offered aid to community colleges and career education programs and initiated a student grant program for low- and middle-income students known as Pell Grants. Ironically, Edith Green voted against the very law that she had worked so hard to craft, disagreeing with a provision on the distribution of student aid. The passage of Title IX was not the only event in Washington that month that would have major historical consequences. In a further irony, Nixon signed the bill just one week after the burglary in the Watergate complex that would end his presidency two years later.[13]

The key provision of Title IX is a mere thirty-seven words long: "No person in the United States shall, on the basis of sex, be excluded from participation in, be denied the benefits of, or be subjected to discrimination under any education program or activity receiving Federal financial assistance."[14] Title IX applies to every aspect of education throughout an institution, not just a specific program receiving federal funds; while it is now associated almost entirely with the issue of athletics, its scope also includes admissions, counseling, course offerings, financial aid and scholarships, facilities and housing, health and insurance benefits, and discrimination based on marital or parental status. The penalty for noncompliance is the potential cut-off of all federal funds.[15]

Like many laws, Title IX's mandate was left deliberately broad, in part because if lawmakers had made it more specific, it likely would have lost the consensus of support necessary for passage. Bunny Sandler is convinced that many politicians voted for the bill because they were thinking, "Oh, this is nice for the ladies. Let's do that for them," without fully thinking through the implications of what they were supporting.[16] Bella Abzug, who won election to Congress in 1970, seconded this view: "We put sex discrimination provisions into everything. There was no opposition. Who'd be against equal rights for women? So we just kept passing women's rights legislation."[17]

Given that athletics would become the "catalyst" that "pulled the other issues with it," even though sports had hardly been mentioned in the legislative history, it is important to reconstruct as fully as possible how and when this transformation took place. Borrowing an analogy from the Senate Watergate hearings, which were unfolding as the Department of Health, Education and Welfare (HEW) struggled to determine the parameters of Title IX, Senator Howard Baker famously asked, "What did the President know and when did he know it?" A similar question can be asked about athletics: when did it dawn on people that Title IX would apply to physical education and athletics? More broadly, when did it become clear that Title IX had the potential to radically challenge the status quo of how schools structured and funded their athletic programs? Unlike Watergate, there is no conspiracy or smoking gun here, just a group of actors inside and outside the government following the implications of this wide-ranging law to its logical conclusion: that some of the most glaring inequities in higher education were in the area of athletics and that legally they must be addressed.[18]

Because of the complexity of the issues and the controversies that surfaced, it would be two years—not until June 1974—before draft regulations were published, and another year—not until July 1975—before they were officially approved. The lack of regulations meant that there was basically no enforcement on the part of the federal government for the critical first three years of the law's existence, since HEW took the stand that it could not enforce the law until the regulations were written and approved. Note, however, that the law itself was in force as of July 1, 1972, and during this interim period complaints were filed with HEW and lawsuits initiated based on the law.[19]

At first officials at HEW seemed to be moving forward with all deliberate speed. In late July, J. Stanley Pottinger, head of its Office for Civil Rights (OCR), wrote to representatives of various education advocacy groups inviting them to informational meetings about Title IX the following week. The idea was to consult with them before regulations and administrative decisions were finalized and keep them apprised of major issues and problems. Margaret Dunkle, recently hired by Sandler to be her assistant at the Project on the Status and Education of Women at the Association of American Colleges, attended the August 4, 1972, informational meeting. According to Dunkle's notes (and she took very good notes), athletics was not prominently mentioned at the meeting. But it must have come up in passing, because less than a week later she was back in touch with the OCR with more information about the issue. Sharing examples of how interest in women's athletics was already on the rise, she pointed out that women activists were concerned that any "separate but equal" facilities be truly equal and asked that "special care should be taken to assure that any policy be sex-neutral both on its face and in practice."[20]

Margaret Dunkle's involvement in concerns regarding athletics so soon after Title IX's passage confirms that the issue was there from the start. What is missing is any foreboding of what a hot-ticket topic it would become. While it seems to have occurred to a few people (Bunny Sandler estimated no more than ten) that athletics would be covered, no one yet grasped Title IX's potentially revolutionary impact. While sex discrimination in education was generally invisible, discrimination in sports was simply not on the radar. Even Sandler, who was in the thick of events, remembers thinking only that the law might mean a few more activities for girls at annual school field days. As she later commented, "If those of us close to Title IX did not fully realize its impact, especially on sports, how could others have known what it would be?"[21]

In October 1972, HEW attorney Gwen Gregory began to grapple with how to apply Title IX to athletics. Like so many others before and after, she began by seeing if it was possible to use the integration model developed for civil rights for the seemingly parallel issue of discrimination in sports. She quickly discarded that approach. (See chapter 5 for the implications of this lost moment.) Since women cannot "compete as a class with men," they "would not be treated equally if forced to compete equally." In other words, just opening all men's teams to women—the equivalent of integration—would mean little since only the most exceptional female athlete would be able to qualify for a men's team.[22]

Was the alternative, then, "separate but equal" teams for men and women? This concept was anathema to many activists because "separate but equal" was precisely the practice that civil rights legislation was designed to overturn. If separate could never be equal when it came to race, why would it be any different for women in sports? And yet women's sports were at such an embryonic stage of development that practically no one could envision a playing field where women and men competed equally. This conundrum, which of course is the puzzle of modern feminism—how to provide equal opportunity for women while also recognizing their differences from men—made the process of writing regulations for athletics extremely challenging, even before male athletic leaders entered the picture claiming that equal participation opportunities for female athletes would bankrupt the existing system.

One way to simplify the sports question just a bit was to distinguish physical education classes, intramurals, and recreational activities from competitive athletic programs. Here HEW adopted the approach known as formal equality that it applied to the rest of Title IX and education: "men and women should be treated alike if they are similarly situated for purposes of the policy or practice that is being challenged." With the exception of sex education classes (which were traditionally an uneasy part of the physical education program), instructional gym classes and other recreational opportunities would no longer be strictly segregated by sex. Even this amount of athletic integration was controversial, however, especially among female physical education leaders who worried about girls being injured or bullied by rough boys in coeducational activities. These gym teachers also worried about losing their jobs as programs were combined, a valid fear, as it turned out. While there were always some parents and administrators who did not like the idea of coed gym classes, this has in fact become the norm as a result of Title IX.[23]

The question of competitive athletics was trickier. In an October 1972 memo to her boss, Gregory proposed a general statement to cover the field: "As it appears that women cannot compete as a class with men in most athletics, such activities should be provided separately for men and women in most cases. However, if it can be shown by an institution that women are not limited by their physical ability from a particular sport, then and in that event, such institution may conduct the sport on a coeducational basis." Pottinger agreed, provided there were some references to specific areas of equal treatment, such as incentives to participate, budgets proportionate to numbers on teams, equal access to facilities and support services, and athletic scholarships for both men and women.[24]

In general terms, therefore, several months after the law's passage, HEW had moved quickly toward staking out a stance on how Title IX would apply to athletics that was not too different from the final regulations: make physical education instruction coeducational, but in most cases keep competitive athletics teams separate for men and women accompanied by a commitment to more equitable access to opportunities and resources. But these tentative formulations remained strictly in-house, and therefore of no help at all to schools and institutions trying to figure out how the law applied to them.

An early (perhaps the first) mention in a general circulation magazine that Title IX might apply to athletics appeared in October 1972 in *Ms.* magazine, which had debuted the previous winter. Under the header "How to Make Trouble: It's Time for Equal Education," NOW's legislative vice president, Ann Scott (who probably had attended one of the informational meetings at HEW in August), proposed an affirmative action plan to implement Title IX in schools and on campuses that included a section on athletics. Under areas for review, she highlighted whether women were being denied the opportunity to participate in certain sports; what the per capita expenditures were per sex; and whether women received athletic scholarships. Noting that "legislation lives or dies by how it is enforced," Scott urged readers to contact HEW's Office for Civil Rights and members of Congress about holding educational institutions accountable to the intent of Title IX.[25]

Then the forward momentum stopped. Regulations were said to be forthcoming, but the waiting stretched to months and eventually years. Anne Grant, coordinator of NOW's Education Task Force, told Margaret Dunkle in January 1973 that she had heard Pottinger was holding back on Title IX guidelines "because he wants to water-down athletic guidelines." In February, Bunny Sandler updated Columbia law professor Ruth Bader Ginsburg that regulations were expected in March, which she said meant "April, May, June. . . ."[26] In April, Dunkle, who was by now spending much of her time at the Project on the Status and Education of Women on the sports issue, reported to Bunny Sandler about an off-the-record meeting where she learned that the regulations would not be out until June, which she said meant September. As Dunkle said later that month in a speech to the American Association of Health, Physical Education and Recreation, "Perhaps all women athletes should be mountain climbers because the plight of women in sports programs is clearly an uphill struggle."[27]

An important milestone in public awareness about discrimination in sport was a three-part *Sports Illustrated* series by Bil Gilbert and Nancy Williamson called "Sport is Unfair to Women" that appeared in May and June 1973, four months before the Billie Jean King–Bobby Riggs match. Gilbert had gotten interested in the subject as the father of three athletically inclined daughters; faced with limited options in his community, he helped start an Amateur Athletic Union (AAU) track club for girls, which he had profiled in an earlier feature for the magazine. When he pitched the idea for a series on women and sport to a magazine not noted, then or now, for its coverage of women, "Editorial authorities were dubious to say the least," he later recalled, but they finally gave him and his coauthor the go-ahead. The first article opened with this forthright—and often quoted—statement: "There may be worse (more socially serious) forms of prejudice in the United States, but there is no sharper example of discrimination today than that which operates against girls and women who take part in competitive sports, wish to take part, or might wish to if society did not scorn such endeavors." One long-distance runner said opportunities were so limited that "most of us feel that being second-class citizens would be a great advance."[28]

Originally Gilbert did not think Title IX would have a lot to do with the story, but the final article mentioned it prominently, quoting Gwen Gregory as saying that guidelines would be issued by July 1973 (another deadline missed) and even giving the address of HEW to file complaints. Appearing in the most popular sports magazine in the country, the series documented the gross disparities between men's and women's athletic programs across the country and helped to begin to spread the word that a new federal law mandated equitable treatment in athletics.[29]

By this point male athletic leaders and the National Collegiate Athletic Association had gotten wind that the draft regulations were going to cover athletics. Why had it taken so long? Since athletics programs did not receive federal funding, it simply had not occurred to many people that they would be included. Unlike the coverage of the events leading up to the passage of the original law, there had been very little public discussion in the *New York Times*, the *Washington Post*, or the *Chronicle of Higher Education* as the drafting process went forward in the second half of 1972 and into the first half of 1973. The first mention of athletics being covered did not appear in the *Chronicle* until November 1973.[30]

Billie Jean King became a public player in the Title IX story around this time. Much in demand after her successful demolition of Bobby Riggs in September, King put her sports celebrity to good use on Capitol Hill when she testified before the Senate Subcommittee on Education on November 9, 1973. This appearance is probably what she remembered when she claimed to have lobbied for Title IX, but she actually spoke in favor of the Women's Educational Equity Act of 1973 (WEEA), a bill sponsored by Senator Walter Mondale and Representative Patsy Mink. The legislation authorized grants to administrators and institutions to develop nonsexist curricula, personnel training programs, and vocational and career counseling, as well as to expand and improve physical education programs for women. In other words, the WEEA was designed to fund projects that would implement the general goals of Title IX. Either way, King was a big hit, still fresh from what she jokingly described to the awe-struck senators as "that match against Roberta Riggs the other day."[31]

Billie Jean King's testimony spoke less to the arcane details of the bill than to the general stereotypes and problems that women faced in sports. For example, she recalled "one morning at the breakfast table asking my father what a good sport would be for a woman, and right there now that I reflect back, I realized I was already a product of the conditioning that goes on." She spoke out against the tiny budgets allocated to women's sports, questioning why the benefits of sports were basically denied to half the population—the female half. "By the time a girl reaches high school or college she is often well programmed to think of sports as extraneous," she said in her prepared remarks, before adding spontaneously, "There are so many women who have potential to be athletically inclined, and they are just afraid, but if through these educational programs, if you do fund athletic programs and girls find out it is fun, they find out that they are accepted, in fact they are looked up to, this will change everything." The Women's Educational Equity Act did not pass until August 1974, but Billie Jean King's testimony certainly brought welcome attention to the issue as well as confirmation of the momentum building around women's sports.[32]

Title IX really burst onto the national scene in early 1974, when the NCAA launched a tremendous lobbying campaign against what it identified as a grave threat to the status quo in college athletics. Up until that point, it had been mainly women's groups and education advocacy organizations advising HEW on the implementation of what was seen primarily as an education bill; now the NCAA aggressively inserted its point of view into the debate. The first six months of 1974, therefore, were when Title IX stopped being a general education law known mainly to Washington insiders and began to build a national reputation, pro and con, as "the sports law."

The National Collegiate Athletic Association, established in 1905, had long been the dominant organization in intercollegiate athletics, administering programs and organizing national championships for its member institutions, and, starting in the 1950s, transforming itself into an economic powerhouse through its tight control of television rights to college sports, especially football. For all intents and purposes, it could have been called the National Collegiate Men's Athletic Association, since by custom and (as of 1964) explicit rule, it confined its attention to male student athletes. Women's collegiate sports in turn were tightly controlled by physical education leaders who downplayed competition and promoted a vision of participation and play instead of elite varsity competition.[33]

Starting in the 1960s and intensifying in the early 1970s, the NCAA began to get nervous that it might be exposing itself to legal challenges because it offered no opportunities for women to participate in intercollegiate athletics. Yet when the issue of women's athletics was raised at the January 1972 NCAA convention, there was general agreement that women's sports were beyond the realm of the group. Women's athletic leaders in the Association for Intercollegiate Athletics for Women (AIAW), a newly constituted governance structure, agreed with that position, more than willing to be left alone to run their programs wholly apart from what they viewed as the NCAA's corrupt model of sports. This dual structure thus suited the interests of both male and female athletic leaders: the women could have their programs and, most importantly, their autonomy, and the men could have theirs too, albeit on a much larger, more prestigious, and definitely more commercial basis. Title IX—as well as broader developments in sport and society—threatened to upset this fragile division of labor.[34]

From the start, football loomed over all Title IX discussions. "The problem is that you're thinking in terms of equality for men and women," a Title IX opponent once told attorney Margot Polivy. "Well, I'm all in favor of equality for men and women but it's not just men and women, there's men and women and football players."[35] Because of football's high costs and huge rosters (upward of eighty-five scholarships, plus as many as fifty additional walk-on players), it was usually the biggest item in a school's athletic budget, far overshadowing the spending on all other men's sports and the tiny women's programs. Football programs enjoyed such a mystique in local communities and on college campuses, as well as with alums, that they were practically sacrosanct.[36]

Football's seeming invincibility was also aided by the myth that football's gate receipts and revenues paid for the rest of a school's athletic program. This myth was not backed up by facts then or now. For example, analysis of NCAA figures from the 1970s showed that fewer than one in five varsity football programs generated revenue at least equal to operating expenses. If schools were forced to dramatically expand participation opportunities for girls and women, critics asked, where would that money come from without hurting men's programs, especially football? Money and control fueled the Title IX debate, although there was also an undercurrent of hubris from the male athletic establishment that they "owned" sports and considered women as nothing more than unwelcome interlopers in their exclusive domain. In any case, changing business as usual where sports were concerned was not going to be easy.[37]

In early February 1974 an Associated Press story quoted Peter Holmes, the new director of the Office for Civil Rights, as saying that the federal government expected to issue regulations soon (yet another delay) that would help ensure "that women have an equal opportunity to participate in competitive athletics." Showing how the media often trivialized the tenets of modern feminism, the *Washington Post* headline read, "Federal Rules Will Give 'Em a Break, Ma'am." *Sports Illustrated*'s "Scorecard" feature on the story warned that the guidelines might "emasculate college sport" by requiring "equity between men's and women's activities" and singled out proposed measures such as equal pay for coaches and equal access to scholarships as especially "extreme." Then *Sports Illustrated* gave a telling example of the other extreme that prompted such legislative scrutiny in the first place: with a multimillion dollar budget for men's sports, the University of Oklahoma was willing to make only an additional $1,500 available for women's sports for the spring term. Repeatedly in the debate over Title IX, media coverage designed to support the status quo in men's sports had the unintended consequence of publicizing just how unfair that status quo was.[38]

In a February 21, 1974, letter to the chief executive officers of member institutions, the NCAA launched its counteroffensive. Calling it a matter of "critical concern," the NCAA noted, "If these regulations are ultimately given the force of law, the administration of the athletic program of virtually every NCAA member will be dramatically affected," and urged all institutions to contact HEW with their objections. The NCAA lobbying had an impact. In mid-March, the *Chronicle of Higher Education* reported that the guidelines, primarily because of questions about their impact on college athletic programs, had been delayed yet again.[39] One month later, the *Chronicle*'s Washington Notes reported "persistent speculation" that HEW might decide to exempt revenue-producing sports such as football from the guidelines.[40]

In many ways the NCAA and the male athletic establishment act as the villains in this story of the early days of Title IX (thankfully they later changed their tune somewhat), but in retrospect they unintentionally played a critical role in ensuring the viability of the law. By prominently entering the debate in 1974 and consciously seeking public support for their anti–Title

IX stance, they helped bring this law out in the open, which in turn made it much less likely that it could have been amended or repealed behind the scenes by a few lobbyists and their Congressional supporters. By creating a corps of supporters as well as detractors, the NCAA made sure that any changes in Title IX would be actively—and publicly—contested.[41]

On May 20, 1974, the Senate inserted itself into the debate, passing on a voice vote an amendment sponsored by Senator John Tower of Texas that would have exempted "an intercollegiate activity to the extent that such activity does or may provide gross receipts or donations to the institutions necessary to support that activity." In effect, the Tower Amendment would have exempted revenue-producing sports from Title IX's coverage, a very serious threat to Title IX's overall viability where sports were concerned.[42]

Once again Billie Jean King lent her name to the cause, writing to selected senators on stationery from her new magazine *womenSports* to ask them to strike the Tower Amendment because it would hurt women in college sports. Claiming that the amendment would "allow intercollegiate athletics to continue to discriminate against women," she reminded senators that the "inequities for women athletes in colleges are tremendous," with spending for men's programs sometimes outpacing that for women's by a ratio of 1,000 to 1. "Indeed, the treatment of women in intercollegiate athletics is one of the worst examples of sex discrimination in our educational system." On June 12, 1974, a House-Senate conference committee dropped the Tower Amendment from the education bill, a huge victory for Title IX supporters and personal vindication for Billie Jean King.[43]

King's lobbying against the Tower Amendment, like her earlier testimony in favor of the WEEA, demonstrated her willingness to take time out of her incredibly busy tennis schedule (in 1974 she was still ranked number one) to speak out on political issues close to her heart. Then, as now, she received far more requests to speak than she could ever fulfill, so she had to pick her battles carefully. No doubt she had help from women's advocacy groups in drafting statements for her signature, but in the end what she said was less important than the fact that she lent her name. King's generosity in sharing her celebrity on behalf of Title IX and women's sports helped build support for the law just as much as the work of lobbyists on Capitol Hill.

On June 18, 1974, almost two years to the day after Congress had originally passed Title IX, Secretary Caspar Weinberger announced the publication of draft regulations setting forth how the federal government proposed to enforce the law. HEW planned to solicit comments from interested citizens and organizations and then finalize a regulation to be submitted to the president for approval. Showing the complexity of the underlying issues, the government took over 12,000 words to explain a mere thirty-seven.[44]

The *Chronicle of Higher Education* called the draft guidelines "a lawyer's dream but a client's nightmare." Committed to the goal of equal opportunity in athletics, the draft guidelines provided no definition of what equal opportunity meant but did set out a list of steps and changes schools were required to take. Discrimination was not allowed in physical education classes or athletic programs, although sponsoring separate teams for members of each sex based on competitive skill was allowed as long as there was no discrimination in equipment, supplies, "or in any other manner." Schools were required to determine student interest at least annually to see in which sports members of each sex would like to compete. Under affirmative efforts, institutions were required to inform members of the previously limited sex (i.e., women) of the availability of opportunities and "provide support and training activities for members of such sex designed to improve and expand their capabilities and interests to participate in such opportunities." The final section stated clearly, "Nothing in this section shall be interpreted to require equal aggregate expenditures for athletics for members of each sex." That last section was clearly a sop to the NCAA.[45]

It is worth noting what these and future draft regulations did not do: they did not set specific quotas or guidelines to guarantee that minority women received their fair share of participation opportunities.[46] In general Title IX practiced a race-blind approach to expanding opportunity that was mainly concerned with increasing the absolute numbers of women athletes relative to men, rather than a commitment to expanding opportunities for minority women; it opened slots but did not have a strategy for insuring that those slots represented the diversity of women. In the 1970s black female athletes benefitted as schools added popular sports such as basketball and track and field where African American athletes already had a strong presence. Later, however, as schools continued to add sports to stay in compliance, black athletes often lost out to "white-girl sports" such as ice hockey, soccer, rowing, and lacrosse, which were not available in many urban or black communities. This outcome was a direct legacy of the decision in the 1970s not to require affirmative action measures or quotas to structure which women actually benefitted, but instead to let the athletic market determine the talent pool. And that athletic market, like the free market in general, was far from fair and equitable.[47]

The summer of 1974 was a busy one in Washington. On August 9, after Senate hearings leading to an impeachment vote, plus an adverse Supreme Court ruling, Richard Nixon resigned from the presidency because of the Watergate scandal. One of the issues that new president Gerald Ford inherited was Title IX. By October, HEW had received close to 10,000 comments on the proposed regulations, an unprecedented number. Even though athletics took up less than 10 percent of the regulations, that subject generated over 90 percent of the comments. As HEW Secretary Caspar Weinberger later quipped, "I had not realized until the comment period that athletics is the single most important thing in the United States."[48]

Even though NOW and WEAL offered different critiques of the proposed guidelines, all the women's groups agreed that the regulations were a step in the right direction.[49] The NCAA argued the opposite. Calling the regulations "arbitrary government in its most naked form," the NCAA called the proposed regulations "so vague, ambiguous and obviously lacking in comprehension of the realities of administration of college athletics as to represent a deterrent, rather than an aid, in the development of athletic opportunity for women."[50]

HEW was caught in the middle. Given the undeniable existing discrimination that was being uncovered, it was legally obligated to try to find a way to promote more equal athletic opportunities for women. At the same time it was engaged in a major public relations battle with athletic groups, and it had to seem responsive to their concerns. In such a situation, nobody was going to win big. In the short term, the more controversial athletics got, the more it helped the NCAA in its attempts to convince HEW to water down the provisions. In the long term, however, the controversy helped the cause of gender equity by building a popular base of support for the law, which helped in turn to insulate it from crippling amendments or repeal. Such popular support also put pressure on the federal government to enforce its wide-ranging provisions.[51]

In March 1975, word leaked that the White House staff was reviewing revised guidelines, and in April the guidelines were officially submitted to President Ford for his review. The headline in the *Chronicle of Higher Education*, "HEW Softens Bias Stand," captured the significant watering down that had occurred. As always, HEW was trying to find a middle ground in a complex area where there weren't obvious winners or losers. The NCAA was not assuaged. After Weinberger's press conference announcing the final regulations, a lawyer for the NCAA was quoted as saying: "This may well signal the end of intercollegiate athletic programs as we have known them in recent decades."[52]

The main changes involved both procedure and policy. The new regulations allowed high schools, colleges, and universities a three-year grace period to deal with changes in athletic policies (elementary schools received a one-year extension), such as implementing the integration of physical education classes and requiring that women be allowed to try out for a men's team if a women's team was not available. (The extension was clearly a concession to the NCAA.) The regulations added a new (and troubling, to women's groups) distinction between contact and noncontact sports: schools were now allowed to exclude women from teams in contact sports, even if there was no separate women's team. This too seemed politically motivated: allowing girls to participate in contact sports such as wrestling and football was quite controversial and could undermine support for the law. Earlier requirements that schools be required to conduct an annual survey of student interest were dropped, and the language calling for remedial action to make up for past discrimination was weakened.[53]

Balanced against those drawbacks—and there is no denying that in most ways the final regulations were far weaker than earlier drafts—were what the regulations did accomplish. They took a general concept of equal opportunity and identified tangible, concrete areas where it had to be addressed in order to be in compliance with the law. This so-called "laundry list" (originally developed by Margaret Dunkle in 1974) included provision of equipment and supplies, scheduling of games and practice time, travel and per diem allowances, coaching, locker rooms and facilities, medical training and services, and publicity, among others. More broadly, the regulations set as a compliance standard "whether the selection of sports and levels of competition effectively accommodate the interests and abilities of members of both sexes." Furthermore, for the first time the regulations set a deadline for institutions to be in compliance.[54]

There was one final hurdle to clear. After the final regulations were signed by President Ford on June 3, they went back to Congress for approval. Due to a rule change since the legislation originally passed in 1972, education regulations, which previously would have gone into effect on publication in the *Federal Register*, now were open to Congressional amendment or disapproval for a period of forty-five days. With the NCAA still actively lobbying against the Title IX regulations and various measures pending in Congress that could have potentially crippled its impact, it is not too melodramatic to say that Title IX faced its most serious threat to date in June and July of 1975.[55]

In early June a broad coalition of thirty national organizations, many of which had been instrumental in the passage of the Women's Educational Equity Act the previous August, met to discuss their stand in defense of the law. (By the fall this group had officially become the Coalition for Women and Girls in Education, with Margaret Dunkle serving as its first president. The group is still active in the Title IX fight today.) Hardly anyone was fully satisfied by the final regulations. Bunny Sandler's assessment was both blunt and realistic: "Sure they could have been stronger, but they wouldn't have gotten anywhere. That's the political process: it's what's possible." After a clear consensus emerged that weak regulations were better than nothing, the group dedicated all its collective resources to making sure that the regulations survived what looked to be a rocky forty-five days ahead.[56]

In June there were efforts in both the Senate and the House to send the regulations back to HEW for further review, which was just a cover for more delay. Representative James O'Hara of Michigan organized six days of hearings during which representatives of the NCAA and the American Football Coaches Association argued that since the so-called revenue-producing sports did not directly use federal funds they should not be covered by the regulations. Responded one feminist activist, "Since when is making money an excuse for discrimination?" O'Hara seemed to have the momentum when his subcommittee disapproved two sections of the regulations (on self-evaluation and on the grievance procedure), but the full committee sent them back for more review. In a show of solidarity, supporters packed the hearing room wearing bright yellow buttons that said, "God Bless You, Title IX."[57]

A simultaneous threat came from a rider tacked on to an education appropriations bill by Representative Robert Casey of Texas which would have barred HEW from requiring the integration of physical education classes. This amendment had easily passed the House back in April by a vote of 253-145 but floundered in the conference committee, which sent it back to the floor for another vote. Just prior to the vote, Representative Patsy Mink of Hawaii, who was managing the floor debate against the rider, received word that her daughter had been in a serious car accident and she immediately left. This time the vote was much closer (212-211), but the physical education exemption still passed. The Senate, however, voted it down the next day by a lopsided margin of 55-29. Beaten, and with Mink back from her daughter's bedside, the House convincingly defeated the amendment 215-178 three days before the regulation was scheduled to take effect. With the major amendments defeated, and in the absence of any serious effort to scrap the legislation entirely, the Title IX regulations went into effect on July 21, 1975.[58]

The passage of the Title IX regulations confirmed the importance of second-wave feminist organizations as powerful political forces in Washington. Well-organized, disciplined, and committed to their cause, feminists' clout was especially critical in crisis situations such as the last-ditch efforts to scuttle the regulations. Even though sports were not a major priority for many of these women's groups, they incorporated the issue into their agendas when it became so prominent in the Title IX debate. For example, the *Washington Post* reported that the Casey Amendment had been voted down in the House after members bowed to "week-long pressure from hundreds of women's rights lobbyists." Maybe it only seemed that many. Said one of those "hundreds": "There were only twenty-seven of us, but we were a talky bunch."[59]

The attention that athletics drew to Title IX had another, unintended, result. For every NCAA jeremiad predicting the end of football, the public also learned what second-class citizens women athletes were at all levels of the educational process. Discrimination in athletics produced clear and quantitative inequities that were so blatant they could not be denied. There is nothing abstract about men getting twenty new basketballs while women get the hand-me-downs, or female athletes piling into their coach's station wagon while men travel by chartered bus or plane. Public awareness of the plight of women athletes increased their legitimacy and helped spread awareness of the broader issue of sexism in all aspects of educational life. Even though in many ways sports "hijacked" what was a general education bill, this outcome was neither surprising nor ultimately detrimental to the overall goals of the law.

When Billie Jean King beat Bobby Riggs, hardly anyone outside of a small circle of Washington activists and HEW bureaucrats knew about Title IX. While women's sports were aggressively entering the national consciousness through events such as the Battle of the Sexes, the role of this specific law was still muted, uncertain. All that changed in the next two years, in large part because of the controversy that the athletics section of the law caused. Whereas in 1973 the phrase "Title IX" would have drawn only blank stares, by 1975 it was finally beginning to enter the vernacular as a symbol of women's new rights, athletic and otherwise. Bunny Sandler noticed the ripple effect: "it gave a tremendous impetus to women on campus—and to some men too and to students—to say, 'What's going on here is illegal. This violates Title IX.'"[60]

In March 1976 members of the Yale women's crew team staged a dramatic protest that drew national attention to the glaring inequities facing women athletes and the potential of Title IX to change those conditions. Lacking access to shower facilities during their off-campus winter workouts, members of the women's team were forced to wait, cold and sweaty, on a bus for half an hour while the men's team showered in the facility's only locker room before jointly returning to campus. Angered at Yale's slow response to their call for proper facilities, nineteen members of the crew team, led by captain Chris Ernst, strode into the office of Joni Barnett, the director of Women's Athletics, and stripped off their sweat suits to reveal naked bodies with "Title IX" written on their backs and chests in blue magic marker. The story was picked up by the *New York Times* and other newspapers around the country. Soon after, the women's crew team got its showers.[61]

ONE INTERESTING ASPECT of the history of Title IX is how little its implementation changed between the Republican administrations of Richard Nixon and Gerald Ford and the election of Democrat Jimmy Carter in 1976. Carter had a somewhat contested relationship with women's rights activists, and he never made Title IX enforcement a high priority.[62] Republican HEW secretary Caspar Weinberger had a point when he said, "The most effective enforcement of all is a public which supports the law." So did his Democratic successor, Joseph Califano, who was reportedly frustrated by the contentious battles over Title IX implementation: "Why did I have to be Secretary when this mess came up?"[63]

The Department of Health, Education and Welfare had three main responsibilities in administering Title IX: 1) explaining the law to schools and colleges and advising the public of its rights under the law and what to do if those rights were denied; 2) investigating charges of discrimination filed by citizens; and 3) initiating investigations to make sure the nation's 16,000 school districts were in compliance with the law. Obviously the delay until the summer of 1975 in finalizing regulations severely limited HEW's ability to publicize and carry out its mandate. "To get Title IX regulations was like pulling teeth with your fingers," recalled its Senate sponsor Birch Bayh. And yet even before the regulations were published, the department could have drawn on its general experience in handling civil rights complaints to rule that suspect practices such as barring girls from shop courses, offering six sports for boys and none for girls, or expecting female coaches to volunteer their time while men were paid were clearly prohibited by Title IX. Instead it tried to avoid taking controversial or politically sensitive stands, of which Title IX had more than its share, especially where athletics were concerned.[64]

In 1974 the Legal Defense and Education Fund of the National Organization for Women established the Project on Equal Education Rights (PEER) to monitor progress in the enforcement of federal laws against sex discrimination in schools, including Title IX.[65] Frustrated by the inability of HEW to provide adequate documentation of its efforts or results, in 1976 PEER initiated an analysis of every complaint regarding sex discrimination in elementary and secondary schools filed between June 23, 1972, and October 1, 1976. (Even though PEER excluded colleges and universities from its study, the enforcement patterns there were likely similar or possibly worse.) The title of PEER's final report, *Stalled at the Start*, foreshadowed its negative assessment. While the report covered all aspects of education, athletics drew special scrutiny: "The disparity in support for boys' and girls' athletic programs is perhaps the single most visible piece of discrimination in American education."[66]

In the period under PEER's study, HEW managed to resolve only one out of every five complaints filed, with two- to three-year delays not uncommon. More than a third of the complaints filed during 1973 were still unresolved three years later. This was not a question of tens of thousands of complaints flooding the office: HEW, with over one hundred people in eleven regional offices in addition to the staff in Washington, received 871 complaints for elementary and secondary schools and resolved only 179 in the four-year period surveyed. While the largest number of complaints concerned employment discrimination against women, the second-largest category was athletics.[67]

According to PEER's case-by-case analysis, investigations were cursory, usually consisting of little more than writing a letter to the school superintendent and then considering the case closed if he (and in those days, the superintendent was almost always male) claimed to be addressing the problem; rarely did HEW regional officials pay a site visit to investigate the complaint. Haphazard enforcement and failure to act on complaints undermined public and institutional respect for the law. In May 1974, the local chapter of the National Organization for Women filed complaints involving three school districts in Beaver County, Pennsylvania, to which the school districts were given thirty days to respond. Two replied but then did not hear anything again from HEW for almost two years; the third district never answered. Jeanne Doyle, the NOW activist who had organized the complaint, observed, "When we first filed our complaint, the school people were really nervous. Today, when you talk to someone in the school district, they just smile. They know nothing's going to happen." A HEW staffer confirmed that "Title IX is dead in a district that's been treated that way." And if HEW took two years to respond to a complaint, how serious could the threat of losing federal funds be?[68]

Without clear leadership from Washington, it was just too easy for school districts to ignore or feign indifference to the law. For example, the 1975 regulations required that schools do a self-evaluation within a year, but very few schools made more than a cursory effort, or if they did, they did not forward the results to HEW. And even though HEW repeatedly said that the three-year adjustment period to end in July 1978 was not a waiting period (elementary schools only had one year; that deadline passed in July 1976) and that institutions must immediately begin taking steps to bring themselves into compliance with the law, many schools made only the most superficial changes or put them off entirely.[69]

In a pattern that would continue throughout Title IX's troubled enforcement history, institutions said repeatedly that they could not go forward because they were confused about what the law required, especially where athletics was concerned. Cal Papatsos, the women's athletic director at Queens College, put it this way in 1976: "The tragedy is that when Title IX initially came out in 1972, it set high expectations because HEW promised all things to all people. Since the final regulations came in effect, I've been up and down the eastern seaboard and the only action I can see is people trying to figure out what it is. I see most people in a holding pattern." In some ways this was a valid concern, since there were major ambiguities about how the law would play out. Just as likely, however, when institutions claimed they didn't understand the rules, what they were really saying was that they didn't want to make the required changes in the first place.[70]

Schools and universities often had starkly different views of what was required. Some of the most apocalyptic language, not surprisingly, came from those with the most vested interest in the status quo. Alabama football coach Bear Bryant announced, "I'm all for women's athletics but if we had to split our budget, it would bankrupt us." (HEW never considered requiring equal total expenditures on men's and women's athletics.) Athletic Director Jim Kehoe of the University of Maryland, where the women's athletic budget hovered around 2 percent of the total, offered a similar mix of support and intransigence: "While I support philosophically the principle of equality, as a practical matter it just won't work." As a result of such foot dragging, it is probably safe to say that no college or university in the country was in full compliance with the law when it officially went into effect on July 21, 1978, six long years after its initial passage.[71]

In December 1978 HEW took yet another stab at explaining how the athletic policy would work, publishing draft guidelines and asking for comments by February 1979. These proposals raised a storm of controversy in much of the athletic community because they proposed to use an "equal per capita" expenditure benchmark to compare men's and women's athletics, by far the most radical proposal yet to have come from Washington.[72] By March HEW had received over 700 responses, nowhere near as many as the 10,000 it got when it was drafting the initial regulations in 1974–75 but still a sizeable number, all with their own opinions and arguments about why the proposals would or would not promote equal opportunity for women athletes or potentially bankrupt existing sports programs, or indeed whether athletics should be covered in the first place. With the potential for damaging riders to HEW appropriations bills working their way through Congress, Title IX's fate once again hung in the balance. The *Chronicle of Higher Education* called it a "giant game of 'chicken.'"[73]

Like the major shift between the draft regulations circulated in 1974 and the final ones adopted in July 1975, HEW's final Intercollegiate Athletics Policy Interpretation showed major differences from its earlier incarnation. The most obvious change was dropping any references to equal per capita expenditures, which had proven a problematic way to measure equality. Among other things, because per capita expenditures were tied to present levels of participation, they tended to perpetuate past discrimination rather than encourage new opportunity slots. Instead colleges were required to provide "proportionately equal" scholarships for men's and women's athletic programs as well as offer "equivalent" benefits and opportunities in other aspects of sports.[74]

In the long run the main significance of the December 1979 policy interpretation was the articulation of what came to be known as the "three-prong test." Under this test, an institution was deemed in compliance with

Title IX if it met any one of the three prongs. The first prong required that participation opportunities, especially scholarships, for male and female athletes be substantially proportionate to their general enrollment in the educational institution. For example, if male students made up 55 percent of students, then they should receive approximately 55 percent of the athletic opportunities, with the remaining 45 percent allotted to women. This emphasis on proportionality was a compromise, pushed by the NCAA and the Football Coaches Association. Two other options had been to require that athletic opportunities be split evenly at fifty-fifty or that athletic expenditures be equal for the men's and women's programs. At the time male undergraduates earned significantly more bachelors' degrees than women (56 percent to 44 percent in 1972), so athletic directors probably breathed a sigh of relief when the proportionality option was chosen, because that goal seemed much easier to reach than fifty-fifty parity. In the long term, however, this compromise backfired when women became a majority of college undergraduates in the 1990s.[75]

The two other routes to compliance concerned the key issue of "interest" on the part of the underrepresented sex, in this case, women. Many athletic administrators as well as leaders of the NCAA argued that the disparities between men's and women's programs were not necessarily the result of discrimination but caused by longstanding societal factors that meant women were less interested in participating in organized sports than men. Women's sports leaders such as Donna Lopiano dismissed this reasoning out of hand: "There's never been a question of enough interest. If you build it, they will come."[76] Reflecting the latter point of view, the second prong required that a school show that it had a history and continuing practice of program expansion to meet the interests and needs of women; the third prong required demonstration that the school's programs "fully and effectively accommodated" the interests and abilities of the underrepresented sex. With small changes and tweaking over the years, these same standards are still the main guiding principles for all Title IX litigation and compliance reviews today.[77]

At the same time the 1979 policy interpretation for athletics was being formalized, another battle was coming to a head: one between the National Collegiate Athletic Association and the Association for Intercollegiate Athletics for Women over formal control of women's athletics. In fact the two stories were intimately connected. The promulgation of the policy interpretation confirmed that, like it or not, athletics were going to be part of Title

IX enforcement. Its political and legal options exhausted, the NCAA stepped up its efforts to maintain control over intercollegiate sports in general by unilaterally announcing in 1980 that it planned to offer national championships in most women's sports starting with the 1981–82 season. Like many other aspects of the battle over Title IX, this power play was about money and control. As AIAW lawyer Margot Polivy noted, "When the budget for women was ten thousand dollars, no one cared how it was spent. When we added two zeroes, it became a power issue."[78]

The NCAA had been eyeing women's sports throughout the 1970s but nothing concrete had come of it. At various points the AIAW and the NCAA discussed a possible merger, but nothing came of those talks either, in part because of the vastly different resources and goals of the two groups and also because of ongoing ill will from the NCAA's anti–Title IX lobbying. The AIAW was only interested in a merger between equals, with an equal split in decision making and continued oversight over the field of women's athletics. Such guarantees were not forthcoming. For the NCAA, merger would really be a submerger: taking over and folding the AIAW's programs into theirs. Think of it as a hostile takeover, and not just by any athletic organization but by one of the most vocal and persistent leaders in the fight to weaken Title IX. Representative Pat Schroeder described the NCAA's strategy in this way to delegates at the 1980 AIAW convention: "First they tried to eat the sheep. Now they've seen the light and want to herd them."[79]

Actually the moment when the battle was lost may have occurred several years before the NCAA made its fateful announcement that it was moving into the field of women's athletics. The tipping point was the result of one of Title IX's unintended consequences: the merging of previously separate men's and women's athletic departments. Note that there is nothing in the law or the regulations that mandates this outcome, but it was often the first step taken by schools as part of their Title IX compliance. By 1979–80, 80.5 percent of all women's programs were run as part of a single administrative structure that included both men's and women's programs, invariably under the control of a male athletic director. The newly designated position of "Senior Woman Administrator" became a glass ceiling above which few women could rise. Without their former power base, and lacking control over the daily content and rhythms of women's sports, women athletic leaders were already deeply disadvantaged when the NCAA made its move. In many ways the NCAA's subjugation of the AIAW just replicated on a national scale the pattern that had already taken place at hundreds, probably thousands of athletic departments across the country as the larger, more powerful male divisions absorbed—and co-opted—the smaller, formerly autonomous female departments.[80]

By the time the NCAA made its move in 1980–81, the chance for an independently run women's athletic structure had passed. Separate teams for girls and women prevailed, but not separate administration and governance. As the Women's Sports Foundation noted, "The tragedy is that it is altogether possible for women to win the battle for equal opportunity and lose the war by turning over the control of women's sports to others." The Association for Intercollegiate Athletics for Women closed its doors on June 30, 1982. Once again the male model triumphed, although in this case it wasn't without a fight.[81]

THE FIRST DECADE OF Title IX's existence represented a time of momentous change for women and sport. Seemingly overnight, American sportswomen found participation opportunities that would have been unthinkable just five or ten years earlier. Even if the law was not being actively enforced for most of the 1970s, it was a powerful tool in the struggle for gender equity in sports because it allowed advocates to put pressure on schools and budgets knowing that a federal law was behind them. As Bernice Sandler observed in 1981, the very existence of Title IX "is a good example of how having a law in place leads to a voluntary change. The vast majority of institutions have not made all the changes we would like, but they have made some changes."[82]

To ascribe all the breakthroughs and progress to Title IX, however, is both inaccurate and simplistic. Some of the biggest jumps in participation and funding happened before Title IX was passed or before its impact on athletics was widely known, which was not until late 1973 and early 1974. In addition, some changes, at least limited ones, were going to happen anyway precisely because the inequalities in sports were so extreme that they could not be ignored. Even the most diehard traditionalists would be hard pressed to argue that it was fair that women and girls received only 1 percent of sports budgets. As sports historian Kathryn Jay observed, "Sports had become too important to American society to exclude half the population."[83]

Since so much progress occurred without active prosecution of the law, some critics have concluded that Title IX wasn't all that important, that many of these changes would have happened on their own.[84] And yet given the intransigence of many athletic directors, school administrations, and NCAA officials, it is hard to imagine that as much progress would have voluntarily occurred in this initial period without Title IX. In addition to suggesting that some change was inevitable, the threat of losing federal funds was also a powerful incentive for action. Even though in hindsight we know that the federal government never seriously considered resorting to this drastic option, institutions did not know this at the time. In Donna Lopiano's memorable image, "It was more like a guillotine in a courtyard. People were afraid of it. For a while, people did things because they felt they had to." These were optimal conditions for change and progress in women's sports.[85]

Just as significant was the influence of a strong and vibrant feminist movement that put issues of gender equity squarely on the national agenda. In the climate of expectations fostered by the revival of feminism, especially in the first half of the 1970s when so much progress for women occurred, the momentum was on the side of those who were calling for change in the gender status quo. Even though second-wave feminism never made sports a high priority, this supportive backdrop aided advocates who were pressing for changes in sports and recreation programs across the country. To use a metaphor from cycling: sports drafted in feminism's forward momentum. Absent the symbiotic connection between the women's sports revolution and the explosion of modern feminism in the 1970s, it is quite likely that the story of Title IX would have been far less dramatic.

The remarkable progress achieved in this initial take-off period shows how much could happen when a new federal law intersected with increasing demands for change in a supportive political climate alongside a certain reservoir of good will to make amends for past discrimination and neglect. Put another way, the existing sports structure had enough wiggle room in the 1970s to accommodate women—up to a point. Then the progress stalled. It took less than a decade to get girls' high school participation rate from 7 to 32 percent of the total; thirty-five years later, according to the Women's Sports Foundation, female athletes on the high school level had only made it to 41.2 percent. Law professor Diane Heckman coined the term "glass sneaker" to refer to this plateau.[86]

While it may not be possible to prove empirically, there seems to have been enough flexibility in the system to meet many of the initial demands for more opportunities for women's sports without seriously impacting the status quo. Many of these changes were more cosmetic than substantive. Add teams, but don't pay the coaches; give girls uniforms, but not for home and away games, and don't replace them every year; upgrade girls' intramural teams to varsity status but still expect them to raise travel funds through bake sales; schedule girls' games for 3 p.m. on Thursday rather than prime-time Friday night. The looming deadline for Title IX compliance added a sense of urgency to implementing these changes. By 1978—the year Title IX went into effect—most of the easy fixes had been applied. After that point the numbers, both participation opportunities and budgets, continued to inch up, but by gradual increments, not huge spurts of growth. Margot Polivy put it this way in 1981: "We're not going back to being barefoot in the kitchen, but we're not going to see the growth continuing, either."[87]

Numbers from both the high school and college level confirm the existence of Title IX's glass sneaker. After great leaps forward early in the decade, there were already noticeable signs of a slowdown by 1978–79 after Title IX finally went into effect. For example, high school participation figures show that the sharp upward climb peaked in the following sports in 1977–78: basketball, field hockey, gymnastics, swimming and diving,[88] tennis, indoor and outdoor track and field, and volleyball. In sports such as basketball, field hockey, gymnastics, and outdoor track and field, the number of girls playing in that year was an absolute all-time high; in others, the peak numbers from the late 1970s were only matched much later in the 1980s or 1990s. (See figure 1.) A similar pattern is seen in women's intercollegiate sports. (See figure 2.) Obviously outside factors affect the popularity of individual sports (the steady rise of soccer confirms this) but the overall trend is incontrovertible.[89]

Once again, much of this is about money. School administrators and athletic directors were not necessarily opposed to women's sports as long as they could add resources and participation opportunities for women without having to cut into preexisting programs for men. Those two goals coexisted fairly well for most of the 1970s, as budgets for both men's and women's sports increased. According to a study by the AIAW, the average men's athletic budget in a NCAA Division I institution rose from $1.2 million in 1973–74 to $1.6 million in 1978–79, an increase of $424,000. Meanwhile the average total women's budget in the same schools for 1978–79 was $276,000. In other words, the increases alone in men's budgets were more than 50 percent greater than the new resources given to women.[90]

With Title IX regulations finally in effect in 1978, most institutions needed to make some harder choices. And who was in charge of making these decisions? Male administrators and athletic directors with a vested interested in

FIGURE 1. Women's sports participation, high school, 1969–1982.

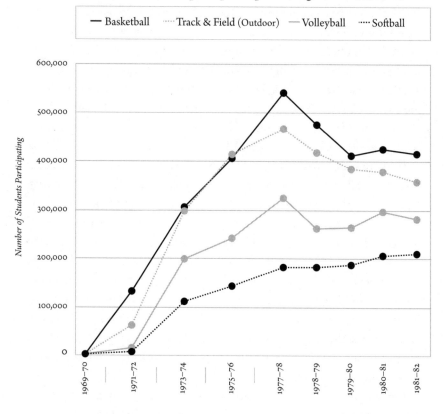

Source: National Federation of State High School Associations
Participation Figures, 〈http://www.nfhs.org〉.

FIGURE 2. Women's sports participation, collegiate, 1966–1982.

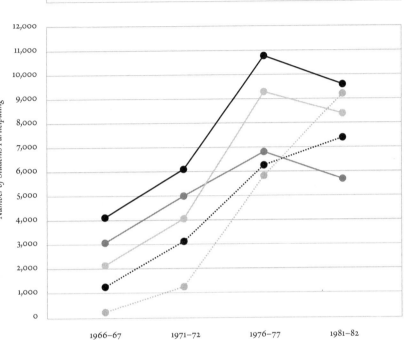

Source: National Collegiate Athletic Association, *The Sports and Recreation Programs of the Nation's Universities and Colleges, Report #7* (1987), 24–25.

the athletic status quo—"In short, the persons who have been most guilty of sex bias are the ones who are first in line to direct its elimination," according to an update by Candace Lyle Hogan in *womenSports*. Around this time the precipitous decline in women in athletic leadership positions that was a byproduct of Title IX kicked in, robbing women physical education leaders of an independent power base to serve as advocates for gender equity. This, combined with the escalating battle between the NCAA and the AIAW, muted the voices calling for continued program expansion for women and girls.[91]

Despite what seemed like revolutionary breakthroughs in the 1970s, in retrospect it is clear that this progress did not go anywhere near far enough. As Bernice Sandler pointed out ruefully, when budgets for women's sports go from zero to 20 percent it only means "things have gone from absolutely horrendous to only very bad." What was it going to take to break through the glass sneaker and get the percentage closer to fifty-fifty parity? Never again would the numbers for women surge the way they did in the 1970s; never again would the battle be fought in such a supportive political and social climate. From now on, it would be a long, slow, contested slog toward the still-elusive goal of gender equity in sports. Without Title IX, that struggle would have been much longer and even harder.[92]

Billie Jean King was already approaching thirty when she beat Bobby Riggs in the Battle of the Sexes in 1973, and she must have known that her playing days would soon be drawing to a close. Her first retirement—after winning Wimbledon in 1975—didn't stick, but she was already devoting increasing time to a variety of business and charitable undertakings while cutting back on her tennis schedule. "I still feel that playing my best on a given day, I can win every match—provided I can concentrate totally on my tennis," she said in early 1976. "As my life now stands, I will devote four months a year totally to tennis with the New York Sets in World Team Tennis competition. The balance of the year will be filled with business commitments, *womenSports*, television commentary with ABC and time off." Reflecting on her options, she said, "It's really great that the sport has produced enough to allow me . . . this choice. I wish this was true for everyone."[1]

Billie Jean King was always clear on the importance of women being able to make a living as athletes: after all, this was the whole thrust behind the establishment of the women's professional tennis tour in the early 1970s. King fervently believed that women's professional opportunities should not be limited to tennis: "Little boys have so many opportunities. They can picture themselves being a baseball player, basketball player, hockey—wherever professional opportunities are open to boys, that's what they can dream about in a realistic way." Her childhood memories were far less expansive: "When I was a little kid, I had to follow Mickey Mantle's batting average. I never had any woman to emulate in politics or anything." She wanted little girls to dare to dream on equal-opportunity terms and proudly offered her career as a model and inspiration.[2]

This is where Billie Jean King's story and that of Title IX converge. In her own career she was working toward the same general goal as the legislation: challenging and eradicating all forms of discrimination in athletics so women could finally have a sporting chance to play on equal terms with men. To accomplish this goal took education, advocacy, political engagement, and even entrepreneurship. Just as she had done in the Battle of the Sexes, Billie Jean King dovetailed her personal and professional priorities with building support for women's sports in the society at large. Not coincidentally, many of her actions also benefitted Billie Jean King personally, either financially or in terms of enhancing the public visibility and celebrity she craved. To her mind, this was a win-win situation: she got to pursue a lucrative career while also acting as a role model for women athletes everywhere. Not surprisingly, her unbridled ambition and drive also opened her to criticism that she was mainly out for herself.

After her victory in the much-hyped Battle of the Sexes, Billie Jean King suddenly found herself flush with cash. Even though the money available in the 1970s seems like peanuts compared to today's multimillion-dollar tournament purses and lucrative endorsement contracts, its scale was unprecedented at the time, especially for a female athlete. The *Wall Street Journal* estimated that King grossed $500,000 in 1973 from her tournament winnings, the residuals from the Bobby Riggs match, as well as a string of endorsements that included Adidas, Wilson tennis rackets, Colgate toothpaste, Aquanet hairspray, Phase III soap, Bonnie Doon socks, and Sunbeam hair curlers. The following year her income approached $1 million. Billie Jean King's "open pursuit of money and fame" appalled many in the tennis establishment and subjected her to inevitable criticism and resentment, which she simply shrugged off as sour grapes: "They love you when you're coming up. But they don't like winners. And they especially don't like me because I talk about money all the time." She concluded triumphantly, "I'm mercenary. I'm a rebel."[3]

Her coconspirator in these mercenary rebellions—what could easily be called "Billie Jean King, Inc."—was her lawyer husband, Larry, or as he unapologetically signed autographs "Mr. Billie Jean King." As he said in 1980, "You've got to make a choice when your wife is involved in sports. You can not be involved at all, you can be a nay-sayer or you can come up with solutions. As it happens, Billie Jean's forte is identifying the problem and mine is identifying the solution." Just as ambitious and focused when it came to business as she was in tennis, Larry King functioned as a tennis promoter ("I've probably promoted more women's tennis tournaments than anyone in the world"), lawyer for the Women's Tennis Association, entrepreneur (with a chain of tennis camps called TennisAmerica and as copublisher of *womenSports*), and real estate developer.[4] As Frank Deford deadpanned in a *Sports Illustrated* profile in 1975: "The lasting vision of Larry is of him standing in a World Team Tennis ticket booth, trying to sell lifetime subscriptions to *womenSports*, as a friend walks by and calls out to him: 'How's the condos going, Larry?'" Like his superstar wife, he rubbed many people the wrong way and often seemed oblivious to his tendency to conflate what was good for tennis with what was good for Billie Jean King, Inc. But he was enormously useful to his wife's career, and she could never have accomplished so much, on and off the court, without him as her trusted partner and financial advisor.[5]

In the years immediately after the Bobby Riggs match, Billie Jean King used her newly won clout and financial success to embark on new ventures, both business and nonprofit. Dennis Van der Meer, who partnered with the Kings in TennisAmerica, observed her unusual priorities: "Most athletes want annuities and pension plans, but Billie Jean is sticking her neck out and putting her earnings back into the tennis industry." In addition to exploring alternative streams of income, she was also interested in linking her name with ventures that could help her to maintain her public celebrity and her undisputed role as the best-known female athlete of her time.[6]

One of her earliest projects was founding a sports magazine for women called *womenSports*, which debuted in June 1974. That same year saw the beginnings of the Women's Sports Foundation, an advocacy group dedicated to expanding and protecting athletic opportunities for women and girls. The year 1974 also marked the debut of World Team Tennis (WTT), a new venture designed to break out tennis from its country-club setting and make it into a popular team sport on a par with baseball, football, or basketball. Billie Jean King didn't stop with tennis. In the 1970s she actively promoted the establishment of a women's professional softball league and cheered the efforts to set up or expand professional leagues for women in sports such as basketball and golf.[7]

With these ventures, Billie Jean King was thinking not only about her professional future but about how to maintain the momentum of the women's sports revolution until her goal—and that of Title IX as well—of equal access for all men and women was reached. She joked she could already hear the sportswriters saying, "Here comes Billie Jean on another crusade—doesn't she ever get tired?" Even though her grandiose visions might be met with skepticism, so many of her dreams for tennis had already come true that she forged ahead with equanimity. As she said in 1975, "No one believes in World Team Tennis. Nobody believes in *womenSports*. Everybody looks at you like you're crazy and you say, 'Am I crazy?'... Most people don't believe anything until after the fact." Even if her role in most of these ventures was more the visionary founder and celebrity cheerleader than a hands-on participant or administrator, Billie Jean King found the decade of the 1970s a fertile climate for her experiments in sports entrepreneurship and self-promotion.[8]

ABOUT NINE MONTHS before the Battle of the Sexes, Billie Jean and Larry were driving across the Bay Bridge from Oakland to San Francisco when she began complaining about *Sports Illustrated*'s lack of coverage of women athletes. After listening to her rants, Larry calmly suggested that she do something about it by starting a magazine of her own. Thus the idea for *womenSports* was hatched. Billie Jean King later put its founding in more personal, if somewhat self-centered, terms: "The thousands of hours I've spent practicing these last 19 years and the thousands of miles I've run on the courts have brought me to a secure position financially. Sure, I've got a sports car, a house on the beach, all the material things I could want. I've even achieved almost all the goals I set out for myself insofar as tennis is concerned. But for some time now, there has been a gnawing, nagging feeling that there was yet one more thing I had to do." By the time the magazine debuted in the summer of 1974, she was positively giddy with anticipation: "I've never had so much fun in my life." She was all of thirty years old.[9]

Starting any kind of magazine is a risky proposition: according to the *New York Times* in 1974, two out of five new magazines started that year were likely to fail. Bankrolling such a magazine would entail a substantial financial risk for the Kings, one that their investment advisors warned against. Better try real estate instead, they suggested, reminding them that *Sports Illustrated*, the premier success story in the world of sports journalism, did not even turn a profit until ten years after it was founded in 1954. In addition, neither of the Kings had the least experience in publishing, or as Billie Jean later admitted, "we didn't know a by-line from a center spread."[10] Tennis associate Jerry Diamond captured the combination of idealism and impetuosity behind the idea well, calling it "a wonderful concept—a women's *Sports Illustrated*—but about ten years before its time. When it came out, women's sports were just emerging. Rather than say, 'hey, let's wait a few years, let this run its course,' nope, they just went ahead and did it."[11]

Billie Jean King was not the first—or the last—to think there ought to be a magazine devoted to women's sports. In March 1973 twenty-six-year-old Marlene Jensen started the *Sportswoman*, with none other than Billie Jean King on the first cover. The magazine was originally planned as a quarterly, but the response was so strong that it immediately moved to six issues a year. Available by subscription only, its circulation was only 5,000, but Jensen saw great potential for growth. But when she approached fellow Californians Billie Jean and Larry King for financial backing, they told her they planned to "do it bigger and better" and turned her down.[12]

By the time of the Riggs match in September 1973, word was out on the street that Billie Jean King was planning to publish a sports magazine for women. The *Wall Street Journal* referred to the forthcoming magazine as "Ms. Sports," although that is the only public reference to such a title.[13] Even without the shared title, the influence of *Ms.* magazine on this venture is clear and omnipresent. When Billie Jean and Larry were in the planning stages, their most influential mentors were Pat Carbine of *Ms.*, John Mark Carter of *American Home*, and Ellen Merlo, a former managing editor of *Motor Trend* who was now with Phillip Morris.[14]

Ms. debuted as an insert in a late December 1971 issue of *New York Magazine*; its first stand-alone issue followed quickly in January 1972, dated Spring 1972 in case it had to sit on newsstands for months. Instead it sold out in eight days. The magazine quickly became the popular embodiment of second-wave feminism, with a circulation of between 400,000 and 500,000 and readership near 3 million. Like all new ventures, *Ms.* struggled financially, but it managed to forge an incredibly strong link to its readers and subscribers. It wasn't just that *Ms.* filled a niche: it aimed to be part of the revolution in women's lives symbolized by the revival of feminism. *WomenSports* aimed to fill a similar role for those who were passionate about sports.[15]

Whether *womenSports* was modeled on *Ms.*, *Sports Illustrated*, the *Sportswoman*, or something else, Billie Jean King had a clear vision of why her magazine was necessary. As she told the *Wall Street Journal* at the time of the Riggs match, "No one knows woman athletes as personalities. Women athletes need a vehicle to communicate with others as well as with themselves." In her debut publisher's letter in the June 1974 issue, she articulated her vision more fully: "I am proud to be a woman athlete. My hope is that through *womenSports*, many more women will take pride in their performance in sports and take pride in the enjoyment a well-toned body can bring them. If athletics is beneficial for men, which I believe it is, if sports competition builds character in men through discipline, which I also believe, then athletics must hold the same benefits for women." Setting her sights high, she aspired to make *womenSports* "not only a service to other women, but a magazine of which all women can be proud."[16]

Billie Jean King was listed on the masthead as publisher, but other than her monthly publisher's letter (which copublisher Larry often drafted), the editorial content was under the control of Rosalie Wright.[17] That boundary failed, especially at first, to keep *womenSports* from seeming like all Billie Jean King, all the time. The first issue was especially embarrassing, even to the tennis star herself. King was mentioned forty times in a ninety-six-page magazine and appeared in six of the twenty advertisements, plus graced the cover, which had the consequence of making the magazine seem like a promotional vehicle for the tennis star. A creative—and peeved—reader from Harrison, New Jersey, sent in a collage containing every one of those mentions. Somewhat sheepishly, the editors replied: "*WomenSports* is not intended to be a showcase for Billie Jean King, but since at this point, there are few equally famous women athletes, Billie Jean is naturally the advertisers' choice. By exposing the public to other great female athletes, we hope to rectify the situation, resulting in future commercial endorsements by other women sports stars."[18]

In some ways, however, the pendulum swung too far the other direction: the editors adopted an unofficial policy of minimizing coverage of the tennis star, which had the consequence of making it seem like she did nothing in the wider world of sports except write monthly publishers' letters. The editors finally relented when they realized that "covering women's sports without covering Billie Jean has seemed like trying to cover national politics without mentioning the President." In May 1977 she was back on the cover with a featured story called "The Bodacious Billie Jean King" about her decision to compete at Wimbledon after prematurely retiring from competition the year before. In this case, it seemed only fair that her magazine would get the scoop.[19]

The demographics of *womenSports'* readers contained few surprises. Results from a readers' survey that appeared in the December 1974 issue confirmed that 98 percent of readers were women, three-quarters of whom were between the ages of eighteen and thirty-four. Fifty-five percent were college graduates; 65 percent lived in their own residence; and 60 percent worked as teachers or other professionals. Confirming a pattern seen at *Ms.*, readers devoured the magazine from cover to cover, typically spending between one and two hours reading its various articles and features. Presumably these well-read copies were then passed along to friends, increasing the readership.[20] In October 1974 the editors reported distributing 300,000 copies to newsstands, but this proved a fairly ineffective way of reaching new readers, who consistently reported great difficulty finding the magazine for sale. Competing for shelf space and attention on newsstands against more well-established competitors was just one of the challenges faced by this fledgling enterprise.[21]

What was it like to read *womenSports* in its early days? The magazine offered its subscribers and readers who managed to find it on newsstands a glossy, upbeat selection of articles and features devoted to women in sports that in many ways was not all that different from a traditional women's magazine such as *McCall's* or *Redbook*: "a glossy cover photograph, an ad on the back cover, a rhetorical style that emphasized a personal tone, and a table of contents with titles of self-help articles." Except that in this case the self-help was about sports. Because the magazine had a three-month lead time, the content emphasized profiles and features rather than coverage of actual sporting events, meaning that *womenSports* could never compete with a weekly such as *Sports Illustrated*, which combined its trademark longer profiles with stories about what had happened in the world of sports the week before.[22]

Since traditional media outlets such as newspapers and *Sports Illustrated* rarely gave the topic of women's sports more than a passing mention, sports-minded readers welcomed an entire magazine devoted to this one topic. But it was not simply a women's magazine, mainly because of its clearly articulated political stance on women's sports. For example, the very first issue in June 1974 featured extensive coverage of Title IX. Calling the law "37 words that will change the world," Ellen Weber noted that "HEW is about to do for women's athletics what the 19th amendment did for women's rights." In addition to regular features on Title IX, the magazine alerted readers to the need to support funding for the Women's Educational Equity Act (WEEA), covered the ongoing struggle between the AIAW and the NCAA over control of women's athletics, and provided trenchant criticism of American amateur sports opportunities as well as specific critiques of the United States Olympic Committee, the main governing board.[23] However, with the exception of two features during the bicentennial year of 1976—an insert on the Equal Rights Amendment in concert with other women's magazines in July and a guide to the 1976 election in November—the only "politics" was the kind that had a specific link to sports.[24]

In this respect there is a clear difference from the wide range of issues found in *Ms.*, which was first and foremost a feminist magazine. Interestingly, even before *womenSports* debuted, the coverage devoted to sports in *Ms.* was already on the upswing. The first *Ms.* sports article, "See Jane Run," which chronicled the obstacles facing Olympic runners, ran in January 1973; the first sports cover was July of that year, featuring—no surprise—Billie Jean King. When *Ms.* covered sports, it tended to focus on questions of equity foremost: access, bias, prize money, and the like. It ran early articles on the sexual harassment of female athletes by male coaches and "how to" articles about challenging your local little league or school department to provide better access to sports resources for girls. It also covered Title IX and the battle between the AIAW and the NCAA. According to one reckoning, the sports coverage in *Ms.* increased 320 percent between 1972 and 1977, comprising 2.5 percent of total editorial space. The consistent inclusion of such articles confirms that sports, athletics, and Title IX were definitely on the agenda of second-wave feminism in the 1970s, even if never a top priority.[25]

While the mere fact of publishing a magazine devoted to women's sports in the 1970s comprised a feminist statement, the format of *womenSports* and the presentation of its features were more traditional, by design and intent. Again, a comparison to *Ms.* is instructive. The *Ms.* cover story on Billie Jean King that ran in 1973, aggressively titled "Billie Jean Evens the Score" and written by sportswriter Bud Collins, very much portrayed her through the lens of feminist politics by focusing on questions of equal rights and prize money and her conflicts with the USLTA as part of the general radicalization of King herself and professional tennis in general. When *womenSports* featured Billie Jean in its first issue a year later, the article had a far less feminist thrust. Titled "How To Win," it talked mainly about her training regime and her motivation for winning. "Maybe the reason I love to win is because it hurts so much when I lose. And I can't stand the pain." How do you get to be a winner? "To be a winner you must have total self-awareness. You've got to be aware of how much training your body needs, how much practice you need, and how much time you need to prepare yourself mentally." The contrasting tone of those two Billie Jean King profiles captures the difference between a feminist magazine and a more traditional magazine devoted to women's sports to a tee.[26]

Because it was not providing coverage of actual events, *womenSports* tended to focus on a variety of sports, using its pages to introduce top athletes and teams to fans and participants alike. Tennis obviously received a lot of coverage because of the link to Billie Jean King, but over the first few years practically all major sports played by women in the United States, including softball, surfing, running, volleyball, soccer, basketball, field hockey, and skiing, received prominent features that focused either on the sport or on a leading athlete associated with it. (Of course the problem for a magazine like this is what to do when it has profiled all the major sports. Editors have to start over again and think of new ways to write the same article for both new and recurring readers.) No doubt influenced by Billie Jean King's own priorities, the magazine gave special attention to the attempts to set up women's professional leagues.[27]

Like any other magazine, *womenSports* also had regular features that readers could look forward to in every issue. "Foremothers" offered profiles of pioneering women athletes from history, including golfer Glenna Collette Vare, tennis player Hazel Wightman, and swimmer Gertrude Ederle.[28] Starting in October 1975, the magazine offered a guide to which schools offered athletic scholarships to women, a clear outgrowth of Title IX that permanently changed the practice of reserving such scholarships only for men. By 1977 this yearly feature had grown so large that it was sponsored by Hanes Hosiery, maker of L'Eggs pantyhose. Said Billie Jean King, tongue in cheek: "We appreciate their energy on behalf of women's sports—and it's been sheer pleasure working with them," a reference to one of their most popular products.[29]

Probably influenced by *Sports Illustrated* and also by Billie Jean King's grudge that she had to share her Sportswoman of the Year award with Sportsman John Wooden in 1972, the magazine in 1975 decided to select its own "womanSport of the Year." Totally surprising the editors, the athlete who got the most votes was not a superstar such as Chris Evert or Olga Korbut but Linda Jefferson, the star halfback on the Toledo Troopers pro football team. Jefferson won as a result of a concerted get-out-of-the-vote campaign by her fellow players and their loyal following among Toledans, including the mayor and the entire city council.[30] The editors professed to be fine with this outcome, but the next year they changed the rules so that readers had to vote from a slate of candidates, which produced more traditional choices—Chris Evert in 1976 and figure skater Dorothy Hamill in 1977. Following their editorial policy, Billie Jean King was deemed ineligible for the award.[31]

One of the most prominent features each month was letters from readers: the magazine always devoted at least two pages to their comments, sometimes more. Once again, *Ms.* magazine blazed the trail: its July 1973 issue published five pages of letters, far more than the skimpy offerings in traditional women's magazines such as *McCall's* or *Good Housekeeping*. Like *Ms.*, *womenSports* editors invited its readers to think of it as "their" magazine. "More than anything else," Billie Jean King told readers in its second issue, "I want *womenSports* to be a vehicle for all women to use in communicating the joys and frustrations of being involved in sports. In order to make this your magazine, you have to help. Please write us and let us know what's on your mind. Let us know what you did or did not like in each issue."[32]

In response, readers wrote back with ringing endorsements and testimonials of how excited they were to finally have a magazine that took women's sports seriously. Readers repeatedly shared their own versions of the "click" moment so prominent in second-wave feminism when they encountered— and often surmounted—sexism or prejudice standing in the way of the full enjoyment of their athletic potential. And they poked fun at the traditional male world of sports coverage: one reader reported that since *womenSports* debuted, she had been using *Sports Illustrated* to line her kitty-litter box. But when the magazine failed to live up to readers' notions of what a magazine on women's sports should be, they wrote back in tones ranging from disappointment to outrage at the lapses.[33]

These critical letters offer an interesting window on how the magazine was being received and on some of the underlying tensions of trying to publish a commercially successful, advertising-based, feminist-themed popular magazine devoted to women's sports. Why was jockey Mary Bacon pictured from behind wearing a pair of polka-dot bikini underpants that showed through her racing jodhpurs? "Now this is exactly the kind of sexist shit that I've always objected to in the likes of *Sports Illustrated*," wrote a reader from New Hampshire. "Why does she have to be pictured as a piece of ass on your contents page? Please try to get away from this approach." Two readers criticized a picture of surfer Laura Ching showing what the editors had captioned "winning form"—a picture in which she is shown simply standing in a bathing suit. "We realize that you, too, are subjected to social conditioning which condones women as sexual objects," they chastised the editors, "but we would hope that a magazine such as yours—supposedly dedicated to women's athletic achievements—would not stoop to such standards."[34]

Readers were also critical of the advertisements, even though these ads made the magazine possible. "The Speedo ad in your March issue was disgusting," wrote a reader from Summit, New Jersey. "As women, we are again being told that the physical characteristics of our bodies are the main assets in 'competing' for men. The ad is also demeaning to the intelligence of men. . . . Hopefully, as more and more advertising agencies find it unprofitable to use people to sell a product, we will be free of the trash in advertising. Until then, I'll remember the brand name Speedo and not buy its products." Editors regularly shared such letters with the advertising companies, reasoning that they would welcome the feedback. The Speedo company, for example, changed the ad that many readers had found sexist and offensive.[35]

Criticism of *womenSports'* decision to accept cigarette advertising as incongruous in a magazine devoted to women's sports and health was there from the very beginning, with predictable results: Billie Jean King was just as unapologetic about accepting the support of cigarette manufacturers as she was about Virginia Slims' role in bankrolling women's professional tennis. In response to readers questioning the policy of accepting beer and cigarette ads, King countered: "We cannot in good conscience refuse advertising space to these categories. First a new magazine is a very touchy business and survival economically does not allow the luxury of doing without advertising. Secondly, the cigarette and liquor industries have supported sports from the beginning and I, as a professional athlete, would be a hypocrite to accept their help in sports events and turn it down in *womenSports*." Then she added her usual mantra about not smoking herself but believing that each individual had the freedom to decide whether to support specific advertisers. As usual with Billie Jean King, the ends justified the means.[36]

In *womenSports'* defense, it should be noted that *Ms.* accepted advertising for cigarettes and alcohol throughout the decade of the 1970s, seeing this as a matter of individual choice as well as a business necessity. Where they drew the line was when the editors considered the advertising sexist or demeaning to women, such as the "You've Come a Long Way, Baby" campaign of Virginia Slims that was the backbone of women's professional tennis. (They suggested a different slogan: "You'll Go a Long Way.") That decision cost them dearly, according to editor Pat Carbine. Needless to say, a similar decision would never have been made at *womenSports* on Billie Jean King's watch.[37]

In addition to complaints about lack of coverage of specific sports such as bowling or too much coverage of tennis and running, as well as gripes about male writers being assigned to stories instead of women, a consistent theme from readers was the lack of attention to lesbians in sports. (*Ms.* was also criticized for this but had a better track record.) Readers pointedly wrote in to challenge the heterosexual bias of many stories, such as athlete profiles that gave a large amount of space to husbands and boyfriends or quotes from the athletes themselves that denigrated lesbian athletes. For example, jockey Mary Bacon was quoted as saying, "What woman reads about other women unless she's queer?" Even if that was an individual opinion, readers demanded, why not counter it elsewhere in the magazine with positive portrayals of lesbians in sport?[38]

Another reader wrote in criticizing the tone of the magazine as bending over backwards so that readers wouldn't get the "wrong idea" about women athletes, which negated the fact that there were indeed lesbians in sport. "To be a woman in sports is hard enough. To be a lesbian in sports is even harder. But to be denied or ignored by other women athletes and *women-Sports* is the hardest of all." Those exchanges then led another reader to fear that running these letters was merely a tactic to avoid dealing with the issue, which provoked this wishy-washy response from the editors: "*WomenSports* takes a humanistic attitude toward the gay movement—that is to say, one's sexual preference is one's own business. We have yet to be convinced that sexual preference has any direct relationship to athletic performance."[39]

Another undercurrent in readers' letters was the relation of the magazine to second-wave feminism. Obviously its timing and inspiration in the first place linked women's sports with the revival of feminism in the 1970s, but not everyone, including the editorial staff, agreed on how feminist the undertaking should be. Readers ran the gamut. One reader got so sick of athletes distancing themselves from feminism that she wanted to tell them all, "If you have ever become angry because of discrimination toward yourself because you are female—angry enough to complain, to write a letter or to do anything—then honey, you *are* a women's libber." Another reader took race car driver Stevi Cederstrom to task for saying she'd been racing long before "women's libbers" knew how to spell liberation: "Any serious female athlete has a grueling uphill struggle, and she's either going to be a feminist or she's going to be a loser. I hope Ms. Cederstrom drives with her eyes open, because I think she must keep them closed a great deal of the time." And yet for every letter complaining that the magazine wasn't feminist enough, there was another that, in the words of one reader, worried about its "overall attitude and tone of a kind of toughness or crassness that has to alienate many readers."[40]

In general, the magazine seemed more concerned with striking the right balance between the hard-core athlete and the woman who was interested in sports for health and fitness than with taking a stand for feminism. Evidence from the magazine content as well as the frequent staff and publishing changes that roiled its early years suggest a clear trend away from its original feminist orientation, the result of a combination of financial, market, and editorial factors. At first the magazine aggressively used profiles of leading athletes and overviews of emerging sports and legislation to promote an agenda of equal rights and plans for action. "How to Pick up Men and Throw Them against the Wall" was the title of an article on self-defense in August 1974. That summer the magazine advertised a t-shirt with the slogan "*womenSports* has balls." As editor Rosalie Wright said, "We showed women how to make waves." And yet what seemed like flaming feminism in the sports world registered as tame—or worse—to hard-core feminists such as Jan Cunningham, coordinator of the Task Force on Sports for the National Organization for Women. This was item number four on her list of things to do in 1975: "Think a little bit about *womenSports*. Write letters of complaint about their sexist articles."[41]

By the summer of 1975 the magazine faced real problems: undercapitalization, staff cuts, low circulation, and a demographic not broad enough to attract advertisers. As also happened at *Ms.*, there were heated conflicts between the advertising staff, who wanted enough ads to keep the magazine afloat, and those on the editorial side, who were critical of support from companies such as Virginia Slims and who were not keen on Maybelline or Clairol's attempt to use sports to promote their commercialized versions of beauty. One casualty was editor Rosalie Wright, who was fired that summer.[42] At the last staff meeting before Wright was let go, one disgruntled staff member said, "Billie Jean got up and gave a pep talk about match point and how we were all on the line and all these sports metaphors. Then she and Larry talked about more beauty, health, fashion, and travel articles. It sounded like they wanted a sweaty *Cosmopolitan*." In protest six other editorial staffers resigned, practically the whole department. In the fall, the Florida-based Charter Publishing, which also published *Redbook*, reached an agreement with Billie Jean King to take over the publishing side of the business, while leaving her with editorial control. Journalist and freelance writer Cheryl McCall became the new editor.[43]

In 1977 the magazine went through another transition to another new editor—Le Anne Schreiber—and a new location, New York, having previously been published in San Mateo. They were up to 185,000 copies a month, but Carlo Vittorini, president of Charter publishing, admitted, "Our biggest single challenge is awareness that the magazine even exists." For her part Billie Jean King concluded that *womenSports* had become too narrow, too concerned with the serious athlete: "It should appeal more to the active woman who plays a couple of hours of recreational tennis a week, or goes hiking or bicycling on weekends."[44]

By early 1978 things were once again in crisis mode. In January, King told readers in her monthly publisher's letter that she was tired of slow but steady growth and wasn't willing to wait ten years to see her magazine take off. "If I had that kind of patience, I'd be a golfer—or at least be able to outlast Chris Evert in a baseline rally on clay. But let's face it, I'm not that kind of person. For better or worse, I play a serve-and-volley game. I want this magazine to go today." She knew that there were hundreds of thousands of women and girls out there interested in sports—the Title IX participation numbers confirmed this—so she proposed a grassroots subscription drive that enlisted current readers to suggest five sports-minded friends to receive a free copy to jumpstart interest.[45]

It didn't work. Even though circulation was strong and advertising revenues were good, the magazine was running a $1.5 million deficit, which was too much of a liability when Charter Publishing merged with Downe Communications. The February 1978 issue was the last before *womenSports* folded.[46]

Billie Jean King's vision of a sports magazine for women did survive for another twenty years, however, in various incarnations. In January 1979 the magazine was renamed *Women's Sports*, a joint venture of Women's Sports Publications, Inc., and the Women's Sports Foundation. Douglas Latimer was listed as publisher, Margaret Roach as editor, and Billie Jean King as founder, although she no longer played an active role. The magazine, which still maintained its glossy format, was conceived to serve a dual purpose: as the membership publication of the Women's Sports Foundation as well as a general magazine encouraging "more and more women to discover for themselves the added dimensions that participation in active sports can bring to their lives." In 1984 the magazine was rechristened *Women's Sports and Fitness*, and it moved even further away from its feminist beginnings.[47]

What are the lessons of *womenSports* for our broader understanding of sports and feminism in the 1970s? Even when interest in women's sports was exploding in the decade and more women and girls participating in organized sports than ever before, there was not a clear or obvious way to harness this niche. Billie Jean King was a big name, but not big enough to singlehandedly guarantee the success of a venture like this. From a business perspective, the difficulties of launching a magazine from scratch were just too overwhelming, especially for neophytes such as Billie Jean and Larry King. In comparison, *Ms.* magazine drew on a much deeper pool of journalistic experience and talent, as well as a broader base of potential readers, which allowed it to surmount some of its early business hurdles as well as articulate a clearer sense of what the mission of the magazine was. And yet it too struggled.

Part of *womenSports'* difficulty was that the categories of "women" and "sports" were too broad and diffuse. Some women were hard-core, elite competitors, others were interested mainly in recreational activity; some wanted to learn about exotic new sports, others wanted information about lifestyle and fitness issues; certain readers wanted actual news and results from the world of sports, others wanted more self-help articles; most problematically, some already embraced or were willing to embrace a feminist perspective when it came to sports, others saw no relationship at all between the two. As the magazine found, it was just too hard to be all things to all people. Gradually fitness trumped both hard-core sports coverage and feminism.[48]

There are many intriguing parallels between the histories of *Ms.* magazine and *womenSports* in their various incarnations. Both had a prominent celebrity—Gloria Steinem and Billie Jean King—attached to the magazine as a prime asset. Both struggled to reconcile the need to accept advertising, even advertising that was not demeaning to women, with the dependence on companies and products, such as cigarettes, cosmetics, and alcohol, whose health hazards were already well known or that were part of the beauty culture the magazines were trying to subvert. Neither was a traditional mass-circulation women's magazine but instead something of a hybrid, even though each still looked pretty similar to any woman's magazine that might be found on the newsstand. Each developed an unusually close and reciprocal relationship with its readers, who expected such great things from the magazine that they devoured it from cover to cover when it turned up in their mailboxes and weren't shy about letting the editors know when they felt the magazine had let them down.

There are also intriguing parallels in terms of chronology. Each was launched in the flush of feminist optimism in the early 1970s when all things seemed possible where women were concerned, and each was struggling by late in the decade, just as feminism itself confronted a growing backlash. In 1979 *Ms.* became a nonprofit under the Ms. Foundation; in 1987 it was sold to an Australian media conglomerate, and in 1990, after a short hiatus, it reemerged as an ad-free, subscription-supported venture. Similarly *womenSports* reemerged in 1979 with a link to the Women's Sports Foundation, renamed itself *Women's Sports and Fitness*, and survived until 1998 when Conde Nast bought it and folded it into its own women's sports magazine, which promptly folded, as did the attempt to launch *Sports Illustrated for Women* soon after. Today *Ms.* soldiers on alone, not the same feminist magazine that it was in the 1970s—but, as any aging feminist can attest, who is?[49]

ABOUT THE SAME TIME that Billie Jean King hatched the idea that became *womenSports*, she also took the beginning steps to establish the Women's Sports Foundation (WSF), a nonprofit national organization that in its more than three decades of existence has become the preeminent advocacy group for Title IX and women's sports in the United States. As with many of her ventures, this one had personal roots: "When I was growing up there was no organized group that said sports were just as good for girls as boys. Girls and women were on their own." Her vision was straightforward and far reaching: "The Foundation is dedicated to encouraging women of *all* ages and *all* skill levels to participate in sports activities for health, enjoyment, and development." Actually, she often joked, the real goal of the Women's Sports Foundation was not to have one at all: "Because if we were really having equality, we wouldn't need one."[50]

As with the founding of any organization that starts small and later goes on to greater things, it isn't always easy to pinpoint the exact genesis of the group. Larry King had spurred his wife to start *womenSports*, but her two coconspirators for the Women's Sports Foundation were Donna de Varona, the Olympic swimmer who became a pioneering sportscaster for ABC, and skier Suzy Chaffee. Donna de Varona recalls contacting Chaffee after the Riggs match and asking her to set up a meeting for the three of them to discuss a possible foundation, which was followed by de Varona flying out to California at Larry King's urging to discuss the idea further.[51] Another version of the foundation's genesis has the three women realizing the need for an advocacy group for women's sports while lobbying in Washington in late 1973 and early 1974, most likely for the Women's Educational Equity Act then making its way through Congress.[52]

While Donna de Varona always considered herself one of the founders of the organization because of her early role (she also served as its first president), the official incorporation papers filed with the state of California on May 2, 1974, listed only three names: Billie Jean King, Larry King, and their business manager James Jorgensen. The original rationale anticipated the major goals that have animated the foundation ever since, although the balance has shifted back and forth over time in relation to the changing social and political climate:

1 To educate women and the general public with respect to women in sports and women's athletic capabilities and achievements;

2 To promote equal rights and opportunities for women in sports and to educate women in sports and the general public as to discrimination against women in sports;

3 To educate and support women in increasing their athletic good sportsmanship and fair play;

4 To encourage and support the participation of women in sports for their health, enjoyment and career opportunities.

Billie Jean donated $5,000 she had won in a tennis tournament to cover the legal costs. By the time the bills were paid, there was about $500 left in the bank.[53]

After the initial incorporation, the foundation basically remained dormant until early 1976, which is often given as its founding year. This lag was not due to a shortage of enthusiasm or interest, just a lack of cash, time, and leadership. At that point Eva Auchincloss, then the associate editor at *womenSports*, was approached by Jim Jorgensen about becoming the first executive director of the foundation. The editorial staff of *womenSports* was in the process of relocating to New York, but Auchincloss wanted to stay in California, so the idea clicked. From a small office in San Mateo, whose rent was paid by the tennis star, Auchincloss attempted to figure out how a volunteer organization with only one paid staff member—herself—could have an impact. Although she was interested in sports, Auchincloss initially did not identify herself as a feminist; but as the foundation grew under her leadership, her awareness of the links between expanding opportunities for women and girls in sports and the broader feminist struggle for equality in the political and personal realms was cemented.[54]

Billie Jean King summed up the mood and the challenges for the Women's Sports Foundation after the first advisory meeting was held in New York in June 1976: "Everyone present at the meeting agreed that our first priority was to change society's attitudes—there are still negative ideas and prejudices floating around—about women in sports." How could a start-up with limited funds achieve such an ambitious goal? The key, they decided, was mass education: "teaching both children and parents that sports are important for *everyone* and that girls have been missing out all the time." In King's vision, the interrelationship of mind and body was always integral to a total human being who was both female and feminist: "Being a side-liner does not prepare a woman for an active, equal role in our society," she argued. "Being a participant does prepare women for the challenges of the many careers that are opening to them."[55]

Starting out with barely 1,000 supporters, the board set an ambitious goal of membership of 50,000 by the end of 1977, with a clear intent to influence public policy and popular ideas through strength in numbers. Despite a few initial attempts to set up local women's sports associations, the predominant thrust of the Women's Sports Foundation has been to function as a broad-based national advocacy organization representing the collective voice of women and men interested in women's sports rather than a grass-roots effort. Even though the board realized that New York or Washington, D.C., would have been better bases of operation than San Mateo, there was no money for offices or to relocate staff. Not until 1986 did the Women's Sports Foundation leave California for New York.[56]

Part of the foundation's strategy, which still animates the organization today, was to enlist the support of prominent female athletes who were willing to lend their names and prestige to the fledgling organization. The media was interested in these women and therefore would provide free publicity and coverage for events they attended. Donna de Varona and Suzy Chaffee, for example, were especially generous with their time in the early stages: as de Varona put it, "Although we didn't have power or money, we did have visibility." Other athletes who signed on at the start included sprinter Wyomia Tyus, speedskater Diane Holum, diver Micki King, softball star Joan Joyce, golfer Jane Blalock, bowler Paula Sperber, and volleyball player Mary Jo Peppler, with Chris Evert joining Billie Jean King (the chair) to represent the world of tennis.[57]

Many of these athletes had gathered for the first Women's Superstars Competition in Houston in December 1974, an unusual chance for twenty-three elite competitors from a broad range of sports to get to know other female athletes they had often only read about in the newspaper—and to win some serious cash. (The winner, Mary Jo Peppler, took home almost $50,000.) During the hours the athletes spent waiting around while the events unfolded for the sole convenience of the television crews, many expressed an interest in trying to maintain their sense of camaraderie by organizing some sort of loose confederation that spoke for all women in sports. At the time, though, they were too busy with the competition to take any more concrete steps.[58]

The Women's Sports Foundation also drew on the support, financial and otherwise, of prominent celebrities and business leaders. The sports-loving television star Dinah Shore, an influential promoter of the professional women's golf tour, was a prominent early supporter.[59] Joining a bit later but making up for lost time was *Peanuts* creator Charles Schulz, who became a trustee in 1979 and a major contributor soon after. Schulz was especially generous in allowing the foundation and other feminist organizations to use sports-related comic strips (think Peppermint Patty as a pitcher or Lucy telling Charlie Brown he wasn't good enough to play on her team) to illustrate their newsletters and bulletins.[60] The WSF also drew support from leaders in sports-related fields such as television, especially Frank Gifford at ABC Sports, as well as corporate support from Colgate-Palmolive, Bristol Myers, and General Mills. Unlike every other organization from this period founded or dominated by Billie Jean King, no cigarette money seems to have been involved from the very start.[61]

The initial agenda of the Women's Sports Foundation was ambitious for such a small outfit; many of its goals only came to fruition decades later. The foundation envisioned a Women's Sports Hall of Fame to bring recognition to outstanding female athletes and build popular awareness of their contributions.[62] It anticipated offering scholarships, especially for summer camps and for training expenses of aspiring women athletes, as well as sponsoring competitions and clinics to stimulate interest. It planned to compile lists of Title IX athletic scholarships available through colleges and universities and maintain a reference library on a broad range of topics relating to women and sports. It even hoped to sponsor sports medicine research. At the beginning, however, long-term goals and priorities took a back seat to dealing with the basic necessity of creating a viable organization.[63]

The Women's Sports Foundation took a significant step forward in terms of public visibility in 1978. Executive director Auchincloss later gave credit to newly hired fundraiser Holly Turner, who was based in New York: "Thanks to Holly's creative talents, we became the first non-profit organization to marry personalities to corporate interests by designing programs that were attractive advertising and public relations vehicles for the corporation."[64]

Symptomatic of how the organization used publicity and public events to build support from corporate sponsors and individual donors was a three-day benefit weekend in Las Vegas in February 1978 called "All Star Salute to Women in Sports," which culminated in a ninety-minute, late-night special on ABC. (As in the Battle of the Sexes match, the increasingly symbiotic relationship between television and sports was very evident by the 1970s.) The first of many galas held over the years, it drew corporate support from such large companies as Bristol-Myers, Burger King, Coca-Cola USA, Domaine Chandon, Tiffany and Company, and United Air Lines. Two months later the Women's Sports Foundation established the Wade Trophy, named for pioneering basketball player Margaret Wade. The 1978 Wade Trophy was presented to Carol Blazejowski of Montclair State University as the best female collegiate basketball player at an awards dinner in New York City, sponsored by Stayfree (manufacturers of feminine hygiene products such as maxi pads).[65]

The Women's Sports Foundation added lobbying to its agenda when it joined the public fight to preserve Title IX in 1979. Since the organization only became operational in 1976, it missed out on the early battles that roiled Washington in 1974 and 1975 over the failure of the Department of Health, Education and Welfare (HEW) to issue regulations and the various attempts to exempt revenue-producing sports from the law's coverage. In the foundation's early promotional material Title IX was rarely mentioned by name, but that silence changed in 1979 when the Women's Sports Foundation threw itself into the battle to get HEW to enforce the law. Realizing that numbers talked, the group quickly assembled a coalition including twenty-six national sports organizations and eighteen prominent individuals to back a declaration asking for speedy review of the pending athletic regulations.[66]

In September a Women's Sports Foundation delegation including race car driver Janet Guthrie, golfer Carol Mann, Olympic hurdler Lacey O'Neal, and swimmer Donna de Varona went to Washington to meet with President Jimmy Carter and HEW secretary Patricia Roberts Harris. "We're here as a living statement that we want women to be able to grow up as part of the American tradition of participation in sports," de Varona told a news conference. "We want to show the president, Secretary Harris and members of Congress that there is visible grassroots support for Title 9, that it's not just an issue for lawyers, educators or people outside the system." Reflecting his administration's somewhat problematic relationship with the feminist movement, Jimmy Carter made no definitive statements about Title IX but told Donna de Varona that he did support women's sports. From that point on Title IX remained at the top of the Women's Sports Foundation's priorities.[67]

The year 1979 also saw the reincarnation of *Women's Sports* as part of the Women's Sports Foundation's outreach. Subscribers to the magazine probably noticed little change at first besides the addition of an apostrophe to the title (to the eternal consternation of librarians and researchers trying to track it down in library databases), and the fact that Billie Jean King no longer contributed a publisher's letter each month. In what seems to have been a mutually beneficial relationship, the magazine donated editorial and advertising space to the foundation, including a page for a monthly column called "Strides." In return the magazine received editorial and journalistic input as well as an ongoing link with Billie Jean King. The Women's Sports Foundation remained affiliated with the magazine until the publication folded in 1998.[68]

With its grand visions for political and personal athletic change, it was incumbent on the Women's Sports Foundation to find ways to raise money as well as build popular goodwill toward women athletes. In 1980, it debuted its first annual "Salute to Women in Sports" gala in New York City, which raised $70,000 for the foundation, about half the funds needed to carry out their current budget. Showing a strong sense that the history of women's sports did not just begin in 1972 with Title IX, the foundation inducted nine women into the International Women's Sports Hall of Fame. In the pioneer category honorees were Patty Berg, Amelia Earhart, Gertrude Ederle, Althea Gibson, Eleanor Holm, and Babe Didrikson Zaharias. The contemporary category honored Janet Guthrie, Billie Jean King, and Wilma Rudolph. The gala also honored two Sportswomen of the Year: Tracy Austin (professional) and Mary Decker (amateur).[69]

Such gala events, which gave athletes a chance to get together in long dresses and high heels rather than sweat suits and sneakers, served to build the kind of camaraderie among networks of athletes that the Women's Sports Foundation wanted to tap. After all, having a prominent Olympic medalist or Wimbledon champion endorse a foundation initiative increased its cachet and brought welcome publicity. Corporate sponsors proved eager to align themselves with these popular athletes, especially if it would help sell products. Not everyone was enthusiastic about these galas. Sports activist Pat Griffin caustically pointed out that athletes were given free hairstyle and makeup advice before the annual dinner, but "the men attending the dinner are not offered similar help with their appearance." Griffin drew this message: "Female athletes in their natural state are not acceptable or attractive and therefore must be fixed and 'femmed up' to compensate for their athleticism." Like the proverbial half-full versus half-empty glass, these fashion makeovers can be read either as a harmless game of dress-up or a crass cop-out to dominant ideas of femininity and heterosexuality. Obviously it's a little of both.[70]

One of the original purposes of the Women's Sports Foundation was to serve as a clearinghouse of information on women's sports, a place where young athletes or their parents could turn for facts, referrals, encouragement, and strategy. Actually the organization was not the first to have this idea: the credit belongs to the Women's Equity Action League (WEAL). What eventually became SPRINT, a national clearinghouse on women in sports, started out in 1975 as WEAL's Sports Kit, a collection of news articles, studies of sex discrimination in schools and physical education programs, information about Title IX enforcement (or lack thereof), and specific examples of sex discrimination. By the summer of 1978, the Sports Kit contained close to twenty articles and memoranda, accompanied by selected bibliographies on women and sports, as well as audio-visual materials and a chart of federal laws and regulations.[71]

Keeping the Sports Kit up to date was initially a volunteer activity, and as the demand increased, a serious responsibility. In the fall of 1977 WEAL sought and won funding from the U.S. Office of Education under the Women's Educational Equity Act of 1974 to set up SPRINT, its national clearinghouse, with a full-time staff and a toll-free hotline for complaints of sex discrimination in sports and requests for information. (A few of the callers were looking for a new communications company called Sprint that shared the name.) The WEEA funding allowed the clearinghouse to expand beyond its initial incarnation as "a shoebox full of newspaper clippings" to "a roomful of files and a national network of contacts." In 1978 WEAL began publication of a quarterly newsletter called "In the Running," which provided updates on advocacy on women in sports until it expired in 1982 when WEEA funding ran out.[72]

Luckily the Women's Sports Foundation was able to pick up the slack. In 1981 the organization had instituted a toll-free 800 number of its own called Sportsline, made possible by a $5,000 grant from Jess Bell, the head of Bonne Bell cosmetics, who was a strong supporter of women's sports, especially running. The hotline started out in California and then went national in April. The "Strides" column called it a "long-standing dream" for the foundation and enthused, "If you have a sports question, you can call the toll-free number and receive an answer immediately." In its first year, it logged 2,141 calls. This feature is still a prominent service of the organization today.[73]

Although Billie Jean King remained the most prominent female athlete associated with the Women's Sports Foundation, always willing to share her celebrity for the cause of women's sports, she did not play a large role in its day-to-day operation in its early years. By 1982, for example, she was listed only as founder and an honorary member of the board of trustees. A case can be made that Donna de Varona, who served as the foundation's first official president from 1978 to 1984, was actually more critical to the start-up stage of the group than Billie Jean King. As Donna Lopiano later told de Varona, "In fact everyone knows, Billie Jean King included, that if it wasn't for you, the Women's Sports Foundation wouldn't be here today. If it was not for your leadership and Eva [Auchincloss] and Holly [Turner]'s role in staffing the everyday activities of the organization, the foundation would never have developed into the force it is because Billie Jean King was not involved during the crucial beginning years."[74]

The Women's Sports Foundation is an interesting example of the many ideas that Billie Jean King seemed to spray like tennis balls all over a practice court, some of which were good but many of which were not, and most of which either worked or didn't without her active involvement. In other words, she was great at founding things, not so good at staying around to run them. A similar dynamic doomed her broadcasting career in the 1970s, when she proved far too impatient for television work: "My temperament is better suited to charging the net and ending the point—win or lose— than waiting endlessly for the equipment to be set up and the show to unfold." She always preferred her role as the sparkplug rather than the careful, behind-the-scenes institution builder. To her credit, her commitment to people and organizations she cared deeply about never flagged.[75]

Billie Jean King was absolutely right on about the need for a national advocacy group for women in sports in the 1970s, a time when there was still so much to be done in terms of just generating basic participation opportunities, overcoming stereotypes, and building goodwill for what was then the novel concept that women and girls had just as much talent and interest in sports as did men and boys. King was also prescient in envisioning an organization that joined the needs and interests of elite competitive athletes with a parallel purpose of encouraging all women and girls to be physically active, even though the balance between those two constituencies sometimes has been a point of contention. From the start she put her sports celebrity at the foundation's disposal, excelling at garnering financial backing for its initiatives from major American corporations. Not only was supporting women's sports good for public relations, she argued, it was also good for business. After all, female athletes are consumers too. As Nike soon discovered, there was lots of money to be made by telling women to just do it.[76]

Although it rarely used the word, from the start the Women's Sports Foundation had a feminist agenda, precisely because its mission of encouraging participation for women in sports necessitated promoting equal opportunities for them to do so in the first place. And yet its feminism— deliberately—was muted, much more of the liberal than the radical variety, dedicated to working within the existing system rather than mounting an institutional critique of the sports world from the outside.[77] As Donna Lopiano later observed, temperamentally Billie Jean King was very good at playing the middle; her role in presenting the Women's Sports Foundation as a reasonable and moderate alternative to more extreme positions was a calculated political strategy. It was also the essence of liberal feminism.[78]

Over the years the Women's Sports Foundation has grown into a multimillion dollar outfit with national outreach on all aspects of women's sports, which of course makes it a major success story. It has proven especially adept at using print and electronic media to get its message across. But there is still that other side: more than thirty-five years after its founding, there remains a real, demonstrable need for a Women's Sports Foundation to serve as an advocate for women in sports, especially where Title IX is concerned. Billie Jean King's hope for the day when such an organization would no longer be necessary is still a ways off in the future.[79]

BILLIE JEAN KING's final professional undertaking in the 1970s was probably the one closest to her heart: World Team Tennis. Like all her other business and charitable activities, Larry was very much involved from the start, making this a true team effort. Like her other endeavors as well, it was conceived to provide a showcase for the tennis player as her career was winding down. It also promised the potential—never fully realized—of turning team tennis into a profitable and popular undertaking that competed successfully for the consumer sports dollar. "The biggest sports in the world are team sports," Billie Jean reinforced, "and I want to make tennis huge. We're a small universe and that bothers me." Tennis traditionalists doubted the team concept would catch on, but Billie Jean King lectured the nay-sayers: "Most people don't ever think any change in tennis will go, and every change in recent years has gone like crazy. Team tennis will, too." Finally, Team Tennis was a way of putting her commitment to sports equality for women into a concrete, marketable package.[80]

Billie Jean and Larry King's philosophy of World Team Tennis (they added the World because they truly believed this would be a global phenomenon) rested on a desire to make tennis, one of the most individualistic of sports, into a team endeavor, complete with rosters of players and a home base whose citizens could cheer them on just the way they would a local basketball or football franchise. Said George MacCall, the first commissioner: "I think the team concept and the league are Americana. Every major sport is built around these concepts." Following the major sports model, they hoped these fans would be a raucous, engaged audience, like those who had cheered or booed at the Houston Astrodome when Billie beat Bobby, not the traditional stodgy country club set. "Polite applause at tennis matches is ridiculous," said the tennis star. "People are going to be allowed to get up and walk around, boo, scream, do whatever they want. I think it will be more exciting for the players, more emotional to have the fans involved."[81]

One of the real attractions of the team concept for a feminist such as Billie Jean King was the chance it offered for men and women to compete together on a team and have the outcome equally dependent on the efforts of both sexes. "Whatever I do must reflect my values—like equality. People need to see men and women working together to attain a goal—both in leadership and supportive roles. That principle works well with tennis, where both genders work together toward a common goal." Larry agreed: "That's the future, I think. Men and women in professional sports together." Actually tennis already offered a popular precedent: mixed doubles, which in sportswriter Bud Collins's words, "stands alone among major sports in offering women an opportunity to play with and against men on an even battlefield and in the line of fire."[82]

Team tennis took that concept even further: teams would have equal numbers of men and women on their rosters. The format also promoted equality: play was divided into two halves, each featuring one set of men's singles, women's singles, and mixed doubles; the winning team was the one whose players collectively won the most games. Other innovations included doing away with traditional scoring (first to score four points wins), allowing substitutions, a heavy reliance on the tie-breaker, and a multicolor synthetic court surface. The season ran from May through July, with a two-week break in the middle so players could compete at Wimbledon.

The financial strategy behind World Team Tennis worked this way: sixteen franchises were sold at $50,000 each, representing fairly large markets such as Chicago, Los Angeles, San Diego, Detroit, San Francisco, and St. Louis. When John Newcombe, then one of the top-ranked men, signed a five-year contract with the Houston EZ Riders in the summer of 1973, the credibility of the league rose. Yet there was a nagging suspicion that not all the franchise owners were very knowledgeable about tennis as the league prepared for its first draft. Noted Bud Collins caustically, "Nobody has gone into business with greater unfamiliarity since Laurel and Hardy joined the Foreign Legion. Anybody who ever held a racquet was drafted. If you weren't, you should quit the game in shame." From the start the main problem was that attendance never approached the breakeven point to pay the huge salaries needed to lure marquee players to join the effort.[83]

In 1974, Billie Jean King, still a year away from even her first retirement, was one of the biggest draws. She signed on as the player-coach of the Philadelphia Freedom and was delighted when her good buddy Elton John wrote the song "Philadelphia Freedom" to be used as a team anthem. Ever the optimist, she predicted that women would be coaching in other professional sports such as football, basketball, and baseball within five years. Most of all, she was ecstatic about the new format. "I've waited 20 years to see crowds react the way they do at our team tennis matches." That year the Philadelphia Freedom were the runners-up to Denver in the World Team Tennis league championship.[84]

But all was not well. Despite having won the championship, the Denver franchise folded and was picked up by Phoenix. Stories of mishaps, financial and otherwise, in the first season included players not being paid and only 200 hearty souls turning up for some matches. The number of teams dwindled from sixteen to eleven, and only four of the original owners were back. "It was so bad," said the owner of the New York Sets, "that we couldn't even get people out to see how shoddy the product was."[85]

One potential solution was to try to build up the New York franchise on the theory that a strong presence there would garner more media attention and help the league as a whole. In a complicated deal, Philadelphia Freedom owner Dick Butera traded Billie Jean King to the New York Sets, earning a spot as the *New York Times* "Quotation of the Day" with this remark: "It's not an easy thing to let Billie Jean go. I feel like King Faisal giving away his oil wells." Billie Jean King received a reported $600,000 for signing a multiyear contract with the Sets and quickly pronounced herself happy to be a New Yorker, at least for part of the year: "It's a great place to live if you have the money. I have it and I might as well spend it." Sounding like a preacher leading a revival, her enthusiasm for the league remained unbounded: "I guarantee you, in five years every player is going to want to be on World Team Tennis first. They don't understand what it means."[86]

The 1976 season was somewhat better, but the financial situation of the league overall was still dicey. New players signed on, including Rod Laver, Chris Evert, Martina Navratilova, and Ilie Nastase, but this just increased the bloated salaries that were sinking the league. For example, the New York Sets payroll totaled almost $400,000: Billie Jean King ($130,000), Virginia Wade ($90,000), Sandy Mayer ($55,000), Fred Stolle ($55,000), Phil Dent

($50,000), with Lindsey Beaven and Linda Siegelman bargains at $8,500 each. Led by King and Virginia Wade, the Sets won the WTT title that year, a special satisfaction to King because it was the only tennis championship that had eluded her. But with fan attendance still hovering in the low four digits, there was no way to turn the franchise into a viable enterprise.[87]

The whole undertaking was also rife with potential conflicts of interest, many of them revolving around Billie Jean and Larry King. For example, in October 1976 Larry King was named interim president of the New York Sets, where his wife was the star attraction, having just stepped down the week before as president of the league, where his wife was one of the main draws. In 1977 Larry owned interests in the Pennsylvania Keystones and the Golden Gaters in addition to the New York team, and was a major partner in WTT Properties, the league's main marketing arm. Noted one friend: "It's not as if Larry is taking the money from both ends and hurting people. It's just that he's protecting his interests from both ends." Larry rationalized these multiple, overlapping responsibilities by saying his commitment to the entire league would help protect the investments of individual backers, of which he, of course, was one of the most prominent. Through the league's initial ups and downs, he remained totally committed to the concept: "It's a business. And I know this league is going to make money."[88]

In 1977 the league reorganized itself once again, instituting a new draft that aimed to distribute the talent more evenly. World Team Tennis limped along but was basically kaput by the end of the 1978 season, when the re-named New York Apples announced they were folding, and seven of the remaining nine teams followed suit. Larry King captured the logistics of the demise especially well: "The domino theory that failed to materialize in Indochina worked like a charm with World Team Tennis."[89]

In retrospect the reasons are obvious—and overwhelming. World Team Tennis never developed an adequate fan base among tennis players willing to turn out to watch the matches. Nor did team tennis manage to attract enough fans from other sports to build up its spectator base, let alone live up to the notion that fans would root for their "home" team against teams from other cities. The absence of male tennis stars such as Jimmy Connors, Arthur Ashe, and Bjorn Borg also hurt the venture. In the end, though, it was a simple fact of economics: the salaries were way too high for the monies coming in, especially since there was no television revenue except for the final league championship. Here those highly individualistic—and well-paid—tennis players bear just as much responsibility for the league's demise as its flawed business plan or shaky financing.[90]

By the time the first incarnation of World Team Tennis folded in 1978, Billie Jean King found herself at the inevitable point in an athlete's career when it becomes clear that while there will be flashes of brilliance and occasional triumphs, she no longer can count on performing at a peak level of performance every day. Luckily she had already been busy laying the groundwork to capitalize on the revolution in women's sports that had coincided with the height of her playing career. *WomenSports* magazine was ahead of its time—it still is, since there is no mass-market sports magazine geared to women. The Women's Sports Foundation continues to grow, broadening its agenda to include a new focus on overcoming physical inactivity and obesity in young girls; Billie Jean King is still very much its most visible symbol. Even Team Tennis, reborn in the 1980s, continues on a fairly solid basis, with Billie Jean serving as its most enthusiastic cheerleader as she continues to wait for the rest of the American sporting public to catch up to her vision of tennis as a team sport.

You need to win two sets out of three to prevail in women's tennis. In terms of Billie Jean King's main business and charitable undertakings in the 1970s, she won two of those sets—the Women's Sports Foundation and team tennis—and put up a good fight for a women's sports magazine. Not a bad outcome for a tennis player, on or off the court.

Billie Jean King's favorite place on earth is probably Centre Court at Wimbledon.
Here she plays in a singles match at Wimbledon in 1962, where as an unseeded,
somewhat chunky eighteen-year-old player she knocked off top seed Margaret Smith
in the first round. (Library of Congress, Prints & Photographs Division, NYWT&S
Collection, LC-USZ62-120847)

Women of Billie Jean King's generation more often aspired to marriage than careers, but she wanted both. Her husband, Larry, whom she married in 1965, wholeheartedly supported her dream. Their marriage, which lasted until 1987, spanned the explosion in women's professional tennis, but in 1965 they were just two young kids wondering what the future would hold. (Library of Congress, Prints & Photographs Division, NYWT&S Collection, LC-USZ62-115796)

Billie Jean King was never afraid to speak truth to power. In 1970 King and eight other players defied the United States Lawn Tennis Association by setting up their own professional tour sponsored by Virginia Slims. Here Nancy Richey, Billie Jean King, and Julie Heldman hold a press conference on October 7, 1970, to announce their decision. Showing the condescension with which the media treated women at the time, the original caption referred to the tennis players as "girls." (© Bettmann/CORBIS)

In 1971 Billie Jean King became the first female tennis player to earn $100,000 in a year. Hoping to raise the profile of women's tennis, she milked this milestone by donning a crown at a New York event and later received a congratulatory phone call from President Richard Nixon. Note the banner behind her with the first words of the Virginia Slims slogan: "You've come a long way, baby." (© Bettmann/CORBIS)

You can't have a spectacle without the media, and both Billie Jean King and Bobby Riggs were more-than-willing participants in the hoopla leading up to the Battle of the Sexes on September 20, 1973. Here they trade barbs at a press conference the day before the match. When the verbal jockeying ended and the tennis began, it was all Billie Jean, 6-4, 6-3, 6-3. (© Bettmann/CORBIS)

DOONESBURY   by Garry Trudeau

Billie Jean King's victory in the Battle of the Sexes confirmed her status as America's first female sports superstar. A month after the match Garry Trudeau's popular comic strip *Doonesbury* featured a series of cartoons inspired by the event. Here a young Joanie Caucus celebrates a feminist breakthrough at the daycare center where she works. Soon after, Joan Caucus applies to law school, joining the legions of women who seized the opportunities created by second-wave feminism and popular culture moments like the Battle of the Sexes. (DOONESBURY © 1973 G. B. Trudeau. Reprinted with permission of UNIVERSAL UCLICK. All rights reserved.)

Dissatisfied with the coverage that women athletes received in mass-circulation magazines such as *Sports Illustrated*, Billie Jean and Larry King decided to start their own, *womenSports*, which debuted in June 1974. No surprise about who graced its first cover—Billie Jean—but note the back cover advertisement for Virginia Slims cigarettes, symptomatic of the close (too close, many would say) relationship between Billie Jean King, women's tennis, and the tobacco industry. (© Bettmann/CORBIS)

Billie Jean King pioneered the concept of tennis as a team sport, and she has always been World Team Tennis's most enthusiastic supporter. Typical of the way that business and sport overlapped in the King family, Larry also found opportunities in Team Tennis as a promoter and team owner. Here Billie Jean King publicizes her trade from the Philadelphia Freedom to the New York Sets (soon to be the New York Apples) in 1975. (© Bettmann/CORBIS)

The symbol of the first-ever National Women's Conference held in Houston in November 1977 that most captured the popular imagination was a 2,600-mile torch relay that began in Seneca Falls, New York. In this widely circulated image, the torch triumphantly arrives in Houston. Decked out in a bright blue Women on the Move t-shirt, Billie Jean King joins the final mile, along with (from left to right) feminists Susan B. Anthony II, Bella Abzug, and (far right) Betty Friedan, as well as runners Sylvia Ortiz, Peggy Kokernot, and Michelle Cearcy. The torch run made the front page of many newspapers, but sports were not a top priority at the conference. (copyright © Diana Mara Henry)

The revelation in May 1981 that Billie Jean King was being sued by a former female lover brought the longstanding rumors about the tennis player's sexuality messily into public view. Here, with Larry's arm cloaking her in heterosexual privilege, she admits that she and Marilyn Barnett had an affair. Billie Jean King's script—accepting responsibility for the incident and asking for understanding and forgiveness from her fans and supporters—would became standard practice for public figures dealing with embarrassing sex scandals. She remains the rare woman, however, who was forced to deal with this harsh media spotlight. (© Bettmann/CORBIS)

Billie Jean King and fellow tennis great Chris Evert share a moment of infectious celebration at the opening ceremony of the newly renamed Billie Jean King National Tennis Center in Flushing Meadows, New York, on August 28, 2006, while male stars Jimmy Connors and John McEnroe look on with bemused detachment. Just as when Billie beat Bobby in 1973, women athletes proudly claim center stage. Or to put it another way, the girls win. (© Justin Lane/epa/CORBIS)

On August 12, 2009, with her mother, Betty, and her partner, Ilana Kloss, proudly looking on, Billie Jean King received the Presidential Medal of Freedom, America's highest civilian honor, from President Barack Obama. Honored for her battles for gender equity in sports and as one of the first openly lesbian sports figures in America, King once again demonstrated that sports can be a powerful vehicle for social change. (© Matthew Cavanaugh/epa/CORBIS)

Chapter Four Before the Sports Bra

A SHORT HISTORY OF WOMEN'S SPORTS THROUGH THE 1970S

On July 10, 1999, more than 90,000 fans at Pasadena's Rose Bowl and an American television audience estimated at 40 million watched the U.S. soccer team defeat China for the Women's World Cup. Tied 0-0 in regulation and after two grueling overtimes, the game came down to a tense penalty shoot-out. When strong goaltending by Briana Scurry kept the Chinese from scoring, Brandi Chastain kicked the next penalty shot to win the match for the United States 5-4. Overcome with emotion and emulating the universal gesture of jubilant male soccer players, she dropped to her knees and tore off her jersey, revealing an incredibly ripped body and a black Nike sports bra. That iconic image came to symbolize the triumphs of the women's soccer team, and by extension, the new legitimacy of women athletes everywhere.[1]

While much had been written leading up to the match about the connection between the team's players and a younger generation of predominantly female soccer fans, the event also resonated with an older generation of women athletes—those who grew up long before the sports bra was invented. Whatever the sport, they too had wanted to play but never had the opportunities that girls and women of the Title IX generations did. To have dreamed of playing before 90,000 cheering fans on national television would have been absolutely incomprehensible in their sporting days. No wonder, noted the *Pittsburgh Post*, that these older, aging former athletes feel "a bit giddy as they reflect on their careers and lives as pioneers. In a way, the broad-based fascination of the World Cup has become the happy ending every female athlete sought but seldom realized."[2]

Of course, there was a precedent for such giddy feelings: the night Billie Jean King beat Bobby Riggs in 1973. Played before enthusiastic crowds and huge television audiences, both events riveted national attention and sparked nationwide conversations about the status of women in sports. Like the women's soccer team, which came to symbolize the aspirations of female athletes everywhere, Billie Jean King stood for the aspirations of an earlier generation of women at a critical moment in American history. The Battle of the Sexes cemented Billie Jean King's reputation as America's first female sports superstar; the World Cup match extended star status to an entire team.

The charismatic members of the women's soccer team were quickly dubbed "the daughters of Title IX" by the media, but the 1999 World Cup victory is best seen as part of a long and varied tradition of female athletic participation rather than the result of a single piece of legislation.[3] Even though participation and opportunities seemed to explode in the 1970s, the story is more complex than that. Title IX did not invent women's sports. As Billie Jean King's early career showed, there were women's sports and committed women athletes before Title IX—they just didn't get much support or public attention. And changes were already underway before Title IX was passed, laying the groundwork for women's sports seemingly spontaneous emergence in the 1970s. Just as second-wave feminists sometimes acted as if they had discovered sex discrimination, thereby erasing a long history of agitation for women's rights, so too does a focus just on Title IX short-change all that went before in the history of women's sport.

Billie Jean King belonged to a transitional generation of American sportswomen. Her career served as a link between older patterns of extremely limited sports opportunities for girls and women and the glimmerings of a brave new athletic future where women's sports commanded respect and resources (almost) commensurate with men's. The decade of the 1970s was when this sea change began, and, as always, Billie Jean King was right in the thick of it. Her ability to forge a professional tennis career at the same time she emerged as a public advocate for women's sports was deeply influenced both by long-term historical patterns and the contemporary context dramatically unfolding around her in the 1970s.

FOR MOST OF American history, sports have been a male preserve. Competitive athletics were seen as "natural" for men and boys, but somehow "unnatural" or illegitimate for women and girls. Shaped by a popular belief that women's bodies were inherently different from—and weaker than—men's, women's sports developed along a path similar to that of segregated schools in the South before the 1954 *Brown v. Board of Education* decision: separate and definitely unequal.

Even though society consistently discouraged girls and women from discovering physical activity and organized games, such disapproval never fully stopped the female sex from experiencing the freedom and joy associated with sport. American girls found multiple opportunities for vigorous exercise and play, either informally or through schools or recreational leagues. Especially after they reached adolescence, however, girls were often told to pin up their hair, lengthen their skirts, and start acting more conventionally feminine. Sprinter Willye White summed up the tension between athletic competition and femininity in this way: "A female athlete is always two different people. A male athlete can be the same all the time."[4]

The history of women and sports and the history of women's higher education are intricately linked. With the founding of women's colleges in the 1870s, physical exercise became a way to assuage critics who feared that too much intellectual activity would be deleterious to tender female minds. At first students did calisthenics and gymnastics as part of the curriculum, but by the 1890s they began to participate in team sports such as basketball (introduced by pioneering physical educator Senda Berenson at Smith College in 1893), volleyball, softball, tennis, crew, and field hockey. Students enjoyed the chance to be physically active and seemed to grasp from the start that the emancipation of women's minds and bodies were fundamentally linked.[5]

Just as important as developments in the women's colleges were broader changes in society in the late nineteenth and early twentieth centuries that encouraged popular sporting and recreational activities for both men and women. The most important by far was the bicycle craze of the 1880s and early 1890s, when women and men took advantage of improvements in bicycle design to embrace a relatively inexpensive outdoor activity that allowed them to go places on wheels that had never been easily accessible before. Other new recreational sports that caught on were croquet, skating, tennis, and golf, all of which necessitated adaptations in women's clothing so that they could participate more freely. Anticipating the modern emergence of sportswear, the new outfits for sport featured a simplified shirtwaist and somewhat shorter skirt, or sometimes divided trousers or pantaloons covered by a skirt, plus the increasing abandonment of corsets. Note, however, that the focus for women's athleticism is on exercise and recreation, not competition. As men's sporting activities became more organized and popular in the twentieth century, especially in areas such as college football and baseball, competition remained entirely off limits for women.[6]

Swimming posed a special case, because of the challenge of coming up with a bathing costume that didn't actually drown the swimmer in its attempt to preserve her modesty. By the 1890s women swam—or, more accurately, bobbed—in short (midthigh) dresses worn over bloomers and thick stockings, while men bathed in public in one piece knitted suits that reached just above the knees. Australian swimmer Annette Kellerman is credited with developing the first one-piece suit for women, which she proudly displayed in swimming exhibitions throughout the United States in the 1910s and 1920s. Even her early bulky versions were liberating compared to the bathing costumes of old; by the 1920s, a trim one-piece suit was standard apparel for most young women.[7]

The development and acceptance of new swimwear was critical to the emergence of competitive swimming for women in the 1910s and 1920s. Another critical event was Charlotte Epstein's founding of the Women's Swimming Association of New York in 1917, where hundreds of girls and women found opportunities to train and compete in the organization's tiny indoor pool on Manhattan's Lower East Side. Endurance swimming, a field where women have a definite advantage because of their higher body fat and lower center of gravity, was a widely followed sport in the 1920s. Perhaps the best example is the huge media attention showered on Gertrude Ederle when she swam the English Channel in 1926 in a record-breaking fourteen hours and thirty-one minutes, the first woman to swim the channel, and faster than any of the previous men. As Will Rogers quipped, "Yours for a revised edition of the dictionary explaining which is the weaker sex."[8]

The growth of competitive swimming for women was linked to the history of the Olympics. The modern Olympics were revived in 1896 in Athens. While women competed informally in its early years in sports such as golf, tennis, and archery, founder Baron Pierre de Coubertin had no intention of promoting an equal-opportunity sporting event. Even today, women make up a minority of Olympic athletes. The first official American women selected to represent the country were swimmers and divers at the 1920 Olympics, soon followed by sprinters in track and field competition.[9]

As always, women faced hurdles not placed in the way of men. At the 1928 Olympics, the press reported that women competitors were so exhausted by the final of the 800-meter run that they collapsed on the field. Later evaluation of the contemporary coverage, including photographs, challenged this widely disseminated view of female weakness, but it was enough to have the race withdrawn from future Olympics. In fact, the longest footrace that women could compete in until 1960 was 200 meters. American women were a strong a presence at the 1932 Olympics held in Los Angeles, with Babe Didrikson winning two gold medals and a silver in track and field. By 1936, however, American women's participation was declining, even before World War II halted the games in 1940 and 1944.[10]

One reason for this decline was a concerted and highly effective campaign against female competition in the 1920s and 1930s, led, ironically, by women physical education leaders. Girls and women who wanted to compete and win were out of sync with dominant ideologies of both gender and sport. This anticompetitive thrust influenced the history of women and sports up until the 1960s and 1970s, including the early years of Title IX.

In the 1920s, control of the field of women's physical education rested with two interconnected organizations: the Committee on Women's Athletics of the American Physical Education Association and the Women's Division of the National American Athletic Federation, which was led by Lou Henry Hoover, head of the Girl Scouts and wife of future president Herbert Hoover. Women leaders in both groups grew increasingly concerned about the supposed ill effects of competition on their female charges, both physiologically and psychologically. In response they put forward a philosophy, carefully nurtured in schools and physical education departments across the country, that was summed up in the phrase "a sport for every girl and every girl in a sport." This model, formalized in a sixteen-point platform in 1923, emphasized participation and play rather than the competition and winning that increasingly dominated intercollegiate athletics for men: "The Women's Division believes in the spirit of play for its own sake and works for the promotion of physical activity for the largest possible proportion of persons in any given group, in forms suitable to individual needs and capacities, under leadership and environmental conditions that foster health, physical efficiency, and the development of good citizenship." Under this new philosophy elite female athletes found their chances to compete took a back seat to opening the competition to all comers, no matter the skill level. Between 1923 and 1930, the number of colleges offering varsity athletic opportunities for women dropped from 22 percent to 12 percent.[11]

This creed of sport took several forms beyond the discouragement of varsity competition. Schools instituted play days, where students from several schools were mixed together on teams. Telegraphic meets mandated that athletes compete at their own schools and then compare results with competitors in specific events by telegraph or telephone, presumably to dampen the excitement and stress of head-to-head competition. Sports days brought various schools and teams together, but they were as much social as athletic meets. Other manifestations of this different approach to women's sports were special girls' rules for basketball (six players, no roving, limits on dribbling) and outright bans on girls playing contact sports such as ice hockey and football.[12]

The sport of field hockey, which was especially popular in the Philadelphia area, highlighted some of the pesky inconsistencies that often pop up where gender, sport, and competition come together. A rough and strenuous game, field hockey escaped condemnation because it was played primarily in women's schools. Recalled one physical educator after witnessing a game, "And as long as they had tea and crumpets and it was all women, then it was perfectly legitimate."[13] The sport of field hockey further underscores the arbitrariness of gender in sports: it was okay for women to hit a ball with a stick on a field but it was not okay for women to hit a puck on ice with a similar stick, at least not until well into the 1980s. In addition, because field hockey was a sport associated with women's colleges and because players traditionally wore distinctive kilts as uniforms, to this day very few men learn to play it.[14]

While most girls experienced sports in the context of their educational experience, schools and physical education programs did not hold a monopoly on athletics for girls. In addition to opportunities for informal play in their neighborhoods or more organized activities through schools, YWCAS, and settlement houses, more serious female athletes turned to the Amateur Athletic Union (AAU), which first offered national championships for women in swimming in 1916, followed by track and field in 1924 and basketball in 1926. Women also played sports, primarily basketball and softball, on industrial teams, which were sponsored by employers as a way to build employee morale. Babe Didrikson, for example, played basketball for the Employers Casualty Golden Cyclones in Dallas as well as competed for them in track and field in preparation for the 1932 Olympics. Needless to say, physical education leaders strongly disapproved of these AAU-sponsored competitions.[15]

Long before midcentury a definite pattern emerged as to how race and class affected athletic opportunities for women. In general, individual sports such as tennis, figure skating, and golf held higher status and broader public approval than team sports such as basketball or softball. Not coincidentally, these individual sports were more expensive to pursue and thus tended to be available predominantly to elite, usually white, women. Conversely, working-class women found opportunities to play recreational softball or basketball through industrial leagues or the AAU, although African American women faced the additional hurdle of segregated facilities limiting their opportunities to play. Still, with a tradition of more physical and outdoor labor and accustomed to strong women in its midst, the African American community was often quite supportive of its female athletes, especially in sports such as track and field and basketball. In this context athletic achievements became political statements about African American capabilities in a racist society.[16]

World War II disrupted many normal patterns of American life "for the duration," including professional sports, since many male athletes either volunteered or were drafted into the armed services. Concerned about declining baseball revenues, Chicago Cubs owner Philip K. Wrigley established the All American Girls Baseball League in 1943. Over 250 women tried out for the teams, and 60 were selected. For talented competitors such as Rockford Peaches first baseman Dottie Kamenshek, to be able to play professional baseball was the dream of a lifetime. The fact that players had to wear skirts as uniforms (not so good for sliding into second base) and follow strict dress, make-up, and deportment codes to project femininity could not dampen their joy, a story brought to modern audiences by Penny Marshall's 1992 film *A League of Their Own*. The All American Girls Baseball League survived the return of male ballplayers from the war but finally succumbed to changing patterns of sports and leisure in 1954.[17]

In the 1940s, 1950s, and 1960s, the world of women's physical education was a small, insular world—separate from the men's athletic program, dominated by women trained as physical educators, and mainly of interest to and only noticed by the participants themselves. So little was at stake that the men were happy to leave women to rule their fiefdoms with impunity. Following the model developed in the 1920s, physical education leaders were concerned with encouraging sportswomen rather than honing elite athletes, competition was downplayed, and the general participation model still held sway. This philosophy had implications far beyond the gym, as National Organization for Women founder and sports activist Kathryn Clarenbach later realized: "This overemphasis on protecting girls from strain or injury, and underemphasis on developing skills and experiencing teamwork, fits neatly into the pattern of the second sex. Girls are the spectators and the cheerleaders. . . . This is perfect preparation for the adult role of women."[18]

For many girls, their main—and often only—exposure to exercise and sport was in required gym classes at school. Gym teachers ran P.E. classes like army drills, at least in the memories of many unathletically inclined participants, hardly an inducement to the joys of lifelong physical activity. (Of course to budding lesbians, their gym teachers were often the objects of endless fascination and unrequited desire.[19]) The dreaded gym uniforms remembered today by any woman born before 1950—sacklike skirted garments, with bloomer-type shorts underneath, usually in an unattractive shade of blue or green—didn't help. And yet for those girls who loved sports, gym class and intramural competitions were a chance to revel in physical activity.[20]

Well before the feminist and sports explosions of the 1970s, this tightly knit world of women's physical education was beginning to change. Play days were eliminated ("High school girls are bored to death at play days," noted one teacher) and more teams set up. These women's teams were a far cry from post–Title IX ventures, however. They generally lacked budgets and were coached—without compensation—by members of the physical education department; no trainers or supplies were provided. If students had uniforms, they generally made or bought them themselves, and then washed them, of course. Instead of a full schedule, teams might play five or six games a year. To get to away games, the coach drove the team in her own car, and the team saved on expenses by packing as many girls as possible into hotel rooms and bringing their own food. Of course there were no athletic scholarships. Probably the most trusted weapon in the women's sports arsenal was the bake sale.[21]

One clear glimmering of change on the horizon was the 1966 formation of the Commission on Intercollegiate Athletics for Women (CIAW). This group was created to encourage the expansion of opportunities for collegiate women's athletics while also holding on to the more "woman-defined" approach of such groups as its parent organization, the Division for Girls' and Women's Sports (DGWS), and the National Association for the Physical Education of College Women. As part of its mandate to build a governance structure for women's intercollegiate athletics, CIAW began offering national championships in two sports (gymnastics and track and field), with four more quickly added.[22]

The Association for Intercollegiate Athletics for Women (AIAW), founded in late 1971 and operational the next year with 278 charter members, grew out of CIAW's realization that women's intercollegiate athletics needed a permanent, national membership organization to coordinate its activities. Some educators applauded the efforts to expand opportunities in new directions, while others were fearful of change. Like its predecessors, the AIAW shared a commitment to a more participation-oriented, less elitist approach to sports that differed fundamentally from the reigning NCAA model that intertwined competition, winning, and commercialization. As the AIAW stated in a May 1974 position paper, "The sense of enjoyment, self confidence and physical well being derived from demanding one's best performance in a sport situation is a meaningful experience for the athlete. These inner satisfactions are the fundamental motivation for participation in sports. Therefore, programs in an educational setting should have these benefits as primary goals." Another major AIAW goal, in the words of historian Mary Jo Festle, was "whatever the direction of women's intercollegiate sports, it was women who should determine it."[23]

Participation in the Olympics was another area of postwar American society that showed glimmerings of change for women athletes. The cause? The Cold War and the need to stand up to the Russians, especially in the increasingly symbolic medal count. Once the Soviet Union entered the Olympics in 1952, its state-supported athletes enjoyed strong success against American amateur competitors who were basically left to fend for themselves in terms of coaching and training facilities. As *Sports Illustrated* put it on a 1963 cover featuring a Soviet Bloc athlete: "Why Can't We Beat this Girl?" Since women's sports were such a low priority in the United States, American competitors had little hope for success, except in individual cases of outstanding talent such as Andrea Mead Lawrence in skiing, Tenley Albright in figure skating, Donna de Varona in swimming, and Wilma Rudolph in track. A $500,000 grant in 1960 from Doris Duke Cromwell, heir to the Duke tobacco fortune, to encourage training and coaching for potential women Olympians was a hopeful sign of more resources to come, as well as another indication that the most extreme hostility to female competition was receding, at least when it came to elite athletes.[24]

The success of Wilma Rudolph at the 1960 Rome Olympics confirmed the dominant role that African American women played in track and field, a trend that had its roots in the interwar years. As part of their anticompetitive campaign in the 1920s and 1930s, white physical education leaders deemed track events "too physical" for most girls and participation plummeted. Into this vacuum stepped the athletic departments of small, historically black colleges and universities in the South, especially Tuskegee Institute and Tennessee State University, ushering in several decades of athletic dominance by black women track athletes. In 1948 Tuskegee high jumper Alice Coachman became the first African American woman to win an Olympic gold medal, in fact the only American woman that year to bring home gold. Tennessee State Tigerbelle Wilma Rudolph won a bronze medal in Melbourne in 1956 and then three gold medals in Rome four years later; in 1956 fellow Tennessee State alum Willye White won a silver medal in the long jump. Except in the African American community, this link between college sports and the Olympics was an anomaly until well into the 1970s when Title IX–supported scholarship athletes began to predominate in Olympic sports such as basketball, volleyball, and rowing. And yet it foreshadowed another Title IX pattern—the channeling of African American athletes into a tiny number of sports, mainly basketball and track and field.[25]

The publicity Rudolph received as an African American athlete paralleled the attention that Althea Gibson received when she broke the color line in tennis in the 1950s. Unlike track stars, Althea Gibson's athletic talent was not nurtured in a historically black college but in Harlem, where she honed her tournament skills in the all-black American Tennis Association. With the support of Alice Marble, in 1950 she became the first African American to play in the national championships at Forest Hills, losing in the second round. Despite her size (she was five feet ten, very tall for a player at that time) and athletic style of play, her career languished. Her breakthrough came in 1955 when the State Department invited her to be part of a goodwill tour to Southeast Asia. In 1957 Gibson, then twenty-nine years old, won Wimbledon and the U.S. Open, repeating both crowns the next year before retiring from amateur competitive tennis because, in her trenchant observation, "I couldn't eat trophies." Although a reluctant civil rights trailblazer, Gibson's triumphs opened further doors for black athletes and indirectly helped to challenge the racism and segregation of postwar America.[26]

The Cold War and the poor showing of American athletes in the postwar Olympics also provided the backdrop for a new focus on physical fitness in the 1950s and 1960s. In 1956 President Dwight Eisenhower created the President's Council on Youth Fitness with a broad mandate to investigate "whether American youth was adequately and properly prepared—in a physical, mental, emotional, social and spiritual sense—for the challenges that history is presenting to our civilization." Although performance standards were consistently lower for girls than boys (for example, only ten sit-ups instead of fourteen), girls as well as boys were expected to meet minimum standards of fitness as judged by a set of standardized tests. The administration of John F. Kennedy ramped up the focus on fitness as part of its effort to reinvigorate American society with the New Frontier. The overall message of these campaigns that fitness for girls was just as important to the nation as fitness for boys provided yet another boost to the emerging demand for women's sports.[27]

As the 1960s gave way to the 1970s, there were many other stirrings underway for women's sports, although they were scattered and not necessarily seen yet as part of a widespread trend:

- In 1967 Kathrine Switzer registered for the Boston Marathon as K. Switzer and completed the race despite an official's attempt to push her off the course; women were allowed to officially register in 1972.
- Bernice Gera began her quest to be the first female baseball umpire in 1968.
- Mary Bacon and Robyn Smith invaded the male world of jockeys.
- Vicky Brown served as the coxswain of the University of Washington men's crew in 1972 until she was ruled ineligible by the NCAA.
- Joan Joyce and Donna Lopiano led the Stratford Raybestos Brakettes to repeated victories in the Women's National Softball Tournament.
- The Virginia Slims professional tennis tour debuted in 1970.

- The DGWS issued a research report edited by Dorothy Harris on women in sports in 1971 which challenged many of the stereotypes limiting women's participation.
- The New York Board of Regents approved coed competition in noncontact sports in 1971, in effect overturning a 1912 regulation that barred women's varsity sports.[28]

By 1972, the year Title IX was passed and Billie Jean King was named *Sports Illustrated*'s first-ever Sportswoman of the Year, women's sports were ready to pop. Journalist Candace Lyle Hogan captured it perfectly: "Fueled by an almost chemical interaction of a federal anti-sex discrimination law, the women's liberation movement, and what is called the temper of the times, women's sports took off like a rocket in 1972."[29]

IN 1973 ONE OF THE hottest topics across the country besides the up-coming Billie Jean King–Bobby Riggs match was whether girls should be allowed to play Little League baseball. That summer eleven-year-old Maria Pepe of Hoboken, New Jersey, tried out for her local team but never played in a game because the national federation threatened to revoke the team's charter if she did. Supported by the local chapter of the National Organization for Women, Pepe appealed her case to the New Jersey Division of Civil Rights, which ruled in 1974 in her favor with these words: "The institution of Little League is as American as the hot dog and apple pie. There is no reason why that part of Americana should be withheld from girls." In the wake of the New Jersey decision, Little League reluctantly announced in June 1974 that girls would be allowed to play "because of the changing social climate." By then it was too late for Maria Pepe, who had aged out of Little League.[30]

Maria Pepe's attempt to join Little League in the summer of 1973 brought out the best and worst in a country highly polarized by the escalating battle between the sexes. Amy Dickinson, who became the first girl to actually play Little League when her Tenafly, New Jersey, team defied the national organization, pinpointed the absurdities of adult behavior as only an eleven-year-old could: "They interviewed one man who said he was a coach. He said he didn't want girls on his team because he didn't want to be responsible if a girl got hit between the legs with a ball and he had to run out and pull her pants down. I started to think that maybe some of these people have problems." Even though Tenafly took a stand in Amy's support, it wasn't exactly for feminist reasons, as local booster James Tuck let slip: "We just decided we'd rather have a few girls playing than have 360 boys be deprived of playing. . . . Let the girls play and get it over with. Then they'll just disappear."[31]

Tuck wasn't far off the mark: girls did not exactly flock to play Little League baseball. In State College, Pennsylvania, for example, there were only 10 girls out of 205 players on the roster in 1977. Starting in 1974 Little League began its own softball program, whose main effect (and probably its major purpose) was to siphon off the vast majority of girls from baseball. This outcome confirms a pattern often seen in early assaults on the sports status quo: high profile and highly emotional legal cases revolved around girls trying to win access to boys' teams, not necessarily because they wanted to play with the boys but because those were the only teams available. After the successful and well-publicized legal challenges, girls' teams often miraculously materialized overnight, in effect reestablishing the sports status quo: boys competing against boys, girls against girls.[32]

Challenges like Maria Pepe's to Little League baseball were happening spontaneously all across the country in the early 1970s, not just in recreational leagues but also in schools all the way from elementary to college. Some of these challenges were linked to Title IX, but many more were just spontaneous initiatives as parents and students looked with a critical eye at what was available to girls and said, "This is not fair." That, of course, is precisely what Title IX said, too, but public awareness of the law was still extremely limited at this point. Instead, the urgency of these demands was linked to the nature of youth and athletic competition, which transcended a specific piece of federal legislation. Kids grow up fast; they can't just put their athletic careers on hold while a case spends five years working its way through the courts. They want action now.[33]

This sense of urgency helps to explain the dramatic growth in girls' sports participation that was already underway before Title IX could conceivably have had such a broad national impact. Participation figures from the 1960s and 1970s are not always the most reliable, but the general pattern is clear. Schematically, in 1971, one in thirteen high school athletes were girls; by 1973, almost one in five; by 1974, one in four; and by the end of the decade, one in three (32.3 percent).[34] Given that broad public awareness of Title IX's impact on athletics was negligible until the first months of 1974, the earliest a Title IX boost to participation could be expected would be in the 1974–75 season. According to figures from the National Federation of

State High School Associations, the number of girls competing had already increased from 294,015 in 1970–71 to 817,073 in 1972–73, a threefold increase in just two years, and then again to 1,300,109 in 1973–74. The high school increases were especially pronounced in certain sports such as basketball, softball, and track and field. In almost every sport offered, the sharpest increases occurred in the "take-off" period of 1971–74, with continued strong growth until 1977–78, after which the progress leveled off. These dramatic increases occurred at a time when male high school participation rates remained basically stable.[35]

The changes were just as dramatic at the college level. In intercollegiate athletics, 15,727 women participated in 1966–67, a figure that doubled to 31,852 by 1971–72 and then doubled again by 1976–77 to 64,375; correspondingly, women's percentage of all athletes rose from 12.5 percent in 1966–67, to 15.6 percent in 1971–72, to 27.4 percent in 1976–77. Note that unlike high school girls' interscholastic opportunities, which basically started at zero before 1970, college women did have some opportunities by the mid-1960s. Still, they experienced similar patterns of steady incremental growth until 1971–72, followed by a period of explosive growth that lasted until 1976–77. Paralleling the experience in high schools, sports such as basketball, field hockey, volleyball, and swimming peaked at that point and then leveled off or declined, although softball, soccer, and especially track and field continued to climb.[36]

While the changes in women's sports seemed dramatic and revolutionary at the time, in hindsight women's athletics in the 1970s was in many ways more similar to women's sports in the 1950s and 1960s than to what would come later. Ask any female athlete from the 1970s how she would fare in today's competitive athletic climate, and chances are she'll laugh and say she wouldn't even make the team. Female athletes in the early days of Title IX were practically self-taught and self-coached, getting by on raw talent and a strong desire to compete, unlike today when athletes have often been honing their skills in a specific sport in recreational leagues and summer camps since grade school. Before athletic scholarships became the norm, it was still possible to walk on to a team, or sometimes even start one yourself if there was enough interest. In addition, it was not unusual for female athletes to participate in multiple sports, sometimes as many as three per year. These female athletic pioneers from the 1970s probably came closest to the vaunted ideal of student athletes than at any time before or since.[37]

Both reflecting the surge forward in participation opportunities and encouraging it, print media stories exploded about the hot new topic of women and sports. *Sports Illustrated* led the way with its three-part series in May and June of 1973; a year later authors Bil Gilbert and Nancy Williamson followed up with a progress report. *Newsweek* ran a long spread called "Sportswomanlike Conduct" in June 1974. From its inception in 1973, *Ms.* magazine devoted regular attention to the issue of women in sport, providing updates about breakthroughs and challenges from across the country as well as profiles of emerging female sports stars and sports "foremothers" from the past. Even women's magazines such as *Mademoiselle*, *Seventeen*, and *Ladies' Home Journal* jumped on the bandwagon. "Move over, guys," said *Seventeen*. "The girls are coming—in gym classes and on the playing fields. Your high school sports program will never be the same. It will be better."[38]

The new emphasis on sports for women intersected with the fitness craze of the 1970s. The focus on self-fulfillment and personal liberation that characterized the counterculture of the 1960s in turn spawned a new emphasis on recreation and leisure, with sport and fitness seen as positive and enjoyable forms of self-improvement. While only 24 percent of Americans eighteen years and older in 1961 participated in some form of physical activity on a regular basis, by 1979 59 percent of Americans—some 90 million adults—did so, with women's rate of participation climbing more steeply than men's throughout the 1970s. Millions of health-conscious joggers took to the streets, fueling the running craze of the 1970s. Also on the increase were aerobics, swimming, biking, and a range of activities that made exercise the province of daily life for a broad range of women, not just elite high school and college athletes.[39]

The 1970s also represented the peak of tennis's popularity, a factor that goes a long way to explaining the opportunities Billie Jean King both seized and created at the height of her career. In the peak year of 1974, some 41 million Americans played the game, competing for court time at their local public parks or clubs as well as fueling consumer demand for rackets, tennis shoes, and clothes. Tennis tournaments such as the U.S. Open became big draws, both for spectators and the impressive television revenues they generated. Tennis stars such as Billie Jean King, Jimmy Connors, and Arthur Ashe commanded attention in popular culture commensurate with football and baseball stars. For a sport that had until recently been associated solely with stodgy country-club ways, this was a huge breakthrough.[40]

All this activity gave a sense of rapid change, tempered, as always, by

HEW's foot dragging as it debated how to implement Title IX in late 1973 and early 1974. Despite the stalling in Washington, the momentum really seemed to be with women. As sports activist Jan Felshin was quoted in *Sports Illustrated* in 1974, "The day is over when you can tell women who want to take part in athletics, 'Go away, we haven't room. Men are using all the equipment and fields.'" By 1978, Joan Warrington, executive secretary of the Association for Intercollegiate Athletics for Women, could assert, "Women no longer feel that taking part in athletics is a privilege. They believe it is a right."[41]

The AIAW, which went into operation in 1972 just as women's sports began to explode, found itself functioning in an exciting but challenging environment, one not always of its own choosing. Before, women's sports had been a backwater, of little interest except to those in the phys ed department. Now women athletes were players, literally. All the changes underway proved quite unsettling, both for the student athletes and especially for the educators who had spent most of their careers dedicated to a participation-based ethos that set itself deliberately at odds with the prevailing male model of sport. In part this was a generational issue—younger, more political (although not necessarily feminist)[42] activists all hopped up about the exciting new opportunities for women's sports versus an old guard wedded to the status quo, inadequate as it was. The differences were as much philosophical as generational, and they manifested themselves first over the issue of athletic scholarships.[43]

Why would physical education leaders be opposed to scholarships for their students? To their minds giving a student a scholarship based on athletic ability undercut the real reason that students should be coming to college in the first place: to get an education, not to play on a team. Giving female athletes scholarships, they feared, would mean aping a male model based on competition and winning that put the needs of the institution above the needs of the student athlete. So strongly did the AIAW believe in their antischolarship stand that they initially barred any school that offered athletic scholarships (a tiny number in the early 1970s, but there were some) from competing in their national championships.[44]

Female students had different ideas. If their brothers could qualify for athletic scholarships, why couldn't they? Wasn't it patronizing to be told that accepting scholarship money in return for playing a sport would corrupt or demean them? Why shouldn't they be able to make that choice for themselves? Even within the AIAW there was hearty debate over whether scholarships were okay: "That kind of thinking—the kind that says 'if you give a girl an athletic scholarship, she'll be tainted'—has held back women's athletics too long," reasoned one proponent of change.[45]

At first the prohibition against scholarships held, but then in February 1973 tennis players at Marymount College and Broward Community College in Florida went to court to challenge the rule. The *Kellmeyer* case never went to trial, but it accomplished its purpose. Within months, the AIAW reluctantly withdrew its ban. In retrospect, this change was inevitable. Even if students hadn't sued, denying women access to scholarships that men received would surely have been deemed illegal under Title IX, one of the few clear-cut issues in the otherwise murky field of athletics.[46]

The issue of recruiting proved just as troubling to the AIAW. Recruiting excesses in men's athletics were well documented; when they started to happen in women's sports, educators and parents were appalled. The father of a six-foot-tall high school volleyball star compared recruiting to runaway inflation, noting that his daughter had been offered scholarships to seven colleges without anyone even asking about her grades. "Do you think anybody really cares about my kid?" he asked. "They never talked about anything but the volleyball program." On the other side of the equation, longtime physical education leaders were appalled at the entitled attitudes of recruits who basically demanded, "What can you give me if I decide on your school?" "That really bothers me," said Nancy O'Connor, head swimming coach at Colorado State University, in 1976. "I know that's being naïve, but you'd like to see people doing things for the love of it." Reflecting its ambivalence, the AIAW adopted a complicated set of restrictions designed to put steep limits on scouting and recruiting while also grudgingly admitting that these practices were going to take place.[47]

The AIAW transfer policy, which allowed students to transfer to another school without sitting out a year of sports eligibility like the NCAA demanded, also became progressively out of sync with the increasingly competitive world of college athletics. Its justification was noble: the right of a student to seek out a better education. But the transfer rule was ripe for abuse as coaches and administrators attempted to lure female athletes with promises of larger programs and more resources without any cost or penalty to either the school or the athlete. In part this was a straightforward example of supply and demand: the supply of gifted female collegiate athletes in the 1970s was far smaller than the needs of a range of institutions committed to building up their women's programs in response to Title IX.

It was also an unexpected byproduct of the new focus on winning as the justification for all the resources institutions were redirecting toward women's sports. "I'd be dumb to say I wasn't supposed to produce winning teams," said Judith Holland, director of women's intercollegiate athletics at UCLA, in 1976. As big schools stepped up their recruiting, scholarships, and commitment to building successful (i.e., winning) women's programs, smaller schools felt the squeeze.[48]

Within just a few years of the founding of the AIAW, therefore, spurred in part by Title IX and in part by broader changes in the field of sports, a governance model that tried to chart a separate path from the prevailing model of sports organization was already proving itself ill suited to the new demands of the 1970s. Ironically, when the AIAW made a commitment to support Title IX, many of the steps that the organization took to comply with the law, such as sanctioning athletic scholarships and allowing recruiting, moved it further along the slippery slope of accepting a competitive model of sports instead of its woman-centered, women-led approach. As Cal Papatsos of Brooklyn College told *Sports Illustrated* in 1978, "When Title IX came along we had to take the whole bag, and that started the dilemma. Men were getting blazers, so we wanted them too. Women are no different from men when it comes to handling power. When we get it, the same negatives will apply."[49]

Sports Illustrated summed up the philosophical split in the AIAW in this way: "The problem is that half of the AIAW membership wants to run a sophisticated physical-education program for college women; the other half wants to get involved in the business of big-time sports." In a period of explosive growth and under pressure to conform to the dominant athletic model, many women's programs began to look and act a lot like men's, even before the NCAA formally took over the governance of women's collegiate sports in the early 1980s. "It's funny," observed Judith Sweet, athletic director at the University of California, San Diego, in 1977. "Before Title IX, women were saying they never wanted their athletic programs to be like men's. They were not going to stumble into those pitfalls. They didn't want that grind, all those pressures. Suddenly, because of federal legislation, they're doing exactly what the men did." Nowhere were these changes more evident that in the field of women's basketball.[50]

FROM THE 1890S, when Senda Berenson introduced the sport to her students at Smith, to the present, basketball has been the most popular sport played by women and girls. Even though the history of the game now spans more than a century, its story, at least where women are concerned, is hardly one of linear progress. As such, it offers a window on the history of women's sports before and after the passage of Title IX.[51]

As was common with many other sports, rules were developed for basketball to make it acceptable—that is, less strenuous, sweaty, and rough—for the supposedly weaker, more excitable sex. Berenson divided the court into three sections, to which players were restricted; contact was banned, and dribbling limited. In 1936 most schools switched to a two-court, six-player format, but this still made for a slow, plodding game with a lot of standing around while the action was in the other half of the court. In 1962 a roving forward was allowed to cover the entire court, and in 1966 unlimited dribbling added. Finally between 1969 and 1971, the five-player men's game prevailed. These restrictions were done in the name of protecting women from undue exertion and competition, but they could not take away the sheer pleasure that many girls and women got from the game. Novelist Caryl Rivers, who played Catholic Youth Organization basketball in the 1950s, boasted: "If you have played basketball—really played it with pride and passion—you can never really be docile again."[52]

Basketball proved a popular sport in many schools and communities, both white and African American. It was much cheaper for a community or school to support than football, was open to both sexes, and did not place too many demands on gymnasium space. In the 1920s thirty-six states had high school tournaments for girls, and many colleges also fielded teams, including historically black colleges in the South. Reflecting her school's insistence on proper etiquette for African American young women, one Bennett College player from the 1930s remembered, "We were ladies too," before adding subversively, "We just played basketball like boys." Even such subterfuges were not always enough in the anticompetition atmosphere of the 1920s and 1930s. For example, educators concerned that basketball was "too strenuous for young ladies" decided to shut down the program entirely at Delta State in Cleveland, Mississippi, in 1933. "We cried and burned our uniforms," remembered Delta State player Margaret Wade, "but there was nothing else we could do." Delta State did not reinstate women's basketball until 1973.[53]

With the college game under attack in the interwar period, the only way for most skilled players to keep playing after high school was AAU competition, which added a national basketball tournament in 1926. According to historian Robert W. Ikard, the AAU is the missing link in the history of basketball between Senda Berenson and her physical education students at the turn of the century and the revitalization of the game from the 1970s on because of Title IX.[54]

Most of the women competing in AAU events played on industrial teams sponsored by their employers. These teams were especially popular in the South and Texas in the 1940s and 1950s, where they provided cheap and wholesome entertainment for small towns and communities in the days before television. The powerhouses of the game—such as Nashville Business College (NBC) from Tennessee or the Hanes Hosiery team from Winston-Salem, North Carolina—became legendary for their domination of the game and the skill of their players; many consider NBC's Nera White the finest all-round female basketball player ever. Even though many of these women played pickup games using the full-court, five-player format, the AAU still fielded six-person teams. Remembered Hanes star Eunie Futch: "I would have given anything to play men's rules. But the people over in Greensboro [professional educators] said it was too hard on us."[55]

In the 1950s and early 1960s, a time which two historians of women's basketball call "a dark age" for the sport, AAU basketball was practically the only game in town. Perennial contender Hanes Hosiery disbanded its team in 1954, which left Nashville Business College as the dominant force. Then for the first time a four-year-college team, the Wayland Flying Queens, challenged in the AAU. (Remember there were no national collegiate championships until the CIAW and AIAW began offering them.) Wayland Baptist College in Plainview, Texas, was not your usual college team. The players, lavishly backed by prosperous local business leader and Wayland alum Claude Hutcherson and his wife, Wilda, traveled by private Beechcraft airplanes (hence their name), attended school on scholarships, wore spiffy blazers and matching skirts off the court, and were literally treated like queens. Starting in 1954, they won the first of their seven national championships.[56]

Teams such as the Wayland Flying Queens and National Business College also provided the majority of players for the international competitions that began in 1953. Playing in South America or Europe was a wonderful dream for many small-town girls, but the U.S. teams were hampered by lack of support and the difficulties of switching to a full-court game. Just as in the Olympics, which added women's basketball in 1976, a Cold War desire for American women to hold their own against foreign, especially Soviet bloc, competition, worked in favor of changes on the homefront.[57]

The one place where girls' basketball truly flourished was the state of Iowa, a shining beacon of what can happen when girls' sports are given the same kind of community encouragement and support as boys'. Iowa girls' basketball was like Friday Night Football in Texas. When sportswriter and broadcaster Heywood Hale Broun was asked to describe the most exciting sporting event he had ever covered, he chose not the Kentucky Derby or the World Series or the Super Bowl but the Iowa girls' state basketball championship.[58]

Even in Iowa, girls' basketball faced challenges that almost killed it. When female educators called for the abolition of the increasingly popular girls' tournament in 1925, dissenting schools decided to form their own organization, the Iowa Girls' High School Athletic Union (IGHSAU). Why did basketball do so well in Iowa over the next five decades while it declined elsewhere? Having its own organization was critical, especially under the farsighted leadership of its longtime director, E. Wayne Cooley. So too was the generally rural nature of Iowa: basketball flourished in small towns and communities, plus Iowa girls were used to hard labor on the farm, so questions about the strenuousness of the game were moot. In fact, the girls' tournament consistently outdrew the boys'. In the often-quoted baseline pre–Title IX figure of 294,000 female high school athletes throughout the country in 1970–71, 20 percent of them were from the state of Iowa alone! Bucking the national trend, Iowa kept the six-player game until the 1993–94 season.[59]

As the rest of the country abandoned girls' rules, the AIAW came into existence. For the first three years, 1972–74, the AIAW national basketball title was won by the Mighty Macs of Immaculata College, a small Catholic girls' school outside Philadelphia. Girls who went to Immaculata weren't recruited, they didn't get scholarships, and they didn't play in a fancy gymnasium; the nuns banged buckets in the stands to cheer them on and their part-time coach, Cathy Rush, was paid $450 a year. But the players were competitive and talented, and they loved the game. In 1972 the Mighty Macs almost could not go to the inaugural national tournament in Normal, Illinois, for lack of money—there wasn't time to drive, and flying was too expensive. So players sold toothbrushes to raise money; college trustees each adopted a player; and finally they scraped together enough to fly eight players (less than their full roster) and their coach—standby. When they won the tournament by defeating their crosstown rival, West Chester State, the president of the college told them to fly home first-class, no matter what the cost. They repeated as champions the next two years.[60]

In 1975 the AIAW crowned a new champion, Delta State, which beat Immaculata in the finals. What a sweet victory for Delta State's coach, the same Margaret Wade who had burned her uniform in protest when the school shut down her program in the 1930s. "The ball is still round," observed Wade. "I guess that's about all that's the same as it was in my playing days." Showing yet another sign of change, the Mississippi team included both white and black players (Wade's teammates in the 1930s had all been white), including the talented Lusia Harris. Delta State repeated as champions the next two years.[61]

By the mid-1970s, however, the days of a small college winning a national title were fast receding, in large part because of changes brought about by Title IX. Said one Immaculata starter, "It was a very narrow window. I mean, you could see it. You knew it was going to change and it did." As larger college programs began to beef up their women's offerings, largely in response to Title IX, the popular sport of basketball was an obvious place to start. Once the AIAW rescinded its ban on athletic scholarships in 1973, schools could aggressively recruit high school standouts or transfer students. In 1974 Ann Meyers, the younger sister of a male UCLA basketball star, became the first woman to win a full athletic scholarship to the school. In 1978, UCLA won the national title, the first time that a large school was victorious. Never again would schools like Delta State, West Chester, Queens College, or Immaculata contend for the title.[62]

By now women's basketball was well launched on its journey as the success story of the new women's athletics. In January 1975 the first televised women's basketball game saw Immaculata beat Maryland, the same year Immaculata and Queens College filled Madison Square Garden for a closely contested match.[63] Coverage of the 1976 women's basketball silver medal team at the Montreal Olympics also boosted the sport's profile. Rivaling the records of legendary coaches such as John Wooden at UCLA, the seeds of new female dynasties were being laid: in 1974 Pat Head Summit, age twenty-two, took over the program at the University of Tennessee and started her historic rise to prominence as the highest-paid women's coach in history, and the first to crack the million-dollar salary barrier in 2006.[64] As far back as the 1970s, the women's game was already beginning to mimic the men's in terms of level of play, exposure, and fan support, but also in things such as recruitment scandals, declining opportunities for female coaches, and the like. After all, this was what women wanted from Title IX, right? Or was it?

IT IS IMPOSSIBLE to tell either the story of Title IX or the broader history of women in sports without confronting the persistent—and pernicious—pattern of homophobia, that is, the irrational fear or intolerance of gay, lesbian, bisexual, or transgendered people. The labeling of women athletes as "dykes" is a time-tested way of discrediting them and their athletic accomplishments by implying that they are not "real" women; in this view sexual deviance goes hand in hand with female athletic prowess, suggesting that there is something wrong or transgressive about women's desire or ability to play sports. Women who are interested in team sports such as softball and basketball are especially suspect, although individual sports such as golf and tennis are also popularly assumed to harbor large numbers of lesbians. (This perception is often referred to euphemistically by sports promoters as "the image problem."[65]) Whether there are in fact more lesbians in the world of sport than other areas of American life is an open question, but there is no doubt that those who are gay often choose the strategy of "play it, don't say it" as a way of deflecting public scrutiny. Billie Jean King is a prime example: for years she dodged rumors about her personal life and probably would have stayed in the closet indefinitely if she had not been so brutally and publicly outed by a former lover in 1981.[66]

The issue of homosexuality plays out very differently in men's and women's sports. As sports scholar Pat Griffin points out, "While women athletes must constantly prove their heterosexuality, most people assume that male athletes are heterosexual unless they provide evidence that they are not." The ethos of male athletics is one of aggressive, combative, often violent masculinity, where catchphrases like "playing hurt," "never let them see you sweat," or "game face" prevail, especially in sports such as football. In such a context the worst thing a male athlete can be called is the antithesis: pussy, wuss, fag, or faggot, to name a few of the most derogatory epithets. The idea of a gay man who is just as strong and competitive as his straight teammates undermines the core value structure of much of contemporary male sports culture. To provide cover for any suspicion of homosexuality, heterosexuality is enforced and homophobia rampant. As one sports agent said, "Frankly, it would be easier for someone convicted of bank robbery to get a job in the NFL than an overtly gay player."[67]

The widespread association of lesbianism with sports affects all women, gay and straight. Women athletes are encouraged to play up their hetero-sexuality and femininity through grooming, makeup, and other ploys such as ponytails and hair ribbons; boyfriends, husbands, and other heterosex-ual credentials are paraded in public. As early as 1974, Jan Felshin labeled this strategy the feminine "apologetic." Such dodges can have severe per-sonal and psychological consequences for women athletes who basically are forced to pretend they are something they are not in order to partici-pate in the sports and competition they love. Pat Griffin coined the phrase "strong women/deep closets" to capture "the apparent contradiction of physically strong and competent women who feel compelled to hide their deepest personal commitments, families, and love relationships in order to be members of the women's sports world."[68]

Despite these deep closets, lesbians have often found a safe and support-ive haven in the world of women's sports. Because women's sports were generally not highly valued, they provided a welcoming environment for girls and women not interested in traditional gender roles; they also offered an alternative vision of athleticism that was focused less on competition, more on participation. Even if players never talked about lesbianism spe-cifically, it was an "open" secret that there were lesbians in sport. Lesbians new to town often joked that if they found the local women's softball league, they would find a ready introduction to the gay community.[69]

Yet often this space was safe and welcoming only if lesbians stayed quiet and closeted. If they didn't, the repercussions could be quite real. College athletes feared losing playing time, or even worse, their athletic scholar-ships, if they were too open about their sexual orientation, by joining cam-pus gay pride groups or participating in public events with their partners, for example. Unfortunately this hostile environment was sometimes abet-ted by closeted lesbian athletes and coaches themselves who participated in putting other gays down as a mode of self-protection.[70]

Much of the fear around this issue was driven by parents and administra-tors who were unwilling to face the fact that there were lesbians in sport, as players as well as coaches, departmental administrators, and teachers. Pat Griffin is especially critical of "the hypocrisy of championing equality for women's sports yet tolerating discrimination and prejudice against lesbian athletes and coaches." One of the most pernicious tactics was the use of negative recruiting—where a coach, when talking to prospects and their parents, casually let slip that a rival team was known to harbor lesbian players or possibly even a lesbian coach. Pennsylvania State University women's basketball coach Rene Portland took this one step further, running her team on a "no alcohol, no drugs, no lesbians" basis until she was publicly confronted in 1991 and forced to rescind the policy. Alas, this is the same Rene Muth who helped lead the Immaculata Mighty Macs to three national championships in the 1970s.[71]

These rumors built on the longstanding if misleading image of the predatory lesbian out to seduce your daughter in the locker room or on the field. In fact, the fear of lesbian coaches may be one reason behind the trend toward more men coaching female sports, one of the most dramatic changes in the more than thirty-five years of Title IX's existence. While there are isolated examples of female coaches who enter into improper relationships with their players, a far greater problem is sexual harassment of female players by their male coaches. This phenomenon, which has been widely documented in academic studies as well as memoirs by former athletes such as Mariah Burton Nelson and Leslie Heywood, happens both in educational settings and professional sports but has yet to cause the kind of widespread outrage or fear that lesbianism has.[72] As a result, the number of openly gay women coaches remains small, and they tend to congregate in smaller schools and minor sports. At the top of the female coaching hierarchy, the trappings of femininity are very much on display. Case in point: basketball coaches stalking the sidelines in skirts and high heels.[73]

Why weren't women physical education leaders more in the forefront of making sports welcoming to gay and straight players alike? Various factors conspired to limit their ability to provide leadership. The world of athletics in general is a fairly conservative one, and women athletic administrators within this "near-total institution" function in an unsupportive climate for activism or social change. Many of these women had originally gravitated toward sports and coaching long before feminism or gay liberation, and they were still securely in the closet in the 1970s. Already marginalized by their involvement with women's sports and under attack as athletic departments aggressively merged formerly separate men's and women's programs after the passage of Title IX, they feared added disapproval if not outright dismissal from their jobs if their sexual orientations were known.[74]

Over the years, as sports have become a more acceptable outlet for girls and women, in large part because of Title IX, the threat of being labeled a lesbian has lost some of its force, although homophobia still causes many female athletes to hide or be less than open about their sexual orientation.

The biggest change is that the pre–Title IX jock subculture that nurtured many lesbians—and nontraditional girls who weren't afraid to be called lesbians—has increasingly been replaced by a more generic athletic culture where all girls are encouraged, indeed expected, to participate and play. In the words of Lucy Jane Bledsoe, "Wouldn't it be ironic if, by complying with Title IX, schools ruined sports for young lesbians?" Like other unintended consequences of the law, Title IX brought progress for many, but at the cost of diluting what had been a special haven for some.[75]

WITH THE EXCEPTION of the women's tennis tour, the 1970s proved much less hospitable to the take-off of women's professional sports than to the opening of opportunities to women athletes at the high school, collegiate, and recreational levels. Alas, no Title IX legislation required that women get an equal shot at making it as professional athletes. In fact, women's professional sports have struggled ever since to get a toehold in an increasingly crowded field, held back by the lateness of their arrival on the sports scene and the difficulty of attracting corporate and financial backing. These efforts were also hurt by lingering attitudes that once the curiosity factor wore off, women's sports just weren't as interesting or exciting to watch as men's.[76]

The attempts to set up a professional basketball league in the 1970s offer an instructive—and cautionary—tale. Hoping to capitalize on the popularity of the debut of women's basketball at the 1976 Olympics, a group called the Women's Basketball Association (WBA) announced the formation of a league that year. Unfortunately its ambitious marketing plan failed to win support either from the players or, more important, the financial backers it would have needed to pick up the individual franchises. It folded before it ever played a game. In 1978 UCLA star Ann Meyers forged a new path when she was invited to try out for the Indiana Pacers. She earned a contract, but was cut from the team after several months. Soon Ann Meyers was back playing with the girls when the Women's Professional Basketball League (WPBL) got off the ground in 1979.[77]

The WPBL was better financed and conceived than the earlier WBA, but still a hard sell. The league began with eight teams and quickly expanded to fourteen; all of its owners and coaches were men. Women players were paid salaries in the $15,000–20,000 range, sometimes lower; then as now, the women's salaries were far below their male National Basketball Association counterparts. Nor did NBA players have to sleep three to four players to a room to save money, or change in their hotel rooms before games, which on a good day might draw 1,000 spectators, often less. By 1982 the league had folded.[78]

Explanations for the failure of the WPBL ranged from the lack of depth of talent in women's collegiate ball to poor fiscal decisions to lack of television exposure to increased competition for the discretionary sports dollar. Mainly, it was just premature, as events since then have confirmed. After an attempt to set up a small, six-team league in the 1980s, nothing happened on the professional front until the late 1990s when the NBA-sponsored Women's National Basketball Association started up in 1997, crowding out the rival American Basketball League which had started in 1996 but folded in 1998. While the WNBA draws loyal crowds, no one would ever confuse it with the NBA.[79]

Women's softball fared no better in its attempt to sustain a professional league. In 1975 Billie Jean King aggressively recruited other women athletes, including golfers Jane Blalock and Sandra Haynie and tennis player Martina Navratilova, to put up money for the Women's Professional Softball League, proudly announcing with a nod to the upcoming bicentennial: "Women supporting women in a new professional sport is a revolutionary idea." Realizing the need for a sound management plan, King recruited promoter Dennis Murphy, who had been involved in starting up the American Basketball Association, the World Hockey Association, and World Team Tennis. The league's organizers hoped to draw on the deep talent that already existed in softball to build fan loyalty and support. Joan Joyce, for example, was an amazing athlete and dominant pitcher; if she had been a man, she could have made millions in professional baseball. Instead she played for the league for four years until it folded in 1979, the victim of inflated expectations and lackluster support, both financial and from fans. Disappointed but not defeated, Joyce returned to playing on the amateur Raybestos Brakettes.[80]

Basketball and softball were both team sports, which helps explain their fates. The history of women's sports since the 1970s has confirmed again and again that it is much harder to build professional franchises in team sports than in individual sports. "Until team sports are accepted the same way they are for men," argued Billie Jean King in 1981, "we haven't arrived. Everyone talks about our success; all I can think about is, we haven't even started."[81]

Women did in fact fare better in individual sports in the 1970s, although only slightly. Figure skaters such as Peggy Fleming and Dorothy Hamill were able to parlay Olympic medals into careers with the Ice Capades. Women also competed in professional bowling, skiing, and track and field, while the running boom offered women a supportive climate to run races and earn prize money alongside men. Once again, the biggest success story, practically the exception that proves the rule, was professional tennis, aided by the tennis boom of the decade, which provided the fast-growing and popular sport with a large fan base, augmented by consistent (if controversial) corporate support from Virginia Slims. In other words, if Billie Jean King had been a crack softball player, bowler, or skier, she would have had a much harder time creating a persona as a national sports celebrity in those years. Once again, tennis proved the perfect platform for her ambitions on and off the court.[82]

After tennis, the women's golf tour was probably the most attractive opportunity for women professional athletes. The women's pro tour dated to the late 1940s with the establishment of the Ladies Professional Golf Association (LPGA), dominated by the phenomenal golfer and all-around athlete Babe Didrikson Zaharias, as well as stellar players such as Betty Hicks, Louise Suggs, and Patty Berg. After Zaharias's premature death in 1956, Mickey Wright emerged as a tour leader, and the LPGA grew in terms of television exposure, increasing purses, and corporate sponsorship. When Wright abruptly retired in 1965, the growth of the tour stalled until Colgate Palmolive stepped in as the main sponsor in 1972. In addition to the infusion of corporate cash and celebrity support, especially from Dinah Shore, whose name became practically synonymous with women's golf, the game profited from the promotion of new stars such as Nancy Lopez. As golfer Carole Mann noted in 1978, "Five years ago little girls never walked up to tell me that they wanted to be a professional golfer. Now it happens all the time."[83]

Things were also changing in the previously all-male world of NASCAR racing, thanks to Janet Guthrie. Always very much of an individualist (her background was in aeronautical engineering and physics), Guthrie had been racing cars since the 1960s, gaining experience that allowed her to be the first woman to qualify for the Indy 500 in 1977. She qualified again the next year, finishing ninth overall. Overcoming lingering—and often overt—prejudice that women couldn't drive as fast or as well as men, Guthrie put her success in wider perspective: "It was the women's movement of the late 1960s and early 1970s that made it possible for a woman to drive at Indianapolis and Daytona. I was simply the woman at the right place at the right time with the right background, and an overwhelming passion for the sport." In Billie Jean King's opinion, "Brave women like Janet Guthrie made it more acceptable for women to be elite athletes. She dared—no, demanded—to compete at the highest level of her sport in an era when entry and acceptance were a much greater challenge." Access and the right to compete were the watchwords of women's sports in the 1970s; acceptance, respect, and professional viability would take much, much longer.[84]

THIS CHAPTER BEGAN WITH the image of Brandi Chastain in her black Nike sports bra, so it seems appropriate to end this survey of the history of women's sports by returning to that piece of underwear, which, like so much else in this history, had its birth in the 1970s. Even as women's sports participation opportunities exploded in that decade, there was not yet a comparable explosion in gear and equipment for women. In the meantime female athletes were forced to make do with men's shoes in smaller sizes, uniforms that were cut for men's bodies, and a range of compromises and adaptations that reinforced that the norm in sports was male and women were still interlopers. A prime example: Kathrine Switzer ran the 1974 New York City marathon in a tennis dress.[85]

One of the most vexing problems was bras, which were designed for fashion and everyday wear but not for serious athletic activity. For all but the most flat-chested women, going without a bra (the image of feminists as bra burners notwithstanding) was not really an option, for reasons of both comfort and modesty. In 1977 marathoner Lisa Lindahl grew tired of bouncing breasts while she ran. "Why isn't there a jockstrap for women?" she asked herself. The next year she teamed up with Hinda Miller, a professional costume designer, to develop such a product. Their ingenious solution? Sew two jockstraps together. All they needed was softer fabric and better elastic, and the basic concept behind today's sports bra was born. At first they called the product Jock Bras, but when the sporting good stores where they planned to market the product (note: *not* in women's lingerie departments) objected to the name, it became Jogbra.[86]

Marathoner Ellen Wessel had a similar "eureka" moment in 1977 when she grew frustrated by the ill-fitting and poorly designed clothing available to active women like herself: "You go through a period of time thinking you're too fat, too thin, too this or that instead of realizing the clothing is really the problem." With a $7,000 loan, she and Elizabeth Goeke founded Moving Comfort, based in Springfield, Virginia, to design and market running clothing specifically geared to women. Unlike most start-up businesses, they had no cash flow problems at first because, Wessel later joked, they were too stupid to know they should give credit: everything was cash on delivery. With very little initial competition, they developed their product line and refined their business plan. The company doubled in size each year and by 1983 had gross sales of more than $4 million.[87]

Long before Reebok hired Rebecca Lobo or Nike told women to "Just Do It," a band of far-sighted women entrepreneurs saw a niche and began to fill the needs of all those female athletes whose lives were being changed by the revolution in women's sports, right down to their underwear. No wonder a *Washington Post* writer in 1999 described the now-ubiquitous sports bra as "the cloth symbol of Title IX's success."[88]

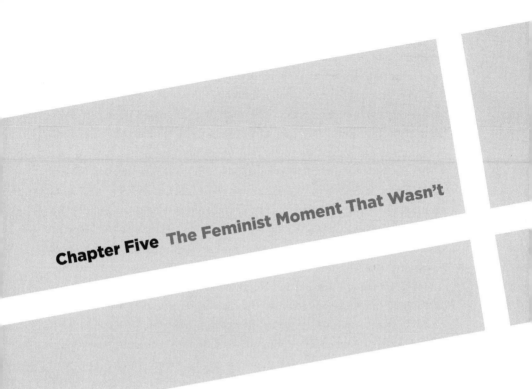

Chapter Five The Feminist Moment That Wasn't

In her November 1977 Publisher's Letter, Billie Jean King alerted readers of *womenSports* to be on the lookout for "the largest gathering of tomboys and ex-tomboys in recent history." She wasn't referring to a sporting event or pre-Olympic competition, but to the National Women's Conference to be held in Houston on November 18–20, 1977, in observance of International Women's Year (IWY). This gathering brought together 2,000 elected delegates from every state in the union, supplemented by almost 20,000 alternates, observers, and members of the press, to debate and eventually pass a national plan of action on women's issues. In many ways the Houston conference was the high point of feminist activism in the 1970s, as women of varying political agendas came together to build common ground. In retrospect, it also demonstrates the growing political power and attraction of the antifeminist narrative, embodied by Phyllis Schlafly's marshalling of between 15,000 and 20,000 women to a counter-convention for those who claimed that the Houston delegates did not speak for them. Here was the moment in the 1970s when it became clear that the category "woman" was far too broad to embrace everyone of that gender.[1]

The symbol of the Houston Conference that most captured the public imagination was a 2,600-mile torch relay that originated in Seneca Falls, New York, the site of the seminal women's rights convention in 1848, to recognize the link between the two historic conferences.[2] Organized by a team of volunteers, including members of the National Association of Girls and Women in Sport, the Road Runners of America, and the President's Council on Physical Fitness and Sports, the event began at a candlelight ceremony in Seneca Falls on September 28, when Judy Carter, the president's daughter-in-law, read a Declaration of Sentiments written by poet Maya Angelou, who was also an International Women's Year commissioner. The next morning Kathrine Switzer, the first woman to officially compete in the Boston Marathon, accepted the torch from a descendant of a signer of the original Seneca Falls declaration. After several miles, she handed it off to Donna de Varona, Olympic gold medalist and Women's Sports Foundation activist. Other runners that first day included Carole Oglesby, a Temple University professor who was the primary sports consultant for the International Women's Year commission, and Betsy East, a physical education specialist and coordinator of the New York state leg who happened to be the daughter of Catherine East, one of the original IWY coordinators.[3]

Over the next fifty-one days, the volunteer corps of runners made their way south and east, clearly identifiable as they ran their assigned miles by their bright blue t-shirts with "Women on the Move" embedded in the IWY logo. Their somewhat circuitous but media-friendly route took them by way of New York City, where they held a spirited rally led by presiding IWY officer Bella Abzug, and then Washington, D.C., where the runners circled Lafayette Park and held another rally outside the White House. Then it was on to Virginia, North Carolina, South Carolina, and Georgia. Other than the usual problems of bad weather, traffic, and sore muscles, the most serious difficulties arose in Alabama, where under pressure from Equal Rights Amendment (ERA) opponents, many of the scheduled Birmingham runners pulled out at the last moment, causing the relay organizers to scramble to recruit substitutes, and in one case, fly in marathoner Peggy Kokernot from Houston to run for sixteen miles. In sweet vindication, it was Kokernot's picture that graced the cover of *Time* magazine's December 5 story about the conference.[4]

Soon the torch relay was back on schedule, moving steadily through

Mississippi and Louisiana and finally into Texas. After a symbolic stop at Babe Didrikson Zaharias's birthplace in Beaumont, the relay moved into high gear as it approached Houston. In the final mile the official runners were joined by a host of supporters, including Donna de Varona, Olympic skier Suzy Chaffee, IWY commissioner Bella Abzug (with customary hat, but wearing pumps instead of running shoes), Betty Friedan, Susan B. Anthony II, and, not to be left out of such a wonderful moment linking her beloved causes of sports and feminism, Billie Jean King. The widely distributed photograph of the runners, arms linked with feminist leaders Abzug and Friedan as well as sports icon King, became the symbol of the "Spirit of Houston."[5]

Billie Jean King thought it was highly appropriate that sportswomen "on the move" served as the image of the Houston IWY conference. Not only did they symbolize the enormous changes underway in the field of athletics, but they also showed how much more remained to be done before women reached equality—in sport, and in all aspects of American society. The prominence of sports imagery at the conference also pointed to another truth about sports and feminism: that while issues of athletic equity were certainly recognized by second-wave feminists, they were not deemed important enough to be a major focus of the Houston plan of action, despite efforts by a small band of sports activists to push the issue. The National Plan of Action endorsed the Equal Rights Amendment, the rights of minority women and lesbians, and support for reproductive freedom, but subsumed all sports questions in the general plank on education, which called on the president to "direct the vigorous and expeditious enforcement of all laws prohibiting discrimination at all levels of education and oppose any amendments or revisions that would weaken these laws and regulations." In hindsight, the Houston conference confirmed that the most dependable way for sports to stay on the feminist agenda was through its association with Title IX.[6]

Even if sports remained a low priority for second-wave feminism nationally (it likely had more resonance on the local level[7]), there were still many points of connection between the powerful ideas of modern feminism and contemporary sports developments in the 1970s. Billie Jean King supplied one of the most prominent links with her outspoken advocacy of more opportunities, resources, and respect for women in sports and for women in general. The National Organization for Women's strong support for the Equal Rights Amendment led it to propose a controversial and far-reaching challenge to the principle of separate but equal where sports were concerned, and legal cases used the Fourteenth Amendment to expand opportunities for women to compete alongside men. Lurking beneath the surface was the question of why it was necessary to so strictly segregate the sexes when it came to sports in the first place. Ironically liberal feminism, which is often criticized for its tendency to work within the system, contained the seeds for a radical approach to sports that would have totally upended the contemporary world of athletics. This challenge did not take root in the 1970s—the feminist moment that wasn't—but the philosophical and practical questions it raised are even more relevant and compelling today.

BILLIE JEAN KING'S initial reaction to second-wave feminism in the late 1960s was decidedly negative: "When I heard that women were marching, burning bras, and picketing things like the Miss America pageant in the politically turbulent 60s, I thought they were foolish." (Her husband, Larry, offered an unintentionally hilarious explanation of why she fixated on the bra-burning: "Billie Jean just couldn't understand why people were burning bras. Billie Jean was really literal. To her, you needed a bra when you played athletics.") Quoted in the *New York Times* the day after mass rallies commemorated the fiftieth anniversary of woman suffrage around the country on August 26, 1970, she said she agreed "with most of the women's lib things, but some of it seems far out. But that might be just for attention. Lord knows, you really have to exaggerate these days to get attention." Her major beefs were the stridency of feminist demands and the necessity to toe the party line: "Women's lib can be so negative, so defensive, so narrow-minded. They think their thing is the only thing in the world for everybody. I have to do things my own way." That last phrase—"I have to do things my own way"—sums up Billie Jean King's philosophy of life as well as her relationship to feminism.[8]

Even as she was increasingly associated in the public mind with women's issues—a process that predated the Battle of the Sexes—Billie Jean King often resisted the feminist mantle, wanting to be seen as an individual and an athlete, not as the spokesperson for a cause. For example, in 1972 she complained to the *Washington Post*, "I won 19 tournaments last year. I was the first woman to win $100,000. *Time* magazine calls and wants to talk about women's lib. I wish they would say, 'We want to talk to you as an athlete.'" Note how her use of the phrase "women's lib" tended to parrot and reinforce the dismissive tone the media had adopted toward this new movement; feminist leaders carefully avoided the term, precisely because of its negative connections. And yet King realized that whenever the terms feminist or women's lib were applied to her, they were usually used pejoratively, so she was well aware of the power of the labels to silence or discredit so-called "uppity" women.[9]

Not surprisingly, Billie Jean King had mixed feelings about the Equal Rights Amendment, the centerpiece of the legislative agenda of second-wave feminism. "Progress is going to continue for women whether the law is passed or not, because society's changing and society will rule," she said in 1976. "But I wish we could just get it ratified and go ahead and get this show on the road. It is so obvious that we should already be equal under the law that it's ludicrous to be debating about a law that should have been there when the Constitution was written 200 years ago." Showing her liberal feminist bent, she sometimes wished it could be called the Equal Opportunity Amendment or the Equal Chance Amendment, as in, "The ERA just gives you a lot more options, and you take it from there." In 1982, the year that the ERA went down to defeat, she still was not convinced that it was necessary or the best tool for change: "If it means the end of discrimination on the basis of gender, then I want it. But I don't believe you can legislate people's minds. I believe that it is persuasion you need, not force. Just because you legislate does not mean people will change."[10]

And yet there is no denying that King had a well-developed sense of feminism. Here is how she defined her views in her 1974 autobiography: "To me, women's liberation means that every woman ought to be able to pursue whatever career or personal lifestyle she chooses as a full and equal member of society without fear of sexual discrimination. That's a pretty basic and simple statement, but, golly, it sure is hard sometimes to get people to accept it." The focus on freedom of choice and equal opportunity, which are the essence of liberal feminism, was the core of her philosophy, as she showed in an interview in *Playboy* in 1975: "If a woman wants to have a career, I say fine, don't put her down for it. But if she wants to be a housewife, right on; if she wants to be a mother, that's beautiful. I want every woman to be able to be whatever she *wants* to be. That's what the women's movement is all about." As a corollary, she always made it clear that similar choices and options should be open to men, in sports and in life generally. "I don't want to see women pressured by society to become housewives and mothers, but I also have empathy for the little boy who doesn't want to be a super-jock. . . . Let the boy do what he wants to do." If the world were set up in reverse where gender was concerned, she once said, she hoped that she would be fighting for the equality of men. Mainly she wanted all people to be treated as individuals, regardless of sex. This too was a key tenet of liberal feminism.[11]

While initially she had not connected her struggles in tennis with the broader movement, Billie Jean King gradually—and a bit grudgingly—made the link: "Although I realized many things were not right in my small but total sphere of tennis, it took me a while to relate them to the inequities that exist in other spheres. I finally realized that these women were not different from me; that what they were demonstrating about was the same thing I was protesting in tennis—lack of equal opportunity." Or as she told *Ms.* in 1973, "At first, when I was becoming aware, I blamed the system, but when I began to analyze it, I realized the 'system' is men." She always credited her husband, Larry, with being the major influence on her developing feminism, far more so than feminist leaders or activists, whom she knew only slightly.[12]

Being linked in the popular mind with the feminist cause helped her advocacy of women's professional tennis and sports in general, but in many ways the women's movement needed Billie Jean King a lot more than she needed them. Given all the other demands on her time, plus a deep-seated individualism bordering on stubbornness, King often experienced the movement's requests as unwelcome intrusions.[13] Still, she generously lent her name and presence to a wide variety of feminist causes. She spoke out publicly in favor of legalized abortion and equal pay for equal work and testified before Congress in support of the Women's Educational Equity Act in 1973. She also lent her name to the National Women's Political Caucus starting in 1972. As she realized, "because of my prominence, or notoriety, or whatever you want to call it, I've got a platform. I'm in a position to be heard out. There are certainly a lot of women who are more intelligent than I am and better informed about things like Women's Liberation, for example, but they can't reach anybody. What I have and what they don't have, simply, is a forum."[14]

Billie Jean King was so much in demand in part because she was the rare athlete who truly saw sports within a feminist framework. Journalist Grace Lichtenstein found out how rare King's perspective was after spending a year on the women's tennis tour in 1972–73. With the exception of King, Rosie Casals, and a few others, the vast majority of tennis players failed to grasp any link between tennis and the women's movement. "They were jocks," Lichtenstein concluded ruefully. "Their minds did not think about those things—they let their bodies do the talking for them." As player Julie Heldman later recalled, "The majority of players didn't want to know about women's lib.... People kept laying women's lib on us, instead of [us] laying it on them."[15]

Athletes' lack of identification with the feminist movement went far beyond tennis. Most successful women athletes had made it on their own by distancing themselves from traditional definitions of female behavior, which did not exactly breed a feminist consciousness or an incentive to refer to women as "we." Said softball player Joan Joyce in 1974: "I've pretty much done what I wanted my whole life, so I don't need feminism." Or as jockey Robyn Smith said in 1972: "I'm not trying to prove anything as a female jockey. I do it because I enjoy it so much, and I think people should do whatever makes them happy." A lot of established professional women, no matter how liberated their lifestyles, had similar reactions to the brash arrival of second-wave feminism on the scene in the 1970s, but the situation was even more acute for athletes who identified themselves in terms of physical rather than intellectual prowess. As golfer Kathy Duggan put it: "We're not talkers. We're doers. What does it matter what the players say as long as they *live* women's lib?"[16]

Nor did the leaders in the field of women's physical education exhibit much interest in the rising women's movement, at least initially. Even though sexual discrimination in sports was probably more extreme than anywhere else in society, these women were so caught up in the need to constantly assert their heteronormativity in the face of general disapproval of women's athleticism that they lacked many of the necessary preconditions for feminist consciousness raising. Already marginalized by their interest in women's sports and actively trying to protect their small enclave of women's athletics, such leaders were reluctant to risk being labeled strident, unfeminine, or worse (i.e., lesbians), which they feared could cost them important male allies, and possibly their jobs.[17]

In many ways the tensions between Billie Jean King and second-wave feminism replicated the classic mind/body split, with King coming down on the action side of feminism rather than the intellectual. "Tennis helps the women's movement just by *doing*. We're *there*, we're visual, like blacks in sports helped their movement. If people see us out there every day, that changes people's minds, not *talking* about it." Referring to Kate Millett's influential but dense *Sexual Politics*, an unexpected bestseller in 1970, King recalled: "I started the Kate Millett book, but I couldn't hack it. That stuff's great for about two percent of women. What I'd rather do is influence one hundred percent of women to see a better life for themselves." And yet King always remained frustrated that leaders of the women's movement, while friendly, too often left sports off the feminist agenda, even though athletes "could have been a great conduit for social change." As she told Bella Abzug around 1982, "You know, the real shame is that women's sports could be so visible. It is such an obvious tool. But you've never used it. No one has." She made similar complaints about failing to use athletes to highlight equal rights issues to Gloria Steinem, who supposedly replied, "Billie, this is about politics." For once, the tennis player trumped the prominent feminist with this spot-on reply: "Gloria, we *are* politics."[18]

Billie Jean King was not the first—or the last—to notice a certain disconnect between sports and feminism in the 1970s. Grace Lichtenstein captured the movement's noticeable lack of interest in sports when she noted in 1974 that while feminist leaders "may have helped liberate women from the kitchen, they did not urge anyone to run out onto the volleyball court." For many feminists, the topic of sports conjured up images of Monday Night Football, not women's softball. All of the major sporting championships such as the World Series, the Super Bowl, and the Masters totally excluded women, and other than Billie Jean King, there were hardly any well-known women from the world of sports to identify with and look up to. Sport was seen as so "male" that many feminists at the time wanted nothing to do with it, even had they been encouraged or welcomed, which they most definitely were not. As Donna Lopiano later put it, "[The women's movement] thought that athletics was a male construct that taught violence against somebody else, inordinate levels of competition—that it was an unhealthy activity for women—and that we were going to follow in the footsteps of men's values, and not the best men's values at all."[19]

The crass commercialism and focus on winning that largely characterized male organized sporting activity were a real turn-off to an emerging feminist movement built around the ethos of cooperation and sisterhood, where the issue of competition between and among women at times functioned almost as a feminist taboo. Here is how the 1973 edition of the Boston Women's Health Book Collective's *Our Bodies, Ourselves* described the contemporary world of sports and women's role in it: "But given the American world of athletics, based as it is on the most aggressive, dog-eat-dog patterns of male competitiveness and greedily engaged in marketing the successful athlete like any other product in our society, we do not want to see women triumphing over women in ugly, masculine ways. Instead of turning talented people into superstars, we favor providing opportunity and encouragement for all."[20] Some feminist softball teams, for example, experimented with rotating positions, letting everyone play equal amounts of time regardless of skill, and treating the other team like sisters by sharing the same bench rather than sitting on opposite sides of the field. Their noncompetitive mantra: "The obsession with winning is a vestige of patriarchy."[21]

Also unappealing was the connection between sport, war, and aggression: many women viewed all three with suspicion and distrust, especially while the Vietnam War still dragged on. Of course, just because sports have traditionally been portrayed as patriarchal and violent doesn't mean that that is the only way they have existed or could operate. "To dismiss sports as a product of a capitalistic, patriarchal society is to accept things as they are rather than work toward things as they might be," Hollis Elkins observed with a note of disappointment in 1978. Donna Lopiano made a similar point even more forcefully: "Why any feminist would deny the validity of participation in a highly competitive activity that produces strong women who are able to resist oppression or who have the guts to uphold principle is beyond me. Sport *itself* is not 'bad.' The values men have brought to it and inserted as 'primary' are an anathema. Don't discard the baby (sport) with the bath water (exploitive values)."[22]

Besides the view of sports as violent and male defined, there is also a lingering suspicion that perhaps sports were not high on the feminist agenda because so many of the early movement leaders were physically inactive and/or had no exposure to or interest in sports. Remember that one of the key slogans of the movement was "the personal is political." Remember also that many of the new movement's leaders were based in New York City, hardly a hotbed of athleticism for women. If a budding feminist happened already to be involved or interested in athletic activity, she would be more likely to make the link between feminist ideology and the practice of sport. If sport was an alien foreign culture, however, then there was little reason to expect that it would find a prominent place on the feminist agenda. As sports theorist M. Ann Hall later put it, "Female bodies have always been central to feminism, but sporting bodies have not," an insight with profound consequences for the revolution in women's sports and women's lives in the 1970s.[23]

THE NATIONAL ORGANIZATION for Women (NOW) offers one example of how the women's movement approached the issue of women and sports in the 1970s.[24] Founded in 1966, NOW did not have a task force on sports in operation until the summer of 1973, when national coordinator Judy Wenning reported 130 members and a goal of having a sports committee in every chapter. Title IX enforcement was the task force's top priority, followed by a long list of goals, including equal access to recreational facilities; elimination of discrimination in all school athletic programs; development of a positive image of women in sports; unbiased media coverage; public support for women's sports development, including encouraging local chapters to help develop programs for girls and women with an emphasis on "health, enjoyment, and physical fitness"; and the encouragement, collection, and dissemination of research on women and sports. That ambitious agenda was matched by a budget of only $705, typical of the way in which NOW task forces were often given broad mandates but little support to carry out their goals.[25] NOW never developed an official sports policy statement, and by 1977 the task force was no longer in operation. NOW later tried to take credit for being in the lead on Title IX ("Passage of this legislation was one of our proudest moments"), but such a statement vastly overinflates its involvement at the time.[26]

With the proviso that sports were never a high priority for NOW at the national level, there is intriguing evidence from the 1970s that the organization was ready to leap into the debate about how best to provide athletic equality for girls and women with a stand on sports that was far in advance of conventional wisdom. While admitting that women might need sex-segregated programs in the short term until they were able to come into their own athletically, NOW activists envisioned a sports program that treated women as individuals. NOW's stance was firm and unequivocal: "NOW is opposed to any regulation which precludes eventual integration. Regulations that 'protect' girls and/or women are against NOW goals and are contradictory to our stand on the ERA. Of course one has to be prepared to answer the question, 'Do you want your daughter to box?' The answer is of course, 'MY daughter is the one to decide that, not HEW!'"[27]

NOW's disavowal of laws designed to "protect" women or treat them differently from men was very much wrapped up in the long and contentious debate about protective legislation that had divided the postsuffrage women's movement practically from the day the Equal Rights Amendment was introduced in 1923. Protective legislation for women emerged in the Progressive era as a way of guaranteeing better working conditions for women. Because of working women's supposed physical inferiority and status as "future mothers of the race," there was support, both judicial and political, for easing their burdens through legislation such as limiting work to eight hours a day, guaranteeing a minimum wage, setting limits on the amount of weight they could lift on the job, and banning night work out of concerns for women's physical safety after dark. While some reformers no doubt believed that working women were indeed weaker and in need of more protection than men, they also had an instrumental reason for focusing legislation only on women: no early twentieth-century court would have upheld such laws for men. In the view of the courts, such laws were infringements on the right of workers and employers to enter into contracts, precisely the reasoning the court applied in *Lochner v. New York* (1905) to strike down a law limiting the hours of bakers in New York State. Just three years later, however, swayed by a brief submitted by Louis Brandeis and the National Consumers' League documenting how long hours damaged the health and family roles of women workers, the Supreme Court upheld a ten-hour day for Oregon's female workers in *Muller v. Oregon* (1908).[28]

When the ERA was introduced in 1923, its language threatened this tradition of protective legislation. Some feminists felt the broad constitutional protection of the ERA was more important than specific laws, while others were unwilling to give up hard-won reforms for an abstract ideal. The impasse stood until the 1930s when New Deal legislation such as the Fair Labor Standards Act of 1938 in effect extended those protections to all workers. Still many women activists, especially those in the labor movement but also including many reformers, refused to put aside their opposition to the ERA. This rift played itself out from 1961 to 1963 in the President's Commission on the Status of Women, which proposed a range of recommendations to advance women's rights but declined to endorse the ERA. The tide was turning, however, and by the late 1960s most women activists had concluded that protective legislation was no longer necessary. In turn, they rallied, although not always enthusiastically, around the ERA.[29]

NOW leaders were steeped in this debate over protective legislation, and it almost certainly influenced their stand on sex segregation versus integration in sports. To their minds, the attempt to segregate women's sports into a separate track because of assumptions about physical limits and inferiority must have sounded distressingly similar to the old stereotypes that had suggested that women workers needed special protection solely because they were women. For example, laws limiting women to lifting thirty pounds on the job (the weight of a small child many a mother has picked up) or preventing the hiring of women with preschool children were not only based on outmoded ideas of women's physical capabilities but also hindered women in the workplace by keeping them out of higher-paying jobs. Instead NOW proposed that women be treated as individuals, not members of a second sex; if any protection or special circumstances were needed, let them be provided on an individual, not group, basis. "SEPA-RATE IS NEVER EQUAL!!!!!" proclaimed Pennsylvania chapter president Ellie Smeal emphatically in 1973.[30]

A good place to see how this stance played itself out in terms of sports policy is with the comments submitted to the Department of Health, Education and Welfare (HEW) in October 1974 on the proposed Title IX regulations. These comments were prepared by the NOW Legal Defense and Education Fund and NOW's Project on Equal Education Rights, with legal advice from the Center for National Policy Review in Washington. Other women's organizations such as the Women's Equity Action League or the Association for Intercollegiate Athletics for Women (AIAW) submitted detailed comments as well, focusing on questions such as equal access, treatment, and resources, as well as demanding leadership roles for women in administering the new programs, but they accepted the basic overall premise behind the existing sports structure. NOW charted a very different course.[31]

While encouraged that the guidelines called for coeducational physical education classes, NOW was disturbed that the section on competitive athletics rested on a "separate but equal" doctrine, "without any indication that we should be working towards the day when absolute nondiscrimination— full integration—is possible." NOW's comments stressed that equality in competitive athletics must address both tangible and intangible factors, including the skill level on a team, since the more skilled the team, the better the athlete. As they put it pointedly: "If men's and women's teams are fully equal, including skill level, *there is no justification for segregation.* Inequality, whether because of differences in past training, interest, or physical abilities, is the only justification for segregation." Reminding policymakers that there was not yet conclusive evidence on whether current differences between male and female athletes were the result of innate physical differences or differences in training and expectations, NOW insisted that the policy rest on a presumption of sexual equality rather than an unproved assumption of sexual inequality.

Certain elite female athletes could already compete with their male peers, but they would be the exceptions. So NOW hedged its bets just a bit, asking that schools also provide guarantees "that where such equality is not now a reality, females will still be assured of an equal opportunity for the physical and psychological rewards of athletic competition." Finally, the regulation should ask recipients to do everything in their power "to overcome the effects of past discrimination with a view toward making complete integration possible as quickly as possible."

How would such a plan actually work? NOW proposed that each school establish a nondiscriminatory "unitary" team open to both sexes "in each sport and at each level of competition in which the recipient wishes to provide competitive athletic opportunities." However, when a unitary team resulted in a predominantly single-sex team "because of discrimination, difference in training, interest, or physical attributes, or any other factor limiting the presence of members of one sex on the team," then the institution must also set up a separate team for the sex so limited. The team must be equal to the predominantly single-sex team in areas such as facilities, coaching, expenditures, and prestige. At the point when the nondiscriminatory unitary team was no longer predominantly single-sexed, there would no longer be a need to field an additional separate team.

The call for a "unitary" team open to both sexes was controversial, especially among leaders in the field of women's physical education who feared that institutions would simply open all the men's teams to women and say that they were legally providing equal opportunities to both sexes. Since only the most talented girls would be able to make the boys' teams, girls might actually end up with even fewer participation opportunities than before. How real a threat this would have been is hard to gauge. Given the explosive demands for access to sports by girls and their parents in the 1970s, it is hard to imagine them being satisfied by having a token girl or two on the tennis or swimming team. In any case, NOW always took pains to say that this was not their only solution. As Anne Grant, coordinator of NOW's Education Task Force, wrote to J. Stanley Pottinger of the Office for Civil Rights in January 1973, "I must emphatically add that a single, integrated varsity team is not our ideal for public athletic programs. It is merely one model which will remove sex discrimination from athletic programs as they are now structured."[32]

The main idea behind the unitary team was to give the gifted female athlete a chance to compete against her peers, who in this case would be boys. These girls were the ones most disadvantaged by a separate but equal approach; correspondingly, they had the most to gain from an integrated, gender-blind policy. NOW was not just interested in the elite athlete, however; its activists also wanted to increase opportunities "to reach the greatest number of students possible."[33] NOW seemed to have in mind a dramatic expansion of intramural sports geared toward developing the skills and meeting the needs of many "average" athletes, male and female, in contrast to men's varsity programs that spent everything on an "elite" few. In this respect, NOW was in line with the philosophy of the Association for Intercollegiate Athletics for Women, which preferred a more participation-based model of athletics for women and men rather than the competitive approach traditionally pursued by the National Collegiate Athletic Association.[34]

NOW clearly believed that there was just a short window of opportunity to make the point about integration. In the past, there had been hardly any sports programs for girls; now it was clear there would be many more. Don't get caught up in separate programs for women, NOW activists warned, because instead of being temporary solutions while girls and women developed the necessary skills and encouragement to compete with boys and men, such programs will become just as entrenched as the system they were supposed to be challenging. A position paper on sports drafted around the same time by the Pennsylvania chapter of NOW made a similar point: "The sexists of the world will push right now for sex-segregated programs and will try to make these attractive to girls because they do not want them to venture forth in the vicinity of their limited, superboy varsity programs. We must not play into their hands." The Pennsylvania chapter drew an interesting parallel to affirmative action: "We all know that a purely affirmative action program which had catch-up attributes must have a 'phase out' stage. We feel that the present separate but equal programs in reality do not have a phase-out stage." As they cogently realized, "we must move quickly into the vacuum of promoting integrated activities wherever possible so that sex-segregated does not become the absolute *de facto* rule of sports in our state." That, of course, is precisely what happened.[35]

What all these NOW positions have in common is a willingness to step outside the box and think about sports in new and different ways. There certainly were benefits to an outsider's perspective when it came to identifying alternatives to old, entrenched customs, but they came with costs, both financial and political. To truly implement the NOW vision of a unitary team, a separate team for the underrepresented sex, and opportunities for a much broader range of intramural athletes grouped by ability and interest would have been prohibitively expensive for schools at a time when they were wondering how they were going to find the funds to start up even rudimentary programs for girls. Women's physical education leaders were especially threatened by the stance on integration because it would wipe out the carefully guarded enclave of women's sports they had painstakingly built over the years. In frustration, sports leaders and school administrators alike accused these NOW activists of not knowing anything about sports, which was not actually that far off the mark. For the most part, NOW's national leaders came to the issue intellectually rather than from actual practical experience or interest in sports or competitive athletics. They approached access to sports as an abstract problem to be solved, rather than a real-world situation with deeply imbedded practices that would be difficult to uproot. In other words, they weren't jocks. Billie Jean King had an even better characterization: she called their approach thinking "from the neck up."[36]

Nor was there ever a real chance that HEW would adopt such a controversial and wide-ranging proposal, given its politically driven need to craft a compromise that addressed the urgent and often conflicting needs of the wide array of sports, education, and feminist constituencies with a stake in the legislation. Gwen Gregory, the lawyer at HEW who was deeply involved in drafting the Title IX regulations on athletics, called the NOW brief "intellectually the best one, without any question," but "completely unworkable in the real world": "it was 50 teams in every sport and that way everyone has a team on which they can play, and they compete for the team. Well, legally, it's wonderful but it's impossible to carry out." Like school administrators, Gregory concluded that the NOW staff in Washington knew practically nothing about sports. In the end, "we just completely discarded it, because there was no way we could require something like that."[37]

It wasn't just HEW's lack of willingness to embrace bold new ideas that doomed NOW's innovative approach. Even if the federal government had adopted the NOW position, it would have proven extremely difficult to implement because the women's sports revolution was still too embryonic to compel popular acceptance for such a radical assault on the status quo. With the inequities in women's sports barely on the radar in the early 1970s, a policy so far in advance of public opinion would have been doomed to failure.

Another reason why the National Organization for Women did not prevail was that the underlying issues were just too complex for a "one size fits all" solution. As competing approaches dueled for support, it gradually became clear that there was not going to be one quick fix, politically or intellectually, to resolve this complicated debate over gender equity and athletics in the 1970s. As Title IX activist Bernice Sandler recalled later, "I and others spent endless hours with brilliant attorneys, policy wonks, athletic personnel, civil rights advocates, federal civil rights personnel, women's rights activists—all trying to devise some sort of a practical solution to the problem, and yet every so-called 'solution' had some grievous flaws within it." It wasn't just for lack of imagination or trying. On the contrary, the impasse was rooted in the fundamental dilemma of modern feminism: how to achieve equality while also recognizing difference.[38]

At times these debates over Title IX seemed like a classroom in Feminist Theory 101. Billie Jean King and NOW activists represented liberal feminism and an equal rights approach, suspicious of old stereotypes that limited women's full participation in modern life and pushing the view that women must be treated as individuals regardless of sex. The National Collegiate Athletic Association represented a traditional patriarchal view that wanted to keep sports for men only, or at most, offer some crumbs to women without disturbing the male-dominated status quo. The Association for Intercollegiate Athletics for Women shaded more toward difference or cultural feminism with their call for women to retain control over women's athletics, their commitment to the preservation of a female ideal that did not simply ape the male standard of competitiveness and exclusion, and their determination to offer sports for a wider range of participants than just elite athletes. In hindsight there is much to credit in the AIAW vision in the 1970s and much to criticize with the liberal feminist rush to integrate women into the existing athletic system without fundamental change. And yet by zeroing in on the limits of separate but equal, especially when it came to the needs of elite female athletes who could play with the boys, liberal feminism made an extremely important contribution to a debate that is still ongoing.

When the Supreme Court overturned *Plessy v. Ferguson*'s separate but equal doctrine and outlawed racial segregation in schools in *Brown v. Board of Education* in 1954, large segments of American society remained unswayed by the court's assertion of full citizenship rights for African Americans. Well in advance of public opinion, the legal decision eventually acted as a force for social change. Women athletes are subject to cultural stereotypes, lack of access to resources and opportunities, and lingering assumptions of innate biological differences that bear more than a passing resemblance to how African Americans were viewed in the 1950s. If sports had followed the model of racial desegregation when the regulations implementing Title IX were first written in the early 1970s, the model of "separate but equal" might have been discarded in favor of one that promoted sports integration, or at least downplayed the differences between the sexes in sports organization. But popular attachment to a binary gender system, in large part because of the assumption of men's physical superiority, meant that the revolution in women's sports since the 1970s did unfold along separate—and decidedly unequal—lines.

Like so many other aspects of this story of feminism and sports, there was a very short window of opportunity in the early 1970s when new thinking might have prevailed. Women's sports were practically a tabula rasa, a blank slate. Instead of setting up a parallel system that mimicked athletic apartheid for women and girls, what if the model had been more along the lines adopted for physical education, which stressed coeducational activities and integration of programs wherever possible? The literature in sports sociology and medicine tells us that human physical activity and skill is a continuum, that the similarities between the broad range of men and women are more salient than their differences at the very top or bottom. And yet even as the rest of society has moved in a more gender-neutral direction, competitive sports remain rigidly segregated by sex. Ironically, at least when it came to athletics, Title IX ended up reinforcing, rather than subverting, the very differences that it was originally passed to correct.[39]

NOT SURPRISINGLY, there was a lot of litigation around the issue of women's and girls' access to sports in the 1970s. Surprisingly, very little of this litigation involved Title IX, mainly because of HEW's dithering about issuing regulations, its delays investigating complaints and setting policy, the extension until 1978 for most schools to be in compliance, plus the inevitable time lag in cases working their way through the legal system. If not Title IX, then what legal recourse did sports activists have in the 1970s? For the most part, the legal doctrine of choice was the equal protection clause of the Fourteenth Amendment. Also useful were state Equal Rights

Amendments. (Affirmative action was not a major player in this story in the 1970s.)[40] These legal challenges grappled with many of the intellectual arguments advanced by the National Organization for Women in its critique of the Title IX regulations. More broadly, these legal cases show what happens when an individualistic, equal rights approach consistent with liberal feminism is applied to sports. With the logic and precedents of legal doctrine bucking up against deeply held conventional wisdom about male physical superiority, the results often pushed the comfort level of the sports world at the time.[41]

The 1970s were a time of enormous change when it came to legal rights for women. A good way to see how the changing attitudes played out in sports is to compare two cases from the beginning and the end of the decade. In 1971, a Connecticut high school girl sued in order to participate on a boys' cross-country team because there was no girls' team. The judge ruled against her in language that suggested that gender stereotypes were just as compelling factors in his reasoning as legal precedents: "Athletic competition builds character in our boys. We do not need that kind of character in our girls, the women of tomorrow." Fast forward to 1978 and an Ohio case involving girls' access to contact sports such as basketball and football. Judge Carl B. Rubin took a broader philosophical view, writing in his opinion: "It has always been traditional that 'boys play football and girls are cheerleaders.' Why so? Where is it written that girls may not, if suitably qualified, play football? There may be a multitude of reasons why a girl might elect not to do so. Reasons of stature or weight or reasons of temperament, motivation or interest. This is a matter of personal choice. But a prohibition without exception based upon sex is not." He concluded with this vision of the future: "It may well be that there is a student today in an Ohio high school who lacks only the proper coaching and training to become the greatest quarterback in professional history. Of course the odds are astronomical against her, but isn't she entitled to a fair chance to try?"[42]

The cases about access to teams in the early 1970s were most likely to succeed when a girl was seeking the right to play on a boys' team in a noncontact sport where no girls' team existed. The prevailing motivation seemed to be not to crack the barriers of male exclusion but simply to win a chance to compete, period. If there had been girls' teams, many of these suits would not have been filed. For example, in a case in Minnesota decided in 1972 (*Brenden v. Independent School District*, which was affirmed in 1973 by the

U.S. Court of Appeals), two exceptionally talented female athletes, Peggy Brenden and Tony St. Pierre, wanted to play on the boys' teams in tennis, cross-country, and skiing. While the court heard evidence about women's physiological differences from men, it concluded it was not relevant in this case: "Because of their level of achievement in competitive sports, Tony and Peggy have overcome these physiological disabilities. There has been no evidence that either [of them] . . . or any other girls, would be in any way damaged from competition in boys' interscholastic athletics, nor is there any credible evidence that the boys could be damaged." According to Eileen McDonagh and Laura Pappano's recent survey, of the forty cases litigated at the state and federal level over male-only teams, courts ruled in 85 percent of them that such teams were not permissible.[43]

One of the most interesting cases involved a suit filed in 1973 by the Commonwealth of Pennsylvania against the Pennsylvania Interscholastic Athletic Association (PIAA). The PIAA had a by-law that unilaterally forbade boys and girls from mixed athletic competition, which overruled any attempts by exceptional girls to win spots on boys' teams. The case hinged on whether the PIAA's rule discriminated on the basis of sex and thus violated the state's Equal Rights Amendment. The Pennsylvania chapter of the National Organization for Women strongly supported the suit challenging the exclusionary standard and applauded the eventual decision, which ruled that the provision did indeed violate the state's ERA.[44]

What was distinctive about the PIAA decision was that it opened contact as well as noncontact sports to all, regardless of sex. This decision gave glimpses of what a legal doctrine that mandated equality and overlooked prevailing stereotypes and rationales might look like. Addressing the question of whether girls should be allowed to play on boys' teams even if there were teams for girls, the court pointed out what really is the most compelling argument in terms of women competing alongside men: "Even where separate teams are offered for boys and girls in the same sport, the most talented girls still may be denied the right to play at that level of competition which their ability might otherwise permit them. For a girl in that position, who has been relegated to the 'girls' team,' solely because of her sex, 'equality under the law' has been denied." The decision also showed what sports looked like when participants were viewed as individuals, not as members of a gendered sex subject to overly broad or paternalistic notions: "The existence of certain characteristics to a greater degree in one sex does not justify classification by sex rather than by the particular characteristic. If any individual girl is too weak, injury-prone, or unskilled, she may, of course, be excluded from competition on that basis but she cannot be excluded solely because of her sex without regard to her relevant qualifications."[45]

Even more important than state Equal Rights Amendments were cases decided under the equal protection clause of the Fourteenth Amendment. Unlike the athletics regulations of Title IX, which encouraged a sex-differentiated view of equality, the equal protection clause of the Fourteenth Amendment mandated that all similarly situated individuals receive "equal protection of the laws." For example, a 1972 Nebraska decision about a girl's attempt to play on the boys' golf team reasoned: "The issue is not whether Debbie Reed has a 'right' to play golf; the issue is whether she can be treated differently from boys in an activity provided by the state. Her right is not the right to play golf. Her right is the right to be treated the same as boys unless there is a rational basis for her being treated differently."[46]

Another thing that the equal protection clause encouraged was a certain skepticism about the differences between the sexes that supposedly warranted separate treatment. As legal scholar Deborah Brake noted, "The core inquiry is whether the asserted differences between men and women, once stripped of archaic stereotypes and overbroad generalizations, are sufficient to support treating the sexes differently, or are instead mere remnants of traditional views about the proper place of men and women."[47]

Title IX's contact sports exclusion is a perfect example of a regulation that is based primarily on stereotyped views and untested assumptions. What possible legal justification is there for saying that no girls should play rough sports such as football and ice hockey or engage in physical contact with the opposite sex in sports such as wrestling? When strictly scrutinized, many of the supposedly immutable facts about the different capabilities of the sexes rest on stereotyped, out of date, or unsubstantiated statements about what are assumed to be these differences. Not the least, the focus on physical difference totally ignores the many other factors besides size that go into making an exceptional athlete, as nearsighted, 5'4" Billie Jean King's career amply demonstrates.

Despite the contact sports exclusion under Title IX, plaintiffs successfully used the Fourteenth Amendment to win women access to contact sports across the board starting in the 1970s and continuing to the present. The earliest battles were fought in baseball, with the successful battle to open Little League in 1973 and 1974 getting the most publicity, but girls also won the right to compete in basketball and soccer, even football, later in the decade. Sarah Fields, who has studied contact sports and the legal system, notes how courts filled the gap created by the Title IX exemption by using the Fourteenth Amendment to win girls access to contact sports, which to her mind "debunks the mythological power of Title IX, and it lauds the legal might of the equal protection clause." Once again, not all the successes in the history of women's sports can be laid at the feet of Title IX.[48]

Finally, the emphasis on equal protection raises the question that was fundamental to the *Brown* decision on segregated schools: when determining whether separate can ever be equal, it is important to take into account intangible as well as tangible factors. In the case of *Sweatt v. Painter* (1950), the state of Texas offered a separate law school for blacks, which it then used to argue that blacks need not be allowed to enroll in the all-white school. The court ruled that even if the two schools were generally comparable in terms of things such as courses and faculty, they still were not equal because the white school enjoyed substantially more prestige.[49]

How might the reasoning in *Sweatt* and *Brown* apply to athletics? Like the practice of segregation in public education, segregating girls on separate teams could reinforce the notion that they are physically inferior and thus unable to compete with boys as a group. Indeed the whole idea behind dividing sports by sex is premised on the inequality of women—if women and men were equal, then there would be no need for separation. Even if athletic resources and opportunities comparable to those available for boys were offered to girls, intangible factors would still color their experiences. Rare cases such as Iowa girls' basketball aside, girls' teams rarely enjoy the same prestige as boys' teams in the same sport or in the sports hierarchy in general. Few male teams would willingly switch places with their female equivalents, which brings us back to the notion articulated in *Brown v. Board of Education* that separate can never be equal. In such a situation women athletes will always be second-class citizens.

The early 1970s were part of a larger legal moment when equal protection arguments were being used to strike down older, archaic laws that had treated women as a class differently from men, mainly on the basis of stereotyped assumptions. As recently as 1948 in *Goesaert v. Cleary*, the Supreme Court upheld a Michigan statute prohibiting women from tending bar unless they were the wives or daughters of bar owners. This statute stemmed from concern for protecting women as a group from the supposedly inappropriate site of male bar culture, an impulse very similar to—and just as demeaning and patronizing as—earlier protective legislation such as *Muller v. Oregon.* In 1961 the Supreme Court in *Hoyt v. Florida* turned down an appeal by a woman who claimed her rights had been discriminated against because she was convicted of murdering her husband by an all-male jury, ruling that Florida's policy of making jury duty mandatory for men but voluntary for women was constitutional. In its most quoted passage, the Supreme Court called women's exemption from jury duty reasonable, not arbitrary, because "woman is still regarded as the center of home and family life."[50]

Such semichivalrous sentiments were increasingly difficult to defend from legal scrutiny after midcentury. Already by 1972, the following practices had been overturned because they violated the equal protection clause of the Fourteenth Amendment: "the exclusion of women from juries; differential sentencing laws for men and women; the exclusion of women patrons from liquor-licensed places of accommodation; the exclusion of women patrons from an all-male 'prestige' college in a state university system; requiring all unmarried women under 21 to live in a state college dormitory when no such requirement was imposed on men; and requiring extended periods of mandatory maternity leave."[51]

The Supreme Court added some extremely important precedents in the period between 1971 and 1975, cases that are arguably as important for the modern women's rights movement as *Roe v. Wade*'s legalization of abortion in 1973. *Reed v. Reed* (1971) overturned Idaho's automatic preference for a male over a female in terms of executorship if the two were otherwise equally entitled to administer an estate. In *Frontiero v. Richardson* (1973), the court struck down a military provision that provided free medical care for the wife of an enlisted man but did not provide the same care for the husband of an enlisted woman. Two years later the Supreme Court relied on *Frontiero* to strike down a social security classification that allowed benefit payments to the wives of deceased male wage earners but not to husbands of deceased female wage earners, in *Weinberger v. Wiesenfeld.*[52]

When applying the Fourteenth Amendment's guarantee of equal protection, courts must select among three levels of review to determine whether the discrimination is invidious: strict, intermediate, and rational basis review. In *Reed v. Reed,* the Supreme Court came close (four out of the five opinions in the majority decisions) to requiring the application of the strict standard by declaring sex a "suspect" classification. This would have meant that like race, alienage, or national origin, there would have to be a compelling state interest (an extremely high standard) to treat women as a class differently from men. In the years since, the Supreme Court has backed away from that precipice, generally applying an intermediate level of review ("substantially related to achieving an important government objective") where sex is concerned, but still continuing its general skepticism about laws based on outdated assumptions about gender and sex.[53]

The importance of the Equal Rights Amendment is that it would have enshrined the principle of sex as a suspect qualification in the Constitution, making it extremely difficult to draw such distinctions when it came to legislation or government action. The whole thrust of the ERA, which read in part "Equality of rights under the law shall not be denied or abridged by the United States or by any State on account of sex," was to treat individuals equally before the law. Any attempt to classify women and men differently on the basis of sex would have faced strict scrutiny. For example, under the ERA it is extremely likely that both men and women would be subject to a military draft. The ERA would also likely lead to the repeal of the exemption of women from combat.[54]

Historians debate whether the women's movement chose poorly when it made the Equal Rights Amendment the main focus of its public activism from its passage by Congress in 1972 until its demise in 1982; the debate revolves around both means and ends. Part of the controversy is whether all the resources and time invested in the fight for state ratification, a fight that got harder and ultimately unwinnable once Phyllis Schlafly and other conservative women joined the fray in mid-decade, could have been better spent on other issues. There is also a lingering sense that the ERA had at best symbolic meaning: that its main purpose was to place a general standard of equality in the Constitution rather than to impact individual laws. If the equal protection clause of the Fourteenth Amendment had already removed most of the outmoded laws that treated women differently, was a constitutional amendment really necessary at all?[55]

The argument looks different when sports are factored in. While it is true that many legal distinctions between men and women had been chipped away by the 1970s, the one arena where old traditions and stereotypes still reigned practically unchallenged was in sports. Whereas society was no longer willing to prohibit women from being bartenders, exclude them from strenuous jobs, or limit their enrollment in professional schools, it was still willing, indeed eager, to embrace a system for organizing sports that was based on the premise that men and women must be classified separately by sex for the purposes of athletic competition. This is precisely the legal approach that the Title IX athletic regulations took. If the Equal Rights Amendment had been adopted, however, it would have trumped a piece of Congressional legislation.

Is there a possible scenario whereby the courts could have left a sex-segregated athletic system in place despite the ERA? According to a report issued by the Senate Judiciary Committee in 1972, the only two permissible exceptions to the ERA would have been the right to personal privacy and situations related to a unique physical characteristic of one sex.[56] The right to privacy would certainly have allowed segregated locker rooms to continue but does not seem widely applicable to other sports practices. No doubt sports administrators would have tried to argue that sex-segregated teams were related to unique physical characteristics of each sex, the equivalent of the bona fide occupational qualification (BFOQ) that the Equal Employment Opportunity Commission (EEOC) allowed in employment discrimination. The EEOC had initially allowed newspapers to continue to divide ads into "Help Wanted-Female" and "Help Wanted-Male," supposedly for the convenience of job seekers, until NOW successfully challenged this practice in court. Eventually the EEOC limited the bona fide occupational qualification to cases of extreme sexual differentiation such as sperm donors or wet nurses, which is not much of a precedent for sex-segregated teams. Combined with the string of equal protection cases already creating precedents for a sex-blind approach to sports, a sex-segregated sports system probably would have had a hard time surviving judicial scrutiny if it came up against the ERA.[57]

Think of it this way. If the Equal Rights Amendment had coasted to approval and become part of the constitution by 1975, as had seemed likely when it was sent to the states just three years earlier, it would have forced HEW and its various constituencies to craft policy with this higher legal standard in mind. Maybe the ERA would have stopped the separate but equal process in its tracks and encouraged the development of an athletic system that was dedicated to the general proposition of integration, not segregation, as the National Organization for Women proposed; less drastically, the amendment might have raised consciousness about some of the unexamined assumptions that underlay the current structure. At the very least, the ERA would have given those trying to expand athletic opportunities for women a much stronger legal weapon to challenge the sports status quo. If this had been the case, perhaps the Equal Rights Amendment would be getting all the credit for the revolution in women's sports today rather than Title IX.

MOST AMERICANS, indeed most citizens around the world, still take it as a given that men and women cannot compete together in sports because men are faster and stronger than women. Why is that allowed to end the discussion? As *USA Today* columnist Christine Brennan points out, "Stating the obvious fact that women athletes are not as strong and fast as their male counterparts is like criticizing men for not having a body equipped to give birth. There's absolutely nothing they can do about it." And yet there is something society can do about it: it can scrutinize the way modern athletics is organized and it can challenge the often untested assumptions and stereotypes that define women as a different—and lesser—category of athletes than men. And one way to do that is to rethink why sports are so deeply divided by gender in the first place. A liberal feminist approach that focuses on athletes as individuals rather than distinct categories of men and women offers a fresh—indeed, radical—perspective.[58]

Billie Jean King grappled with this question throughout her career. "I see the day coming in sports when we will all be competing on the basis of our individual abilities, not our gender. I see that day coming, and I welcome it," she said in 1984. In her view, sports competition should be integrated from elementary school on so that girls and boys grow up learning teamwork together and competing on equal terms. "I believe that in every aspect of sports, women would achieve much higher levels of performance if they entered the crucible of competition with men on an open basis, from the beginning and throughout the educational process." She was certain that if she had had that experience, she would have been "better, faster, and stronger than I am." How good and how strong? "I may not be the number-one tennis player in the men's division, but that doesn't mean I couldn't hold my own somewhere in the men's division. Especially if I had conditioned myself for it for twenty years the way many of the men have." But King didn't stop there. "There's no reason why we can't have teams determined by ability, not gender. We might want to change the rules too. Why should every sport be based on speed and strength? There are other sports that can be created that aren't based on those things."[59]

In these scattered musings, Billie Jean King raised fundamental and potentially revolutionary questions about how sport and gender are organized in modern society. Why are sports divided by gender rather than by ability, size, or other factors? Why do sports privilege male attributes of speed and strength rather than the endurance or agility more common to women? Would a different array of sports bring different outcomes? What if there are in fact more similarities between the athletic abilities of the two sexes than differences? And if some women can hold their own against men, then what is the justification for a competitive structure such as Title IX's that is basically constructed around the principle of separate but equal? That was the basis of apartheid in South Africa, King noted pointedly. Her answer was clear and unequivocal: "'Separate but equal' means women will always be second-class citizens in sport."[60]

Sports historian Barbara Gregorich put it bluntly: "If baseball had been open to women for the last 150 years, we would have already seen female major leaguers. The game is closed not because women can't play, but because men in power don't want women around." In turn, because the current sports system reinforces the differences between the sexes, it serves to reify the notion that men are inherently stronger and faster than women and that any ideas of women being able to compete with men would founder on their physical limitations. Who benefits from this argument? Men, of course, and men's traditional hegemony of sports, although women too for their own reasons have colluded in keeping the sexes segregated when it comes to physical activity. Title IX has also played a key—and often unrecognized—role in propping up this sexist system, especially with its contact sports exclusion: as Eileen McDonagh and Ellen Pappano argue, "The bottom line was that Title IX's permission to segregate contact sports effectively led to universal sex-segregation in virtually all sports." The end result is the same: since the sports world is constructed to maximize rather than minimize the differences between the sexes, how would anyone know what women are capable of?[61]

Other than the Catholic Church or the American prison system, it is hard to think of a modern institution more deeply gendered than sports. As sports scholar Ellen Staurowsky has noted, the "athletic establishment is without peer in higher education and society at large with regard to its use of gender marking. The athletic landscape is literally and figuratively outfitted in symbols of 'pink' and 'blue.'" She points to the persistent use of gender references in team designations (like Tennessee's Lady Volunteers or Delta State's Lady Statesmen), job titles such as senior woman administrator, and of course the existence of men's and women's teams in the same sport. "These symbols serve as signposts, directing attention time and again to a consideration of gender difference," she concludes. Boys and girls are channeled into acceptable sports by gender: football and baseball for boys; gymnastics, field hockey, and softball for girls. Even when they play the same sport, their experience still varies by gender: a slightly smaller basketball, a different lacrosse basket, a prohibition on body checking, or different distances to the target. Needless to say, the men's sport invariably sets the standard while the women play by different, "girls'" rules. With the exception of pairs figure skating and mixed doubles in tennis, feminist scholar Catharine Stimpson points out, "Today, in the United States, men are from football stadiums, women are not."[62]

Mary Jo Kane has noted how sports vigilantly reinforce the notion that differences between male and female athletic performance are grounded in the physical body, which in turn is deployed to provide "incontrovertible evidence of male superiority" because of the emphasis on factors of height, scores, speeds, and distances that seem to confirm this superiority. "It's a short leap from seeing men as physically superior to seeing men as superior, period," notes scholar Susan Birrell. And yet sport, like everything else, is constructed, not natural. Contemporary society values the burst of speed that wins the 100-meter dash over the endurance that wins a 100-mile race, in large part because speed is what men excel at and endurance is more applicable to female bodies. With the conversation-stopping statement that no woman will ever run the 100-meter dash faster than a man, so don't even talk about women's sports as being on a par with men's, it is very hard to look beyond the binaries that divide the world, especially the sports world, into male and female versions.[63]

One way to destabilize male advantage is to redefine sport to focus more on participation and less on winning. Only a tiny number of people will ever win Wimbledon or a gold medal at the Olympics, but that does not stop millions from competing at their own level in sports of their own choice— are they any less deserving to be called athletes? This is what Simone de Beauvoir was getting at in her often-quoted remark from *The Second Sex*: "And in sports the end in view is not success independent of physical equipment; it is rather the attainment of perfection within the limitations of each physical type: the featherweight boxing champion is as much a champion as the heavyweight; the woman skiing champion is not the inferior of the faster male champion: they belong to two different classes." Less emphasis on the first person (usually male) to get to the finish line and more on the back-of-the-pack runners, male and female, would spread out the experience and enjoyment of athletics, rather than just limit it to a winner. Note that focusing on participation rather than winning as the core definition of sport is very similar to the philosophy that reigned in women's athletics from the 1920s until Title IX destabilized the field, so there are historical precedents for this approach.[64]

Another way to challenge male hegemony is to look at how sports are organized. For example, there is a tendency to think of the range of current sports as fixed, even though many of the most popular sports, notably football, basketball, and baseball, date only to the nineteenth century. It is hardly a coincidence, Michael Messner points out, that "the most popular and valued sports (football, basketball, ice hockey) are historically organized around the most extreme possibilities of *men's* bodies." In fact the trend of late twentieth- and early twenty-first century professional sport seems to be toward even more brute physicality, as witnessed by the expanding girth of National Football League players over the last thirty years. Could this hyperemphasis on male size and strength be a reaction to the inroads of women into sports? Mariah Burton Nelson thinks so. In her pithy summation, "The stronger women get, the more men love football."[65]

What this invested belief in male physical superiority does is inflate enormously the differences between the sexes and erase or ignore their commonalities. Mary Jo Kane's pathbreaking 1995 article, "Resistance/ Transformation of the Oppositional Binary: Exposing Sport as a Continuum," offers a different way of seeing and interpreting evidence that is right before our eyes: "In spite of all efforts to the contrary, there exists today a sport *continuum* in which many women routinely outperform many men and, in some cases, women outperform most—if not all—men in a variety of sports and physical skills/activities." It does not necessarily follow, therefore, that every elite male can outperform every elite female or that even marginal males can outperform the best female. And yet if men's and women's sports are kept rigidly separate, then we never have the chance to actually *see* women outperforming men in sports venues. Kane concludes, "The acknowledgement of such a continuum could provide a direct assault on traditional beliefs about sport—and gender itself—as an inherent, oppositional binary that is grounded in biological difference. In short, an awareness of sport as a continuum of physical, athletic competence could serve as an important vehicle for resistance and transformation."[66]

All this has an enormous amount to do with the legacy of Billie Jean King and the lessons of Title IX for the current organization of the world of sports. Most fundamentally, it challenges a strict division into men's and women's sports as often unnecessary, counterproductive, or misguided. What would a competitive sports structure look like that downplayed gender distinctions instead of institutionalizing them? Here are just a few examples of how gender could be deemphasized in sports:

- In sports such as riflery, archery, sailing, and equestrian, where sex is irrelevant, field a totally coeducational team.
- In sports such as track, golf, cycling, or swimming, have men and women compete in separate events and then combine both scores for the whole team. Encourage relay teams or match play that include both men and women. "In the Olympics, why not Carl Lewis passing off [the relay baton] to Flo Jo [Florence Griffith Joyner]?" Billie Jean King asks.[67]
- Remove any restrictions on women competing in so-called contact sports and synchronize the rules so that men's and women's versions of the game are the same. For example, in ice hockey, either allow body checking for women or prohibit it for men.
- Instead of coaching teams separately, have the coaches of the men's and women's teams work collaboratively, dividing up tasks and sharing duties. Ditto those who provide training and medical services. Having women coach male athletes (as Billie Jean King did when she was the player-coach of the Philadelphia Freedom) would represent a huge step in breaking down prejudice against women in sports leadership positions.
- Follow the example of sports such as boxing, rowing, and wrestling, which organize events by weight and size. No one expected lightweight Sugar Ray Leonard to box against heavyweight Muhammad Ali; institute similar categories where size is a significant factor. "It's really simple," Billie Jean King says. "Your body size determines what sports you can do. If you're a boy and you weigh 150 pounds, you're not going to play football; you might become a gymnast."[68]
- Remove unnecessary or arbitrary variations in rules, such as having men badminton players go to 15 points while women stop at 11, dividing basketball periods differently in men's or women's

games, or having different numbers of referees for men's and women's games.

Once you really look closely at how sport is gendered, the list of offenses both large and small is mind boggling. While it is hard to imagine a sports revolution being started simply by changing the length of a basketball period or fielding a mixed-gender archery team, it's a start. Or more to the point: the realization that these gendered assumptions are so deeply imbedded in sports as to be practically invisible is the first step toward unmasking them and then trying to work toward a more equitable system that treats participants as athletes first, and as members of a specific gender second, if at all.

Once again Billie Jean King's beloved World Team Tennis provides a compelling and far-sighted model. With its roster equally divided between male and female players, and the outcome of the match therefore determined equally by the contributions of both sexes, Team Tennis turned an individual sport into a team endeavor committed to the principle of equal representation without distinctions based on gender. "In Team Tennis, if you help your teammate—it doesn't matter which gender—then everybody wins," King reasoned, before taking her conclusion one step further: "That's the kind of teamwork I want to see happen in the business world, in marriage, and everything. Girls and boys have not been together enough, especially in sports." On another occasion she extrapolated how "boys and girls cooperating, side-by-side, against the same opponent" might play out in real life: "Imagine a kid walking into a gym and seeing boys and girls on the same playing field. That's total gender equity." It is, she proudly announced, "the essence of who I am," and a core principle of her philosophies both of sport and feminism.[69]

The organization of Team Tennis seems a self-evident concept now, but King reminds us that it involved "a lot more thought than people realize." In turn she thinks that if people put their minds to it, many other sports could be truly gender neutral. Why not basketball teams made up of two women and three men or mixed relay teams in track? "Try it at the intramural level," she challenges us, "and see what happens." She sees the bottom line as rewards not just for sports but for society as a whole. "The more research that's done, the more we're finding out that segregating boys and girls is not good. I've known that my whole life, but now people are starting to verify it."[70]

At the same time Billie Jean King encourages us to think about sports in less gender-specific terms, she and many others recognize the importance of all-female settings for the discovery and enrichment of sport experience. She strongly endorses research conducted by the Women's Sports Foundation that has demonstrated that if adolescent girls are not given a supportive and friendly atmosphere in which to develop athletic skills and interests, they drop out of sports quickly. These benefits are not limited to young girls. Generations of adult women have also experienced the joy of competing on women's teams, a process that allows them to build self-esteem and friendships while playing a game.[71] Not all separatism is bad.[72]

Again we return to the dilemma of modern feminism: how to recognize and embrace difference while also seeking formal equality. One of the major tenets of second-wave feminism was freedom of choice: women should be free to pursue any life courses they chose, unencumbered by stereotypes or traditional gender expectations. In terms of sports opportunities, many women will continue voluntarily to participate on women's teams for all the benefits they confer. But they should have a choice; those female spaces should not be the only options.

And so we come back to the question that has animated this chapter: can separate ever be equal when it comes to sports? When men's and women's programs are placed side by side, and intangible factors such as societal support and respect are measured alongside tangible ones such as money, coaching, and travel, would any male team willingly trade places with its female equivalent? Not likely, confirming how the current setup has failed to provide true gender equity despite the huge increase in participation opportunities for women since the 1970s. Separate programs undercut the chance to think about athletics as a whole, instead setting up an "us versus them" polarization where men's and women's teams become direct competitors for an increasingly limited pool of resources. Finally, separate programs are unfair to the talented female athlete who can compete at the highest level if given a chance. As that sympathetic Ohio judge said back in 1978, "Babe Didrikson could have made anybody's team."[73]

One of the main reasons why it is so important to encourage those female athletes to aim high and not be held back by assumptions that they can never be as good as men is that seeing any woman perform at a high level will help to undermine the lingering notions of male physical superiority that have been the underpinnings of sport for most of its recorded history. As Ann Crittenden Scott predicted in *Ms.* back in 1974, "By developing her powers to the fullest, any woman, from Olympic star to the weekend tennis player, can be a match for any man she chooses to take on. More importantly, she will inherit the essential source of woman self-confidence—pride and control over a finely tuned body. That alone would be a revolution." When women compete and hold their own against men, it threatens and undermines the binary opposition that insists that the sexes are fundamentally different, and by extension, that women are the second sex, the other. Until women compete with men, the mystique of male superiority will be not challenged.[74]

Those barriers have fallen in almost every aspect of modern life—except sports. Seeing a woman being sent into the game as a field goal kicker for the New England Patriots, playing second base for the Chicago Cubs, or making the cut at the Masters could be a national consciousness-raising moment similar to the one that Billie Jean King provided when she trounced Bobby Riggs in 1973. Until Riggs netted that final backhand volley to end the match, many traditionalists still clung to the belief that men were naturally women's athletic superiors. King's convincing victory demolished that myth. Moments like these, past and future, shatter old stereotypes and open our eyes to previously unimagined possibilities of female athleticism and equality.

The National Organization for Women was ahead of its time in 1974 when it called for gender integration in the world of sports, but the idea looks significantly less radical today. More than thirty-five years of Title IX have shown what the female body is capable of—pretty much anything that the male's is. Ironically, Title IX has also made it significantly harder to envision such a brave new athletic world precisely because the sports revolution it sparked unfolded in an athletic system so rigidly divided by gender. Reconciling these dual legacies—the unleashing of women's athletic potential versus the inadvertent (or perhaps not so inadvertent) reinforcement of sex segregation in sports—will be a major challenge as the women's sports revolution continues to evolve.

Chapter Six The Perils of Celebrity and Sexuality
THE OUTING OF BILLIE JEAN KING

Americans have grown distressingly familiar with this scene: a male public figure, usually an elected political leader or prominent government official, calls a press conference to take responsibility for a scandal, usually involving sex, while his wife, looking like she has been run over by a truck, stands stoically at his side, offering her silent support. While attention focuses on the contrite statement of the perpetrator for whatever behavior hurt his family and probably will cost him his job, the real curiosity is about what is going through the wife's mind as she faces this most public form of humiliation. Why is it always the wife who stands by her man, commentators ask? What would it look like if the tables were turned?[1]

Larry King knows what it's like. In 1981 he stood loyally by the side of his superstar wife as she admitted that she had an affair with her former secretary, Marilyn Barnett. When her former lover sued the tennis star, the American public suddenly knew what had been an open secret for years in the tennis world: Billie Jean King was a lesbian. King admitted the affair but distanced herself from any outright affirmation of her sexual orientation, then and for many years afterward. Despite her illustrious athletic career, she hated the thought that she would be remembered and categorized solely for what she called a "very private and inconsequential episode."[2]

The outing of Billie Jean King by her former lover was more than just a private affair, and it was hardly inconsequential. The undercurrent of homophobia in women's sports is the backdrop for understanding why the revelations that Billie Jean King engaged in a lesbian affair, as opposed to admitting a drinking, drug, or gambling problem or some other socially unacceptable behavior, had the potential to be so explosive and destructive. The issue of lesbianism in sports—"a silence so loud it screams"—was the proverbial elephant in the room that nobody wanted to talk about. When the cover of a respected athlete such as Billie Jean King was blown, it sent tremors through the carefully constructed public artifice that was women's sports. As golfer Carol Mann Hardy said at the time, "If I were a lesbian, I'd be scared stiff." Even today the number of openly gay athletes, male or female, is tiny, suggesting that "locker-room closets" are perhaps the most difficult to escape of all.[3]

Billie Jean King's outing occurred at a transitional moment for gay history and the media's infatuation with the private lives of public figures. Without Marilyn Barnett's suit, it is likely that King would have been able to continue to lead her closeted existence indefinitely. The controversial phenomenon of outing public figures dates to the 1990s, long after her playing days were over. Until then, there was certainly plenty of gossip about suspected Hollywood figures, politicians, and athletes, but everyone seemed to act within a set of informal, unwritten rules that can be summed up in the phrase "don't ask, don't tell." In other words, there was a zone of privacy—often called "inning" to distinguish it from "outing"—that allowed gay public figures to lead discrete lives without fear that their names would end up in the gossip columns the next day.[4]

At the same time a competing phenomenon was picking up steam: the emergence of a media-driven celebrity culture that threatened to obliterate the blurry lines between public and private. The rise of infotainment, twenty-four-hour cable channels, gossip networks, and the like broke down the older reticence that, for example, dictated that Franklin Roosevelt was never photographed in a wheelchair, allowed Hollywood film stars such as Cary Grant and Rock Hudson to stay safely in the closet, and looked the other way at tales of John Kennedy's womanizing. Such private behavior was simply not seen as newsworthy as late as the 1960s. By the time Billie

Jean King was outed, however, this new celebrity-obsessed culture was well established. The tennis star accepted the fact that her personal life was a public issue: "It may not be fair, but that's the way it is. Anyone who's in the limelight accepts it." And yet she was totally blindsided by the emotional and financial repercussions of her former lover's suit.[5]

The public disclosure of Billie Jean King's homosexuality came at a scary moment for the fledgling women's sports revolution. After the great leaps forward earlier in the 1970s, progress had slowed at decade's end as women's sports reached the equivalent of its glass sneaker. The feminist movement, stung by the failure of the Equal Rights Amendment and the shifting national mood symbolized by Ronald Reagan's election, was also vulnerable to a conservative backlash. While women's professional tennis was on a reasonably sound basis, the tour still worried about the public relations impact of a scandal involving its best-known (if not always best-liked) star. Personally, Billie Jean King feared that her endorsement and promotional opportunities would evaporate just as her playing days were ending. What a way to end my career, she must have thought, and possibly take the whole women's sports revolution down with me.

In the 1960s and 1970s Billie Jean King served as a trailblazer for the professionalization of tennis and as a symbol of the new roles of athletic women, Title IX, and feminism in general. By contrast, she wasn't ready yet to take on the mantle of gay rights, certainly not in 1981 after being so violently and publicly outed. When she finally tentatively started to publicly identify herself as a lesbian in the late 1990s, she did so within a much-changed social climate that offered increased visibility and acceptance for gay men and lesbians, young and old alike. "I can tell you that in the 70s, there was this huge fear about coming out," she recalled about those earlier times, but now she embraced gay pride with gusto. When Billie Jean King was named a recipient of the 2009 Presidential Medal of Freedom at a White House ceremony hosted by President Barack Obama, she was honored not just for her activism for gender equity in sports but for her role as "one of the first openly lesbian major sports figures in America." What a distance she—and American society—had traveled since 1981.[6]

MARILYN BARNETT first entered Billie Jean King's life in 1972, an incredibly busy and complicated time in the life of the tennis superstar and her husband. "Those couple years were so intense," King recalled in 1982. "Making women's sports acceptable, and making women's tennis, particularly, into a legitimate big-league game was a crusade for me, and I threw my whole self into it in ways that exhausted me emotionally as much as they did physically." Larry too remembered it as probably the most hectic time in both their lives, but not necessarily the most productive for their marriage. He was busy with his myriad business ventures and soon embarked on a fairly public affair with Australian tennis player Janet Young. Connected through tennis, their lives were increasingly disconnected everywhere else.[7]

Looking back on those years, King often uses phrases like "lost soul," "going through hell," or "a mess" to describe her emotional state. Confused and ashamed of her sexual feelings for women, she failed to take responsibility for her actions because she feared what the disclosure might mean to women's tennis and her life as a sports celebrity. When she once haltingly tried to talk to her mother about her sexuality, she couldn't find the words, not that her mother would have been willing to have this conversation. Nor was Larry, who conveniently managed to deflect his wife's pleas to get out of the marriage by ingratiating himself even more deeply into her business and personal life. Her dissembling about her sexuality was symptomatic of a larger personality trait: her lifelong desire to be all things to all people. At base she wanted to be loved by her friends and family, as well as by all her fans, an impossible standard. Miserable and trapped in a web of lies, she remembered, "My whole world was in flux."[8]

Into this vortex stepped a twenty-three-year-old hairdresser named Marilyn Barnett. She first met the twenty-eight-year-old tennis star in May of 1972 when she styled her hair at a well-known Beverly Hills salon. Several months later they ran into each other at a party and renewed their acquaintance. Friendship drifted fairly quickly into a sexual relationship, not Billie Jean King's first. "I had very soft boundaries when it came to sexuality," she later admitted when thinking back about her twenties. "When you're playing tennis and you're busy every day, it's a great way to put everything on the back burner." Barnett begged King to let her quit her job as a hairdresser and accompany her on the tour, and by the spring of 1973 Marilyn was on the King payroll at $600 a month, serving as a combination travel agent, companion, and advisor. "She was a bad choice for me," King later told journalist Selena Roberts, "but I was very vulnerable at the time we met. She was dangerous. I was screwed up."[9]

Far from hidden, Barnett was especially prominent around the time of the Bobby Riggs match in September 1973, usually identified as King's traveling secretary. The night of the match she was prominently seated at courtside, along with King's coach, Dennis Van der Meer, and her husband, Larry, even though it was highly unusual for "friends" to be on the court during a match. If members of the press knew or suspected King's irregular lifestyle, no one said so in print, or at least not directly.[10]

In this light it is interesting to revisit Grace Lichtenstein's *A Long Way, Baby* (1974) for what she does—and does not—say about the relationship. The year the journalist spent following the women's professional tennis tour coincided with the height of the affair, and Lichtenstein found it impossible to write about Billie Jean King without including Marilyn Barnett in the story. Calling Marilyn a "high priestess of the Billie Jean sect of worshipful admirers," she characterized her as "a wispy flower-child of a woman with streaky blonde hair who favored print halter-dresses" and knew next to nothing about tennis. Noting that Billie Jean spent far more time with Marilyn than her husband, she called them "a strange, totally contradictory, but apparently very compatible pair." She did note, however, that the relationship could take "ominous shades," such as the time Marilyn dropped some autographed cards and Billie Jean ordered her to pick them up "in a scene right out of *The Killing of Sister George*," a not-so-subtle reference to a 1968 movie about three lesbians. Later in the narrative Lichtenstein made a clear reference to the gossip about the relationship and Billie Jean's "disinclination to spend time with her husband," although in the epilogue she noted that Billie Jean and Larry seemed more together as a couple than they had for quite a while. For her candor Grace Lichtenstein found herself persona non grata on the women's tour.[11]

In fact, Billie Jean King had long been dogged by rumors about her sexuality, even being asked pointblank whether she was a lesbian. While this is a common journalistic practice today, it was quite unusual in the 1970s. For example, when discussing the question of lesbianism in tennis, she was asked by an interviewer for *Playboy* magazine in 1975, "You're not a lesbian yourself, then?" to which she replied: "My sex life is no one's business, but if I don't answer your question, people will think I have something to hide, so I'm in a bind. I'm damned if I answer your question and damned if I don't, but I'll give you the answer: no, I'm not a lesbian. That's not even in the ball park for me." Frank Deford's profile of King in *Sports Illustrated* later that year, titled somewhat incongruously "Mrs. Billie Jean King," noted that interest in her private life "borders on raw inquisition." And yet she still held on to her heterosexual privilege, thanks to a complicit spouse and a less intrusive media.[12]

In 1974 Marilyn convinced Larry and Billie Jean to buy a $135,000 beach house in Malibu, which she used extensively, even after her duties as a traveling secretary were phased out. By the end of that year Barnett had gone back to work at the Jon Peters Beauty Salon in Beverly Hills and was no longer inseparable from the tennis star, although in her March 1975 *Playboy* interview King still called Marilyn her best friend. According to King, their relationship ended in 1975 or 1976, but Billie Jean and Larry let her continue to live rent-free in the Malibu house, all expenses paid by the Kings' business manager.[13]

By 1979 they had had enough and formally asked Barnett to leave the house, which had now appreciated in value to $550,000, but she refused to budge. Emboldened by letters from the tennis star at the height of their relationship as well as credit card receipts and paid bills that she had kept, Barnett threatened to go public if they continued to try to evict her. When her blackmail attempts failed, in May of 1981 she sued for title to the Malibu house and half of King's income from 1973 to 1979, which was estimated at more than $1 million. If King hadn't been a public figure with a large disposable income and celebrity profile, there likely never would have been a lawsuit. Nor would legions of reporters have shown up at the obligatory press conference announced by Barnett and her lawyers to spread the inflammatory story all over the media. The gossip- and scandal-driven celebrity culture quickly moved into high gear.[14]

Billie Jean King first learned of the lawsuit from a *Los Angeles Times* reporter's query while playing a tournament in Florida. Picking up her phone messages after an early-round loss, she recalled her reaction when she heard the news: "I went into shock. My heart was pounding, my skin tingling. I thought I'd been hit by a truck. I don't think I'll ever get over the shock. I'll have to work on it for the rest of my life." After first issuing an emphatic denial calling the allegations "untrue and unfounded," two days later King admitted having a lesbian affair with her former secretary but insisted that it had been over for quite a long time. "I made a mistake," she told a packed news conference, flanked by her husband, Larry, and her stunned parents, "and I will assume responsibility for it. I only hope the fans will have compassion and understanding." Cloaking herself in heterosexual privilege at the event, she called Larry "my husband, my lover and best friend" and allowed him to drape his arm around her chair the whole time she addressed the assembled journalists.[15]

Tennis players are performers, and once again Billie Jean King put on a performance: the initial denial, then public confession and acceptance of responsibility, followed by a request for understanding and space in her time of trouble. If this media strategy doesn't seem unusual to us today, it is because there is almost a script now for public figures to seek redemption when things go awry. Not out of choice but necessity, Billie Jean King was one of the pioneers of this confessional mode of handling public relations.[16]

King stayed on this message relentlessly: in the obligatory post-revelations interview with Barbara Walters on ABC's 20/20 watched by 20–30 million Americans; in the candid tell-all with Larry ("Larry and Billie Jean King Work to Renew Their Marriage—and Put Her Affair Behind Them") in *People* magazine;[17] and finally, as soon as it could be rushed into print, in a self-justifying autobiography cowritten with Frank Deford that journalist Selena Roberts later charitably called a "candid lie" but Jonathan Yardley of the *Washington Post* dismissed at the time as "so blatantly self-serving that it can only win its author more enemies than friends."[18]

Still, King obsessively worried how her actions would affect other people. "You can talk about yourself as an individual, but whatever you say always affects other people, like pebbles in a pond," she said at the time. "There's that rippling effect. I always worry that I may be hurting someone else." She was obviously thinking about her parents, who had already been devastated to read about her 1971 abortion in the newspaper rather than hearing about it from their daughter herself. While they stood by her in public, King's parents remained deeply shaken by the revelations about her affair with Marilyn Barnett for years afterward.[19]

Larry King never seemed fazed by the questions about his unconventional marriage and he never wavered in his public support for his embattled wife, encouraging her to go public with the truth when Marilyn Barnett sued in 1981 and pledging to stay by her side in the aftermath. "I love Billie Jean and I would say that ultimately, if she could be happy, then I would be happy too. That may be too philosophical or too detached for most people, but that's how I feel," he told *People* magazine. Some found his assertions that he bore part of the responsibility because he had been so preoccupied with business hard to fathom, and others were offended by his statement that he would have been much more upset if his wife had had an affair with another man, conveniently forgetting to mention that he had had affairs with other women. A lot of people simply assumed that Larry was gay too. But most observers had long ago given up trying to understand what kept Larry and Billie Jean's marriage intact. "Dammit, what do people want?"

Billie Jean had exclaimed in exasperation in 1975. "I just love Larry. I've gotten to the point I can't say anything else."[20]

Billie Jean's response to Marilyn Barnett's revelations was a model both of candor and obfuscation. As we now know, her relationship with Marilyn Barnett was not the passing homosexual episode she portrayed to the press, but she didn't make the link then between her individual experience and a wider lesbian sensibility. To her, sex was a private act, which could happen with either men or women. She couldn't be a lesbian, she basically asserted, because she didn't feel "homosexual": "If you have one gay experience, does that mean you're gay?" Even when their sexual relationship continued, King clung to the fact that Marilyn had been living with a man right before, adding, "I can't stand women who don't like men." In her mind what she and Marilyn did was different from her image of man-hating lesbians: "Still it was very significant to me at that time that Marilyn and I were only having an isolated homosexual experience, and that we were not participating in a full homosexual life-style, because I'll admit that that insular, segregated way of living puts me off a little." To her credit she added that a typical heterosexual suburban lifestyle had the same effect.[21]

When the news of the lawsuit initially broke, the reactions from the tennis world and sports fans were positive and supportive and remained so throughout the subsequent legal battles and proceedings. The fact that King had been so brutally outed and a past relationship betrayed in such a public manner in a court of law built sympathy: even if people didn't support or condone homosexuality, they certainly could feel the pain that King was experiencing being blindsided by what she thought was a private matter. She was especially heartened by the outpouring of support she received from other female athletes, and not just from the field of tennis. And she was touched by the support that her brother Randy's teammates on the San Francisco Giants gave him, which meant they were behind her too.[22]

Press reaction, from major newspapers and sportswriters, was also generally positive, stressing that her contributions to sport far overshadowed any questions about her personal life. As a columnist in the *Washington Post* said, "It should matter not at all whether she rushed the net as a heterosexual, homosexual, bisexual, or asexual. . . . What matters is that she plays a swell game of tennis. . . . If the tragedy and pain of the Billie Jean King affair does nothing more than put a human face on homosexuality, she will have accomplished quite a bit." Fans reacted in similar ways in letters to the editor of magazines such as *Women's Sports* and *Ms.* King's offer to resign as president of the Women's Tennis Association (WTA) was quickly and firmly declined, and NBC honored its commitment to use her as a color commentator at Wimbledon the following June.[23]

And yet there was an undercurrent of muted criticism about how she handled herself throughout the affair. Shelley Roberts in *Newsweek* called King on her transparent attempt to salvage her career by tagging the affair a mistake, noting the abject way she asked for forgiveness was "in the voice of a little girl caught making mud pies in her best pink organdy Sunday dress." She continued, "I wish you had simply left it at, 'Yes, I did it.' Or ever better, you might have said that regardless of how it has turned out, the affair had been a valid experience for you." Some sports commentators suspected that she was speaking more from her pocketbook than her heart, while others were troubled by the callous way King dismissed the years she spent with her former lover as totally inconsequential. Her statements that the affair was a mistake and would have been just as wrong with a man won her few friends in the gay community. And yet it is much easier to pass judgment from a distance than to imagine how a person might act in such a painful and exposed position. In this situation there were no winners.[24]

Too proud to deny something that had happened, but enormously concerned about its impact on her career and women's tennis in general, King crafted a middle ground that accepted responsibility for her past actions but failed to put them in a wider political context. Central to this was her continued public affirmation of her marriage to Larry, who was by her side throughout the initial breaking story, the trial and subsequent court battles, and all the manufactured publicity. For some this was just a little too pat. As one reader complained to *Women's Sports*, "Did anybody else think Billie Jean's cover pose a little contrived, with hand showing wedding ring held up in front of her face? Yes, Billie Jean King, we *know* by now that you're married and your affair with Marilyn Barnett was a one-time mistake—you've told us often enough."[25]

After the public revelations in May 1981, the case went to trial later that year. The legal doctrine under which Barnett claimed to have a right to sue derived from a 1976 decision by the California Supreme Court that involved actor Lee Marvin and his former live-in lover, Michelle Triola. Tagged "palimony" by the press, the decision ruled that people who lived together and then split up were bound by whatever prior agreements they had made about distribution of property and income, even if they were only verbal. In Barnett's case, she claimed that King had promised her the Malibu house as well as substantial lifelong financial support. Not surprisingly, the press quickly dubbed the suit "galimony."[26]

The Lee Marvin–Michelle Triola case was bandied around a lot in the coverage of the King-Barnett suit, and it is useful to look at what it did and did not do. Marvin and Triola lived together from 1964 to 1970, during which time she gave up her singing career to serve as a companion and homemaker to the Hollywood star. For a year after they broke up, Lee Marvin sent her monthly support payments, but he stopped in November 1971. At that point Triola (who had legally taken the name Marvin in the last year of their relationship) sued, claiming that she had been promised support and that she was entitled to a portion of the assets Marvin had accrued during the time they lived together. The Los Angeles Superior Court dismissed her plea, claiming that the state could not enforce a contract for monetary payments between two unmarried persons. Why? Because such a relationship would constitute prostitution and therefore be illegal. That ruling was upheld on appeal.[27]

In 1976 the California Supreme Court overruled both those lower decisions with reasoning that broadened the definition of nonmarital relationships: "Although we recognize the well-established public policy to foster and promote the institution of marriage, perpetuation of judicial rules which result in an inequitable distribution of property accumulated during a nonmarital relationship is neither a just nor an effective way of carrying out their policy. The mores of society have indeed changed so radically in regard to cohabitation that we cannot impose a standard based on alleged moral considerations that have apparently been so widely abandoned by so many." Michelle Triola therefore did have legal standing to sue Lee Marvin for property assets and income earned during the time they lived together if there was an express or implied contract or "some other tacit understanding between the partners."[28]

That wasn't the end of the matter. The California Supreme Court sent the case back to Superior Court, where it finally went to trial in April of 1979, with results far less favorable to Michelle Triola. The judge denied her claim of breach of contract, finding no legal basis for her assertion that she had an oral or implicit contract with Marvin to share assets accumulated during the time they lived together: "To accede to such contention would mean that the court would recognize each unmarried person living together to be automatically entitled by such living together and performing spouse-like functions, to half of the property bought with the earnings of the other nonmarital partner." The judge did award Triola the sum of $104,000 for "rehabilitative purposes," an outcome that allowed both Triola and Marvin to claim victory, but clearly Lee Marvin came out better.[29]

It is not surprising that Marilyn Barnett's lawyers tried to use this California case as a precedent, both in the legal system and in the court of public opinion. The idea was to show that people who lived together had the same rights and responsibilities as those who were legally married. The novelty in Billie Jean King's case was twofold: the relationship involved two women, and one of them was married. By demanding money from Billie Jean, Barnett was in effect attaching Larry's income and assets as well. As a columnist in the *National Review* put it, "She is asking the cuckold to pay for the privilege in an updated version of a Restoration comedy."[30]

Let us review the facts of the case. Barnett claimed that Larry and Billie Jean King bought the Malibu house expressly for her and promised to deed it to her eventually; when they failed to do so and instead said they wanted to sell it, she fought back. Barnett's main bargaining chip was the collection of more than one hundred letters that King had written to her lover, which provided conclusive evidence of the sexual relationship. Showing that the tennis star was not above paying hush money, King's lawyers offered Barnett $125,000 for the letters and her silence, but Barnett wanted more. With King's lawyers fearful that Barnett would just keep coming back to them with higher and more outrageous demands, the negotiations fell apart. In retaliation, Barnett sued. In addition to putting in a claim on the house, Barnett also asserted that King promised to provide for all her "financial support and needs for the rest of her life in the same style and manner commensurate with the life-style of King." In response, King's lawyers countersued to begin eviction proceedings against Barnett.[31]

The legal case was never about sex, titillated as the press was by revelation of the affair. King's admission at her press conference that she had been intimate with Barnett removed the question of whether there had been a sexual relationship. Still the publicity-conscious tennis star was determined to avoid the publication of the letters at all costs. When rumors began to circulate that Barnett might sell the letters to the *National Enquirer* for $25,000, King's lawyers quickly secured a temporary restraining order to prevent their publication. The judge further agreed that the letters would only be read in the judge's chambers, not in open court. When King's lawyers moved to have the case dismissed, however, Superior Court Judge Leon Savitch ruled that there was sufficient law to support Barnett's case, citing the 1976 California Supreme Court decision. King's lawyers claimed that Barnett's lawsuit was different from the Marvin case because that involved a man and woman. In response, the judge pointed out that the 1976 case did not say anything specific about the sex of the parties, so he allowed it to go forward.[32]

The case came to trial in December before Judge Julius Title of the California Superior Court, and stage one (or "set one," as *Newsweek* called it) was quickly resolved in Larry and Billie Jean King's favor. The judge ruled that there was insufficient proof that the tennis star had ever intended to deed the beach house to her lover, and he ordered Barnett to move out within thirty days. Citing Barnett's conduct with the letters, the judge called her actions close to "an attempt at extortion." After the decision, Barnett said, "I'm hostile toward Billie Jean, but I'll always love her." King declined to reciprocate those feelings. "I don't know what I feel toward Marilyn. But one thing I know is, she is not my friend." Asked if she had any ill feelings about "putting Barnett on the street," she replied tartly, "Are you kidding?"[33] A year later, in November 1982, Judge Sara Rudin of Superior Court threw out the rest of the suit (the "galimony" part), in which Barnett had sought lifetime support from her former lover, saying there were no grounds for the action. Ironically just eighteen months later the beach house was so severely damaged by a violent storm that it was condemned and torn down.[34]

Revisiting the case almost thirty years later when questions of civil unions and gay marriages dominate the news, Barnett's suit offers an interesting attempt to extend to gay people some of the legal protections enjoyed by heterosexuals, married or not. Marilyn Barnett never talked publicly about her motivations for bringing her lawsuit against Billie Jean King or connected their personal story to the larger struggle for gay rights in America. At the time she was definitely seen as the less sympathetic character—a betrayer of trust, a blackmailer, a moocher. And yet in many ways she was a pioneer in asking that relationships between two women be given the same standing in courts of law as relationships between a man and a woman. She did not prevail then, but victories in similar cases would not be all that far in the future.[35]

The identity of the other person most deeply affected by the story was not publicly known at the time. In 1979 Billie Jean King had teamed up with a new doubles partner named Ilana Kloss, a South African player thirteen years her junior. "If being around me is going to jeopardize Ilana, I don't want her around," she said when the story broke, referring only to the possible taint that playing tennis with a known lesbian might have on the young player's career. The subterfuge actually went much deeper: King and Kloss were already in a serious off-court relationship. In part to protect Ilana and their privacy as a couple, Billie Jean made a conscious choice to downplay the depth of her sexual orientation and portray the affair with Marilyn Barnett as an isolated, unfortunate event. Simultaneously, she took refuge in her marriage to Larry as a cover, even though she had pressed him for a divorce at several points in the 1970s. Kloss has been King's life partner ever since, but it was years before she was willing to be publicly identified as the other half of this lesbian power couple.[36]

Was there ever really a possibility that Billie Jean King would be totally forthcoming about her sexual orientation after she was so brutally outed? King's repeated statements that the affair was a "mistake," that it didn't mean anything to her, that she was just as comfortable with men as women, suggest not. Billie Jean hated labels of any kind, and she felt especially uncomfortable with being labeled gay at that point in her life. As a perceptive journalist later concluded, "Billie Jean King didn't want to be gay, not then, with so much at stake, not ever, given where she'd come from and who she was. It didn't fit with her plans, her self-image and all that she wanted to do to change the sport she loved." In addition, she felt personally betrayed and humiliated by someone she had been extremely close to, with the public revelations going to the heart of an immensely private part of her life. "Any therapist will tell you that when you're ready, you will [come out]," she said later. "To be outed means you weren't ready."[37]

Temperamentally and politically this wasn't Billie Jean's fight in 1981. She had been a pioneer for women's professional tennis and also for feminism. Being a spokesperson for gay rights would have to wait a bit longer. But there still is an undeniable way in which her outing, painful as it was for her and the field of women's sports, also held the seeds of a more enlightened future where the sexuality of any athlete, male or female, was irrelevant to his or her athletic performance. Golfer Betty Hicks captured this well at the time of Marilyn Barnett's revelations when she said, "Billie Jean King, in full view of millions, divested herself of much of the comfort of her disguises. She is now nearly free, and in attaining that freedom, she may have pointed the way for her sisters."[38]

BILLIE JEAN KING was not the only tennis player battling rumors about her sexuality in 1981. That summer Martina Navratilova ended a very public, two-year relationship with bestselling lesbian novelist Rita Mae Brown. King and Navratilova, competitors and sometimes friends but of different generations and temperaments, took very different approaches to their personal lives. Billie Jean King's grappling with her sexual orientation in many ways belonged to an earlier time when gay people, male and female, were far less visible and much less open about their sexuality. King had been raised in a very homophobic environment and claimed she had never met any lesbians when she was growing up. Her sexuality remained something to be hidden, a secret to be ashamed of. She would have preferred to stay in the closet indefinitely.

Martina Navratilova's attitude was more like, "Yeah, so what?" As she said forthrightly in her 1985 autobiography, "I never thought there was anything strange about being gay." Navratilova came out well before the changes in acceptance for gay people in American society that began to happen in the 1990s and beyond; she simply couldn't pretend to be something she wasn't. Even though her candor cost her endorsements and public support that gravitated toward the more traditionally feminine Chris Evert,[39] there still was so much more money in professional tennis by the 1980s that she had a financial cushion for her unorthodox sexuality. Billie Jean King had to play in nineteen tournaments in 1971 to make $100,000, and her career prize earnings never reached $2 million; Navratilova's were easily ten times that. Still, the difference mainly came down to temperament, as Billie Jean later realized: "Martina has a personality that doesn't ever, ever worry about consequences."[40]

Martina Navratilova was born in Czechoslovakia in 1956 and showed athletic aptitude from an early age. Gravitating toward the sport of tennis, she climbed the ranks of her country's tennis structure, while also feeling the pull of playing tennis in a noncommunist setting with more personal and political freedom. She had a regular boyfriend but also experienced crushes on girls. She first came to the United States to play on the tour in 1973 as an immature teenager, where she was captivated by American consumer culture and especially its food. (She later referred to her "see-food" diet—"Any food I could see, I'd eat," with predictably deleterious effects on her weight and training.) In September 1975, after losing in the semifinal of the U.S. Open to Chris Evert, she made the momentous decision to defect to the United States, even though this meant that she might never see her family in Czechoslovakia again. At a time when Cold War rivalries were still quite intense, her defection was major news. Billie Jean King was the only tennis insider with whom Martina shared her intention in advance.[41]

Young, talented, but cut off from her family and her country, Navratilova experienced a rollercoaster of success and defeat as she tried to find her emotional equilibrium in the aftermath of her highly publicized defection. In 1976 professional golfer Sandra Haynie took Martina under her wing, providing a home in Dallas and a structured atmosphere to discipline and nurture Navratilova's raw athletic talent and appetite for life. By nature quite open and candid (she once told Barbara Walters that she could go to bed with either sex, but preferred waking up with women), she felt emboldened by her move to America to embark on her first serious relationship with a woman. "A lot of it has to do with freedom," she explained in her autobiography apropos of her personal choices. "Once I became a regular on the circuit, I saw a lot of women doing what they wanted to do. That sounds like a political statement when I say it, yet it really wasn't a matter of dogma. I just perceived some women doing what they wanted to do, and felt comfortable in their society." For Martina as well as Billie Jean King and many others, women's sports offered a route to independence and freedom from traditional gender expectations. Still she realized that it was in her interest to keep her sexual orientation somewhat in the closet in order not to jeopardize her application for citizenship. At this point she was still a fairly low-ranked player on the tour, so she assumed this would not be too difficult. As her tennis improved dramatically, so did her public profile.[42]

In the summer of 1979, Navratilova entered into a relationship with Rita Mae Brown, the author of the best-selling lesbian classic *Rubyfruit Jungle* (1973) and a flamboyant character with a reputation as "the Warren Beatty of the women's liberation movement."[43] She and Navratilova bought a twenty-room house in Charlottesville, Virginia, where Brown (who was twelve years older than the tennis star) introduced her to a world of culture and literature beyond tennis. Their highly public affair continued through 1981, when Navratilova moved into a new relationship with pro basketball player Nancy Lieberman, who became her trainer and coach. Rita Mae Brown, who had shown little interest in sports, got her revenge later that year by publishing a thinly disguised roman à clef called *Sudden Death* that featured an unflattering portrait of a lesbian defector tennis star with more than a passing resemblance to her former lover.[44]

On July 20, 1981, Navratilova's long-anticipated citizenship became final, and she was sworn in as a U.S. citizen. Several months earlier the tennis player had given a wide-ranging interview to Steve Goldstein of the *New York Daily News* where she discussed her messy breakup with Brown and her fears that her sexuality would be used against her and the women's professional tour. (Billie Jean King always denied a persistent rumor that she once candidly told an interviewer in the early 1970s that she was bisexual only to have the article killed when Virginia Slims threatened to withdraw its support of the tour if it was published.)[45] Instantly regretting her candor, Navratilova implored Goldstein not to use the material, largely because it might affect her chances for citizenship. He reluctantly agreed, but once her status was finalized, he felt entitled to run the story. Once again she strongly objected, thinking the topic was still too hot after the King-Barnett explosion that spring. But he went ahead with a July 30, 1981, story under the headline "Martina Fears Avon's Call if She Talks." In it she was quoted as saying, "If I come out and start talking, women's tennis is going to be hurt. I have heard if I come out—if one more top player talks about this—then Avon will pull out as a sponsor." Kathrine Switzer, who had parlayed her marathoning into a position promoting women's sports at Avon, saw little consumer outrage at the Billie Jean King and Martina Navratilova-Rita Mae Brown revelations. Avon received only nineteen negative letters, she announced, "less than when we change a lipstick shade." Nevertheless, the next year Avon dropped out as a sponsor of the women's tour.[46]

The summer of 1981 proved an inauspicious time for Martina to talk candidly about this issue. Nancy Lieberman was not willing to be publicly identified as gay, so Navratilova chose the label "bisexual" to describe herself, and averred that Lieberman was straight. (After her relationship with Navratilova ended, Lieberman temporarily reclaimed her heterosexual credentials through marriage.) Nancy Lieberman remained part of Team Navratilova until 1984, when Navratilova embarked on another quite-public relationship with Judy Nelson, a Texas divorcee with two sons.[47]

In many ways this notoriety surrounding the private lives of female tennis players was a byproduct of the conscious decision of the Women's Tennis Association and its sponsors to market the women's professional tour as personality-driven entertainment. By focusing on its leading players as celebrities and public figures whose lives were of interest to the general public, tennis became, in Peter Bodo's words, "as much about the people who play the game as it is about the game itself." Knowing that women's professional sports still had a long way to go to gain acceptance with fans, the tour wanted its image to be one of heterosexual glamour, not lesbianism. Having corporate sponsors such as Avon and Virginia Slims that geared their consumer products toward women reinforced this focus.[48]

Thank goodness for Chris Evert, America's sweetheart and the most popular player for most of the 1970s and 1980s. "I was lucky in that I was the first really feminine, big-name player of the Open era, at least in America, and I carried that to the hilt," she recalled. "I made sure my earrings and makeup were always perfect." Tour player Wendy Overton agreed with Evert's approach: "I think it's important as an athlete to maintain an air of femininity. We should look nice out there. We're entertainers, people are watching our actions. You just don't show up in a pair of dirty old shorts and T-shirt anymore." Billie Jean King later made reference to "the feminization of women's tennis" in the 1980s, a development that she viewed as a positive and necessary step for the continued growth of the women's professional tour. The attempt by women's tennis to present a salable, acceptable feminine image that did not raise red flags about musculature or sexual deviance was not dissimilar to the charm school required of the All American Girls Baseball League in the 1940s or the focus of the Women's National Basketball Association in the 1990s on family fun and personal fulfillment. In each case promoters played up the trappings of heteronormativity to counter the negative stigma associated with women's sports, and the women athletes played along.[49]

Lesbianism wasn't the only challenge that the image-conscious WTA faced in its early years. In 1976 transsexual player Renee Richards petitioned to play on the women's tour, throwing the WTA into an uproar. WTA executive Jerry Diamond later judged Richards's challenge more threatening than the revelations about Billie Jean King's lesbian affair: "I consider that, a transsexual playing women's tennis, much more daring, as far as the public is concerned, than [someone] admitting to a homosexual relationship seven or eight years ago. We survived that, and we'll survive this." The main issue was whether Richards would have an unfair advantage since she had earlier competed as a man. Both Billie Jean King and Martina Navratilova supported her cause and most of the players eventually came around too, but this was not the WTA's finest hour.[50]

Richard Raskind, captain of the 1954 Yale tennis team and a nationally ranked player, was a prominent ophthalmologist, married and the father of a son, who had long harbored feelings that he was really a female trapped in a male body. In the 1960s he began hormone treatments (his friends feared he had cancer as he lost facial hair and body mass) and eventually underwent surgery to bring his body into anatomical conformity with his feelings as a woman. Now known as Renee Richards, she moved to California to start a new life. Hankering to see how she would do on the burgeoning women's tennis tour, she entered a small tournament in La Jolla, California. It is not clear how she hoped to keep her new identity a secret, because her six-foot-two height and distinctive serve caused several people in the small world of tennis, including Bobby Riggs, to guess her secret. When she won the tournament, a local reporter claimed that a "man" had won a woman's tournament, and the controversy entered the public domain.[51]

Having lost her anonymity, Renee Richards now claimed that she wanted to be able to enter major women's tournaments such as the U.S. Open. "I said to myself, o.k., now, damn it, they're putting my private life out in the street. I'm going to pursue every right I possess to prove I'm a woman and a tennis player." The Women's Tennis Association and many women players were not eager to welcome her into their ranks, fearing that her former experience as a player on the male tour and the supposed advantage she held physically would give her an unfair edge. As Rosie Casals put it emphatically, "I'm 100 percent behind Renee in her fight for civil rights. But when it comes to sports, she's not physically a woman. And there's always the chance that one day some 20-year-old male tennis champ will go out and get his plumbing changed and ask for the same right to play. We have to draw the line somewhere. And we decided to draw it here." When Richards entered a warm-up tournament in South Orange, New Jersey, in August 1976 (the tournament director who accepted her entry had played against her as Richard Raskind), most of the top players boycotted the event. Denied entry to the U.S. Open in 1976, she continued to play on satellite tournaments over the next year.[52]

Despite her own struggles with her sexuality and a reputation as an outspoken advocate of human rights and social change, Billie Jean King took a while to take a stand on Renee Richards. "I haven't made up my mind," she said in August 1976. "She may have undergone an operation to become a female but you must remember that she still has male hormones. More than that, she has played men's tennis for 30 years. That is a tremendous advantage. It is an advantage that should be weighed before she is permitted to compete with women."[53]

By the following April, by which time Richards had played in seven tournaments and won $10,000 in prize money, King had reconsidered, and she now welcomed Richards into the women's tour, asking her to be her doubles partner in several tournaments while she worked her way back from knee surgery. "Look, Gladys," King told tournament director Gladys Heldman. "If the doctors say she's a woman, that's good enough for me. No, I'll go even further. If Renee thinks she's a woman in her heart and mind, then she is a woman."[54] Martina Navratilova took a similar stand, although hers was laced with pragmatism as much as principle: "If the real experts said she was a woman, I figured, let her play. Besides, I took one look at her warming up one day and knew she wasn't going to dominate women's tennis—and she certainly wasn't going to dominate me." In her estimation, "Renee Richards looked like, and played like, a pretty good forty-two-year-old male player."[55]

When the United States Tennis Association demanded that Richards pass a chromosome test similar to the sex testing used in the Olympics, she sued. In the end it took an injunction from a New York State court for Richards to enter the women's draw at the 1977 U.S. Open. Richards drew third-ranked Virginia Wade in the first round and promptly lost. The main factor working against Richards was her age, plus the fact that she did not have the fitness or tournament readiness to compete on the professional tour. She continued to play occasional tournaments, winning the women's over-thirty-five title at the U.S. Open against Nancy Richey in 1979.[56] She popped up prominently in the tennis world again when she served as Martina Navratilova's coach from 1981 to 1983, until personality clashes with Nancy Lieberman forced her out. The parting with Navratilova was amicable, however, and as a final gesture of support, Martina loaned Richards money to reestablish her ophthalmology practice in New York.[57]

Despite the WTA's fears, the women's tour has not been swamped by male-to-female transsexuals in the years since, and Renee Richards became something of a historical footnote, despite what she saw as her pathbreaking fight for transsexual rights.[58] Regarding lesbianism, the mantra "play it, don't say it" still primarily holds sway in women's sports. A few female athletes have disclosed their sexual preference while still playing, especially in individual sports such as tennis and golf, joined by an occasional team player such as WNBA star Sheryl Swoopes, but the numbers are still miniscule. More than twenty-five years after Martina Navratilova first came out, she is still the athlete most widely known for the public embrace of her sexuality, not that she has that much company. In her inimitable phrasing, "I don't see any line forming behind me."[59]

The subject of homosexuality remains even more taboo for male athletes, for whom hypermasculinity and aggressive heterosexuality are the accepted—and enforced—norm. As a result, the cases of out athletes have been few and far between. Tennis legend Bill Tilden was arrested on a morals charge in the 1940s after his playing days were over, but he never publicly discussed his homosexuality. The first professional athlete to come out was football player Dave Kopay in 1975, but only after he retired. The few male athletes since who have come out tend to be from individual rather than team sports (diver Greg Louganis, figure skater Rudy Galindo) or retired (baseball players Glenn Burke and Billy Bean). In 1999 Billie Jean King predicted that it would take a male superstar, not a woman, "the taller the pedestal, the better," "a gay Michael Jordan," to break open the resistance to homosexuality in sports.[60] Needless to say, this has not yet happened.

IN THE AFTERMATH OF Marilyn Barnett's revelations, Billie Jean King faced an uncertain future, financial and otherwise. There was literally no precedent or script for a female athlete to continue a career as a sports celebrity after being so cruelly and publicly outed. Because King's playing career was winding down when the allegations surfaced (she was thirty-seven), she was especially concerned about how the scandal would affect her future.

In fact, the publicity had an immediate impact on her financial situation, starting with the $100,000 in legal bills she ran up challenging Barnett's claims. She and Larry later claimed that they lost out on $1.5 million in endorsements, including the cancellation of a $500,000 contract with Murjani jeans and another $300,000 deal with Illingworth-Morris to bring out a Wimbledon-themed line of clothing. Income from television commercials, corporate appearances, and coaching dried up, and the timing of the revelations also threatened Larry and Billie Jean's efforts to get World Team Tennis off the ground again. With much of the corporate world showing cold feet when it came to associating itself with a lesbian athlete, it was clear that she would need to keep playing in tournaments—not for the love of the game as before, but in order to pay the bills and rack up some financial equity for the future.[61]

What would it be like to set foot on a tennis court again—an extremely public and exposed act—after the bombshell that May? The first test was a previously scheduled doubles match in Tokyo with fifteen-year-old Andrea Jaeger. King had immediately contacted Jaeger's parents and offered to withdraw but they and their daughter would have none of it, which meant an enormous amount to the tennis star. So did the warm rounds of applause that she received when she stepped on court in Tokyo and in tournaments to come. Unlike the chilly corporate reception, King found that as far as fans and players were concerned, she could go home again.[62]

In the end Billie Jean King played actively until a month before her fortieth birthday but without the consistency and focus that had once defined her game. For example, in February 1982, just two months after the first trial, she defaulted a first-round match in Detroit to Ann Kiyomura because she literally could not force herself to go through the motions. She began to get her old form back that June at Wimbledon, no doubt spurred on by the pride of playing her hundredth singles match there. She won that match and also beat Tracy Austin, the teenage phenomenon who had won the U.S. Open in 1979 at age sixteen, before losing to Chris Evert in three sets in the semifinals. Then in August she lost in the first round of the U.S. Open to unknown Susan Mascarin.[63] She had similar ups and downs in 1983, reaching the semifinals of Wimbledon again at age thirty-nine but losing to Andrea Jaeger, who was half her age, in less than an hour 6-1, 6-1. King was so used to owning Centre Court that she knew this shellacking was a sign, but it was still so hard to let go: "It's like asking Nureyev to stop dancing and Sinatra to stop singing," she said, before accepting the inevitable. This time her retirement stuck.[64]

No longer being an active player on the tour freed up time for advocacy in other areas. At the top of her postretirement list was participating in "The New Agenda: A Blueprint for the Future of Women's Sports," a conference sponsored by the Women's Sports Foundation and the United States Olympic Committee (USOC) in November 1983. Two years in the planning, the conference "developed in recognition of the need to identify a cohesive plan for the future of women's sports at what appeared to be the close of one phase of the women's sports movement and the beginning of another." Worried about the Reagan administration's commitment to scaling back the role of the federal government, as well as an impending Supreme Court case (*Grove City v. Bell*) that had the potential to severely restrict Title IX, women's sports leaders realized the need for collective action to prevent backsliding. "Unless we continue to fight," said Donna de Varona, president of the Women's Sports Foundation, "we will lose those opportunities."[65]

The Women's Sports Foundation chose Washington, D.C., as the site for the three-day conference because they wanted to demonstrate the breadth and political clout of those who cared about women's sports. To build media interest and represent a range of viewpoints invited speakers included Senators Bill Bradley and Ted Stevens, USOC president William Simon, and Vice President George Bush, as well as Donna Shalala, Diana Nyad, Wilma Scott Heide, and Sally Ride, a crack tennis player long before she won fame as America's first woman in space. As keynote speaker, Billie Jean King exhorted the more than 600 delegates and panelists to spend the next three days "trying to find solutions for the next 10 years." She then delivered a special challenge: "I look forward to seeing in my lifetime, pigtails in the World Series worn by a woman. This is my challenge to The New Agenda. You can make it happen."[66]

An undercurrent of homophobia hung over the conference, spurred in part by the general defensiveness about the role of lesbians in sports as well as the specific fallout from Billie Jean King's recent outing and subsequent trial. Leaders of the women's sports movement worried that foregrounding the issue of lesbians in sport too prominently would cause the loss of corporate support and public goodwill that the conference was specifically designed to tap. An early brochure promoting the conference had, without the approval of organizers, included lesbianism as one of the topics to be addressed. The skittish conference executive board feared that the topic would cause corporate sponsors to withdraw,[67] and references to lesbianism were removed from all subsequent publicity. In the end the issue of lesbianism in sports figured only tangentially in the long list of final resolutions. Judge for yourself: a cop-out avoiding the issue, or a politically savvy way to keep the topic on the agenda without offending corporate sponsors or inviting media attacks? In a nutshell, that is the dilemma of a liberal feminist approach to social change.[68]

By the time of the New Agenda conference, Billie Jean King was settling into a postretirement routine that, while not as lucrative as it might have been before Marilyn Barnett's revelations, nevertheless offered the aging tennis star ample compensation, financial and otherwise. Unlike most players of her era, she had long been involved in the business side of sport, and now that became her main focus, even though she noted that her hard-won credibility in the corporate world came "by the seat of my pants." In 1981 she and Larry had restarted a pared-down version of World Team Tennis; in addition to serving as its biggest fan, Billie Jean became commissioner of the league in 1985 when Domino's Pizza became its major sponsor. King also did promotional work for the Virginia Slims tour and played on its Legends circuit. She did television commentary for NBC and HBO and kept up an extensive speaking schedule. One newspaper article in 1988 compared her frenzied lifestyle to a presidential campaign, which is of course precisely what she wanted. No downtime for her: she always had to be busy, surrounded by admirers, on the go and in the public eye.[69]

Tennis was still the main love of her life, but the sport was changing in the 1980s as a new generation—and tons more money—flooded into it. Even back in the 1960s King had been known as "The Old Lady" on the tour, but now compared to teenaged prodigies such as Tracy Austin and Andrea Jaeger, the label really was true. The rivalry between Chris Evert and Martina Navratilova dominated the 1980s, with Martina holding the edge, but even these two established stars were being pushed by younger players such as Monica Seles and Steffi Graf as the decade ended. Billie Jean King offered an interesting explanation for why the female tennis stars kept coming: "I have often said that women's sports will have arrived *only* when women's team sports are accepted, but until then women's tennis will have a much larger pool of talent to draw on than will men's."[70]

Of course this passing of the torch is inevitable, but older players felt that the newcomers were much more out just for themselves, whereas in their days they had had more fun and felt more part of a community. Mary Carillo called the younger players "coddled and cocooned": "They don't understand what players before them did to make conditions so good for them today. They think all those Jacuzzis and cable TV sets always were in the locker rooms and that the money always was good. They don't understand that they have responsibilities to the sport, to the public, to the media. They just don't get it." Rosie Casals seconded this view in 1983: "The unfortunate thing is that the younger players have difficulty relating to what we went through. We were staking new territory." Two years later Casals was even more caustic: "There is no sense of history and no respect for the older players. They take the money for granted. Everyone is greedy and they don't want to give back anything to the game."[71]

To some extent this was sour grapes on the part of an older generation (a similar generation gap affects feminism), but it was also a comment on how the world of professional tennis had grown so quickly that it was almost unrecognizable to its older players. As Billie Jean King said in 1988, "I think it's difficult because the young ones now make so much money and they're so insulated. We didn't have much money, we had to depend on each other. That was the good side. The downside was that we didn't have the money and opportunities they have now." Reflecting on this gap, King noted that all the players of her generation were still working for a living before adding this afterthought: "And the generation before me looks at my generation like we've got it made, because we made more money than they did."[72]

The bottom line is that in terms of professional opportunities for women, no sport has even come close to producing the number of female stars as tennis, and Billie Jean King deserves a lot of credit for the sport's phenomenal growth. As a reporter observed in 1999, the trailblazing tennis star "has made more money than anyone else. Sadly, for Billie Jean, of course, the money was not made by her personally, but rather by the generations of women tennis players who emerged after she had spent a decade roughing up the authorities in the battle for equality of status and reward." Rather than complaining, King applauded the money that poured into tennis. In 1990 when she was working with teenage phenomenon Jennifer Capriati, a millionaire at the age of thirteen, she reiterated her view that money talks. "I'm glad to see so much money in tennis. Just because we stopped at a certain point doesn't mean they should. The only thing I regret is not making more money at the end of my career."[73]

Billie Jean King was never a very introspective person, but even she could not ignore the passage of time. "I hit my 30th birthday, no problem—same with 40. But 50—whoo, that's very big. For the first time, I'm having a mid-life—well, maybe mid-life-plus—crisis. I've made myself stop and realize that I'm working too hard, that I've got to slow down. I'm trying to balance my days better. That's become a big word to me now—balance. I've learned to say no sometimes." Health problems, including arrhythmia, as well as the loss of her close friend Arthur Ashe to AIDS in 1993, also encouraged her to take stock.[74]

What she hadn't learned to say publicly yet was that she was not ashamed of being a lesbian. The tennis star later told a reporter for a gay newspaper that she felt she had been out since 1981, but that was news to the reporter—and most of the world. After the Marilyn Barnett explosion, King slipped most of the way back in the closet for the next fifteen years. When she and Larry finally divorced in 1987, it received no media attention. She and Ilana Kloss were partners on and off the court, but when it came to public presentations, they were all business. Discreet too—requesting double beds when they travelled together.[75]

Billie Jean King had always struggled with her weight, and in her forties it ballooned to close to two hundred pounds. This weight gain wasn't simply because she had retired from professional tennis, although she did find it harder to be motivated to eat wisely and stay in shape when she was no longer competing. Like many other women, she was using—or abusing—food as a way of dealing with emotional distress, specifically "my struggle to get my family to accept my sexuality." When she realized that only professional help would allow her to overcome her pattern of binge eating, she entered the Renfrew Center for eating disorders for six weeks of intensive therapy. (One wonders what the teenaged anorexics who were the clinic's principal clientele thought of the fifty-one-year-old tennis star joining the therapy sessions.) She started exercising and made physical activity a key part of her life once again. She also forced herself to be more open about her life choices. As she realized later, "Every time I've gotten in trouble— when you have trouble in your life—it's been for not accepting responsibility. Every time I've accepted responsibility for my life—for my finances, for my relationships—usually things start to work out for the better." Soon after she and her parents finally reconciled.[76]

"I always think if I hadn't been so visible maybe I would have worked through this part of my life faster," Billie Jean King told an interviewer in 1998. "But maybe I wouldn't have. Maybe I would have been more in the closet. It's just so scary. I don't think people have any idea."[77] Not that it has ever been easy being gay in America, but in many ways King, born in 1943, grew up during the worst possible time—the 1950s and early 1960s—to be confronting what her society identified as an aberrant and even dangerous form of sexual behavior. At the height of the Cold War, with conformity and heterosexual gender definitions the enforced norm, gays who were open about their sexuality risked rejection by friends and family, the loss of employment, even public disgrace. If homosexuals were mentioned at all in popular culture, they were portrayed as a threat or menace to the American way of life—"something awful, like a horribly contagious disease or some unimaginable perversion," as Steven Seidman put it in his study of recent gay and lesbian life. As a result, homosexuality remained secretive, closeted, out of the public eye, engendering feelings of shame and inferiority.[78]

This was the homophobic climate that Billie Jean King grew up in, and those dark years no doubt abetted her desire to keep whatever transgressive sexual feelings she had safely and securely hidden in the closet. While she always joked that she was about twenty years ahead of her time, unfortunately in this case her timing was off by several decades. If she had been born in 1983 or even 1963 rather than 1943, her coming-out process would have occurred in a much different and more supportive cultural climate.

Although gay activism had its roots in the postwar period, the appearance of the gay liberation movement is commonly dated to the Stonewall riots in 1969, when gay men at a bar in Greenwich Village fought back against police harassment. Throughout the 1970s gay leaders drew parallels with the earlier civil rights movement and tried to build public support for extending the rights of full citizenship to all Americans. They also urged gay men and lesbians to shed their old defensiveness or reticence about sexual life choices by publicly affirming their sexual orientation, which in turn fostered a sense of community. So too did public events, such as the early Gay Pride parades and mass public demonstrations such as the 1979 March on Washington for Lesbian and Gay Rights, which brought 100,000 marchers, gay and straight, to the nation's capital. Despite this increasing visibility, the gay rights movement was far from a national phenomenon yet. Journalist Amy Hoffman, who worked at the pioneering *Gay Community News* in Boston in the late 1970s and early 1980s, recalled "how completely off the map" gay people were at the time to mainstream society: "We simply did not exist, especially as far as the media were concerned."[79]

While gay men and lesbians share much common history, political mobilization and social life often developed separately along gender lines. Just as pioneering gay men in the 1940s and 1950s organized prohomosexual groups such as the Mattachine Society and ONE, lesbians in San Francisco came together in 1955 to found the Daughters of Bilitis. Congregating in urban areas such as San Francisco, Los Angeles, and New York, lesbians began to reach out to each other in the 1950s and 1960s.[80] Soon after, some second-wave feminists embraced lesbian identities as part of a broader political stance against patriarchy. As Radicalesbians wrote in their pathbreaking 1970 position paper "The Woman-Identified Woman," "Lesbian is the word, the label, the condition that holds women in line. When a woman hears this word tossed her way, she knows she is stepping out of line. . . . Lesbian is a label invented by the Man to throw at any woman who dares to be his equal."[81]

Older lesbians, the product of the closeted and more discreet 1950s and 1960s, were often perplexed by lesbian feminists' aggressive political and theoretical agendas. Nor was the mainstream women's movement necessarily welcoming of lesbian rights as part of its feminist agenda. Betty Friedan was especially hostile to the so-called "lavender menace."[82] While Billie Jean King never used such a loaded term, her relationship with the emerging gay liberation movement in the early 1970s was just as fraught. By now a sports celebrity and advocate on behalf of women's professional tennis, she made no public connection between her sexual relationships with women and the nascent gay liberation movement.[83]

One backdrop for the increasing visibility of gays in modern American life was the growing awareness of the enormity of the AIDS crisis. The first story about the disease appeared in the *New York Native* on May 18, 1981, just two weeks after Billie Jean King's press conference acknowledging her affair with Marilyn Barnett. The Gay Men's Health Crisis was founded that same year. But very little publicity or attention occurred until the summer of 1985 when Rock Hudson disclosed that he had AIDS; he died three months later. As legions of gay men succumbed to the disease, the crisis politicized many gay activists, especially younger militants in groups such as ACT UP (AIDS Coalition to Unleash Power). Starting in 1987 ACT UP activists shed the decorum of past generations to stage attention-getting demonstrations and acts of civil disobedience to remind the world that when it came to AIDS "Silence = Death." Coming out became practically a moral imperative in such a crisis situation. As a consequence, the controversial practice of outing public figures began to happen more frequently.[84]

The momentum continued to build in the 1990s, especially after mid-decade, as the walls between the formerly separate gay and straight worlds began to dissolve. Partly this was because of the enormity of the AIDS crisis, but it also reflected a growing acceptance and awareness of the roles that gay people played in all aspects of American life, sports included. For example, the Clinton administration's "don't ask, don't tell" policy in 1993 confirmed that gays were playing important roles in the military. Performers such as the Indigo Girls, Billie Jean's dear friend Elton John, and—in 1997—the biggest of all, Ellen DeGeneres, came out.[85] By the late 1990s surveys found that three-quarters of all Americans knew a gay man or lesbian personally. In turn, such familiarity fostered dramatically rising public support for gay rights in mainstream America as part of a broader shift toward a more multicultural United States where social diversity, not conformity, was valued.[86]

This new visibility and grudging respect—plus, she would add, years of therapy—finally helped Billie Jean King be more open and accepting about her personal choices. "It's much better now," she said at a press conference in 1997. "In fact, if you want to talk about your sexual orientation, the acceptance level is way up. The whole environment has changed." And talking about it she finally was, although Ilana Kloss still held back. For example, a 1998 interview by Michele Kort for the gay publication the *Advocate* was titled, "Finally, after 17 years of dodging the subject, Billie Jean King Comes All the Way Out." King admitted to Kort that she was currently in a relationship but would not give her partner's name: "Someone who's open privately and with probably three quarters of the people around, but not totally. Do I like it? No. Do I respect it? Absolutely. I've been there, done that." Soon King was publicly lending her celebrity to a variety of gay causes—such as the Gay Games, the Gay and Lesbian Alliance Against Defamation [GLAAD], the Elton John AIDS Foundation, and programs to help gay and lesbian youth—with the same fervor and enthusiasm that she had earlier brought to her advocacy of women's tennis and women's rights.[87]

"My sexuality was probably the most difficult struggle I've had in my whole life," the tennis star said in a 1999 interview, "and the one thing it taught me was that until you find your own truth, you really cannot be free." That truth was on display for all to see in a candid documentary, *Billie Jean King: Portrait of a Pioneer*, that aired on HBO in 2006. Backed up by Ilana Kloss's willingness to finally go public about her role in the tennis star's life, King, in her own words, "pretty much spilled my guts" on camera, honestly if painfully discussing her lifelong struggle to accept her lesbianism and make peace with her parents about her sexual choices. While she had talked to journalists about her sexuality in the past, her revelations seemed even more personal and wrenching on screen. At times it felt like sitting in on someone else's therapy session.[88]

The documentary images of the past were stirring—winning the Wimbledon doubles with Karen Hantze in 1961; talking awkwardly with Richard Nixon in 1971 after she made $100,000; throwing her racquet in elation after beating Bobby Riggs in 1973; savoring her Wimbledon singles crown in 1975. In the end, though, perhaps the most moving scenes were the most ordinary—Billie Jean and Ilana laughing and talking with the elderly Bill and Betty Moffitt over a meal or in the aisle of a supermarket. The ease of seeing them all together after so many years of misunderstanding and pain said it all. Billie Jean King was finally a free woman.

Epilogue The Incomplete Revolution

It's going to take me years to even realize my name's on this. I would never in a trillion years think that this would have happened to a woman—only to a man.

—BILLIE JEAN KING

On August 28, 2006, the first night of the two-week-long extravaganza that is the U.S. Open, the United States Tennis Association formally renamed its flagship tennis center in Flushing Meadows the USTA Billie Jean King National Tennis Center. "Mi casa es su casa," King told a capacity crowd of 21,000. "My house is your house. This house is our house." Thrilled to be the center of adoring attention from the assembled tennis fans, King was serenaded in song by Diana Ross and praised in tributes from John McEnroe, Chris Evert, Venus Williams, and Jimmy Connors. Calling her "the single most important person in the history of women's sports," McEnroe graciously showed the distance he had come since the Battle of the Sexes that had propelled King into the national limelight in 1973: "I was a 14-year-old male chauvinist pig when they played, hoping Riggs would kick Billie Jean King's ass. But now, as the father of four girls, I want to say for the record that I'm very happy Billie Jean won." When King was later asked what Bobby Riggs would have thought about the occasion if he were still alive, she offered this answer: "Bobby is going to be saying he is responsible, which is fine. He did have a big influence on my life." For once, King sold herself short. She earned this one on her own.[1]

While public places are occasionally named for women, an honor of this magnitude, especially a sporting one, was unprecedented. When the USTA named its new stadium in honor of Arthur Ashe in 1997, there had been talk about naming a grandstand court for King, but that would have just replicated the old pattern: male star gets the main stadium, female star gets the smaller venue. Nine years later the governing board of the USTA vaulted beyond political correctness by deciding that the most appropriate recognition of King's influence would be to name the entire complex after her. When told the news, Ashe's widow, Jeanne Moutoussamy-Ashe, crowed: "Any time a woman one-ups a man, I'm all for it. That's my chauvinistic side talking. I couldn't be more thrilled."[2]

Let us pause here to realize what a gutsy and honorable decision this was. Perhaps the most dominant trend in sports in the second half of the twentieth century was the increasing commercialization and commodification of all aspects of the game. At a time when the naming rights to stadiums and other sports arenas regularly went on the block to the highest corporate bidder ("the Beerguzzle or Fig Newton Center" in Bud Collins's trenchant dig), the USTA walked away from the millions of dollars that it could have reaped if it had renamed the tennis center for a corporate sponsor. "Think about it," King quipped in wonder. "I didn't pay $10 trillion for this," earning herself a spot as the *New York Times* quotation of the day.[3]

On the most elementary level, the decision to rename the USTA complex in Billie Jean King's honor was tennis's way of saying "thank you" to the star for her enormous contributions to the development of the sport. As far back as the 1960s, she realized that all was not well in the insular world of amateur tennis. She had a vision of a game which, once freed from its country club image, could truly transform itself into a sport of the people. It is too simplistic to say that she caused the tennis boom of the 1970s, but it is no coincidence that the high point of tennis's popularity in the United States overlapped with the height of her career. King served as ambassador for the sport, introducing tennis to new audiences throughout the country and encouraging millions to take up the sport and follow it actively. The Battle of the Sexes played no small role in tennis's growing popularity.

Billie Jean King also played a key role in the professionalization of tennis, and by extension the explosion of money and corporate support that has so reshaped (not always for the better) the world of sports since the 1970s.

The seeds for today's multimillionaire sports stars, their coffers enriched not just by burgeoning prize money but also by celebrity endorsements and other corporate tie-ins, lie very much in her era. Venus Williams recognized the debt. When she won Wimbledon in 2007, the first time in the tournament's history that men and women received equal prize money, she paid special tribute to King, who beamed proudly from the Royal Box. "No one loves tennis more than Billie Jean King," she said with feeling. "I love you. I wouldn't be here if it weren't for you."[4]

Despite all this favorable publicity, as the twenty-first century unfolded Billie Jean King was in danger of becoming yet another aging sports superstar elbowing for space in our collective memory. "The Baby Boomers know me, and maybe those a little older than that," she said before the USTA naming ceremony. "Now, maybe the younger ones will know." The tennis star was on to something. Americans of a certain age (those folks she predicted would be talking at her funeral about where they were the night she beat Bobby Riggs) could easily recall her as a gutsy tennis competitor, tenacious crusader for women's rights, and staple in popular culture from the mid-1960s through the early 1980s. Younger generations, on the other hand, knew her only vaguely, if at all, as an HBO television commentator at Wimbledon or perhaps from Holly Hunter and Ron Silver's made-for-television portrayals in *When Billie Beat Bobby* (2001). As Jon Carroll noted in the *San Francisco Chronicle* in 1998, "her public persona is in some strange middle period, as people slowly forget how good a tennis player she was, and how dedicated a propagandist, and how smart about so many things."[5]

It is time to rescue Billie Jean King from this historical limbo. In the 1960s and 1970s her activism helped to expand opportunities and options for women to participate in sports, in tennis and across the board. She seized the opportunities created by Title IX and the explosion of women's sports to emerge as a true agent for change where athletics were concerned. In turn, by showing what women were capable of when given a sporting chance, she helped chip away at the old assumptions and barriers that had limited women's full participation in all aspects of American life. Few public figures, let alone athletes, can point to such a deep and far-reaching legacy. And yet like most legacies, hers contains an implicit challenge to do more. Seen in this light, Billie Jean King's unfinished agenda stands as evidence of the incomplete revolution that is women's sports, and by extension women's roles in society—of how far we still have to go.[6]

Even though her outsize achievements distanced her from the lives of most American women, Billie Jean King's life choices and options were very much part of the story of twentieth-century women's history. Born in 1943, a time when traditional gender expectations still held sway but cracks were beginning to appear, Billie Jean repeatedly showed the kind of restless, searching quality that was typical of many women of her generation.[7] She was ambitious and wanted to do something with her life beyond just marriage and children, but what? Like so many other women coming of age in the 1960s, she aspired toward something that didn't quite exist yet—the chance for fulfilling work and career. She knew from the start that she was not a prime candidate for a traditional marriage, and luckily she found a husband who was liberated enough to envision marriage on their own terms. She questioned heterosexual norms and experimented with relationships with women. She also faced the kind of sexist putdowns that were an accepted part of the landscape then: the assumption that her tennis career was just temporary until she returned home to raise a family, the inability to get a credit card in her own name, the sexist belief that nobody would pay to watch women play tennis. In her heart she knew all these things were wrong, but she lacked the intellectual or political framework to understand or challenge them. Instead she just gutted her way through these contradictions on her own.

Then in the late 1960s and early 1970s the forceful ideas of modern feminism entered the American mainstream and began to change women's lives in revolutionary ways. Billie Jean King was in the vanguard, but she also profited from this new climate for women in fundamental ways: it allowed her to build a career as a professional tennis player and to lay the foundations for a kind of public sports celebrity that had been previously unavailable to women. Out of necessity as well as inclination, her whole career was linked with advocacy on women's issues; she grasped something that second-wave feminism often missed—that sports are politics and thus an integral part of the struggle for women's liberation. Even though the moment in the 1970s when feminism commanded center stage quickly passed, it left in place a radically different American society, one where an ambitious and talented superstar such as Billie Jean King could create a successful career by devoting herself to the causes that she cared most about: tennis, women, women's sports, and the connections between them.

No matter how charismatic or driven she was, however, Billie Jean King did not single-handedly cause the women's sports revolution. Things were already beginning to change in the insular world of women's sports in the

1950s and 1960s, and the pace of change exploded exponentially in the 1970s. Following an era of dissent and political protest when civil rights dominated national discourse, it was just a matter of time before activists took notice of the terribly unequal resources offered to girls who wanted to play sports. Here the revival of second-wave feminism assumes a central causative role by providing a historical moment when women's issues were suddenly and forcefully thrust on the national agenda. Even though sports were never a top item on the agenda of second-wave feminism, the general questioning of women's traditional roles, responsibilities, and expectations provided an opening to look at sports with new eyes and fresh perspectives.

The other major player spurring the women's sports revolution was Title IX. The passage of the Education Amendments Act in 1972 put the force and legitimacy of the federal government behind the demands for women's sports sweeping the country. The controversy over the law and its implementation publicized what second-class citizens women and girls were in the modern world of sports and gave parents and sympathetic school administrators an important tool for education and change. And Title IX caused results, with dramatic jumps in girls' participation occurring in the 1970s and steady if slower growth ever since. Despite political attacks and attempts to cut back its scope, Title IX has served as a force for gender equity in sports and will continue to do so for the foreseeable future.

The combination of Billie Jean King's advocacy, the supportive climate of second-wave feminism, and the legislative clout of Title IX set the women's sports revolution in motion in the 1970s. The changes that have occurred for women in sports since then are truly staggering. Perhaps the most fundamental is the challenge to the "maleness" of sports: it is now okay for women and girls to be athletes. Wanting to participate in sports, and being good at them (often better than the boys), is no longer seen as freakish or unnatural; women train and compete with an intensity that was unheard of in the 1970s. Women and girls find greatly increased participation opportunities in schools, recreational leagues, summer camps, even professional leagues in fields such as basketball, volleyball, tennis, and golf; they have teams, coaches, uniforms, and playing fields. Women athletes are much more visible in the media in terms of coverage, endorsements, and fan support and have many more professional opportunities to earn a living in sport after leaving school. The groundwork for all these changes was laid in the breakthrough decade of the 1970s.

The downside is that women athletes now often take access to sports for granted. As tennis phenomenon Jennifer Capriati tellingly said in 2002, "I have no idea what Title IX is. Sorry." (Title IX sponsor Edith Green made a similar point in a different context: "The trouble with every generation is that they haven't read the minutes of the last meeting.") Girls and women in high school and college today have lived their whole lives in a post–Title IX land of opportunities, a huge difference from women just twenty or thirty years their seniors. They often have no idea how recent — or hard fought — these gains are. In some ways, Title IX lets everyone off the hook, because the law makes it seem like the problem of girls' and women's access to organized athletics has been solved. Lost in the celebration is the other half of the equation: that Title IX, and by extension, all of women's sports, are a work in progress, and there is still much, much more to be done.[8]

This is where feminism comes in, specifically the kind that Billie Jean King pioneered in her legendary career. There is a tendency now to dismiss feminism as a relic of the past, to talk about the amazing opportunities girls have these days, to act as if the revolution is over and the mission accomplished. Well, it isn't. Confronting how deeply gendered and unequal the whole sports structure remains today is one way to show how incomplete this revolution is, and how much more remains to be done.

Even though many Americans shy away from the "f" word, feminism's underlying concepts are especially relevant to the world of sports. Ask parents whether their daughter should have a right to play ice hockey or wrestle, or have access to the town's playing fields for her soccer practices, and all of a sudden many of the tenets of modern feminism come flooding out: equal opportunity, equal access, fairness and equity, taking girls and women seriously, powerful bodies to match sharp minds. As a sports lawyer astutely observed during a recent legal case, "There is no more radical feminist than the father of an elite girl athlete." Pointing out the inequities that still affect girls and women in sports has the potential to be a national consciousness-raising moment of monumental proportions.[9]

As we move into the twenty-first century and the fifth decade of the women's sports revolution, it is time to put a fresh name on the political and cultural principle that will insure continued progress toward the elusive goal of gender equity in sports. In Billie Jean King's honor, let's call it sports feminism. What does this perspective get us? Based on the mutual realization that sport is good for feminism and feminism is good for sport, sports feminism offers a vision of athletic, activist women who have both an intellectual and physical dimension. Female athletes are what women's liberation looks like: strong, confident women who by showing what women can do athletically change hearts and minds about what women can do generally.

Without denying the amazing changes that have happened since the 1970s, sports feminism looks toward the day when organizations such as the Women's Sports Foundation are no longer necessary and women are not content to have 42 percent of participation opportunities when they make up a hefty majority of students in educational institutions. Instead of being grateful that more girls and women than ever before have a chance to play, it asks why they still don't get the same societal support and resources as men and boys. It asks why the percentage of women coaches is declining, not rising, and why, if men coach women's sports, it is the rare woman who gets offered the comparable chance to coach a men's team. Sports feminism questions an athletic system structured around keeping men and women separate, rather than encouraging them to play and compete together, and challenges any archaic notions of female inferiority by insisting that women have as equal a right to be athletes—with equivalent respect, support, resources, and opportunities—as men. It also challenges the pervasiveness of homophobia in the world of sports, seeking instead a safe space for women no matter what their sexual preference. In other words, it's not content with the way things are; it is always challenging the status quo. Of course Billie Jean King has been doing this her entire life.

Billie Jean King would no doubt find sports feminism too narrow, too confining a legacy. She's for everybody, she says, and so she is. But there is no denying that her actions and example have had the most resonance for women, and that the guiding principles of fairness and equal opportunity that shaped her tennis career and her broader agenda are especially relevant in the larger struggle for women's rights and gender equity. In large part because of the 1973 Battle of the Sexes, Billie Jean King will always be linked in the popular consciousness with the powerful ideas of modern feminism. She fought and won that battle, turning a tennis match into a referendum on gender roles as well as athletic ability. That breakthrough continued to ripple through the rest of the twentieth century and into the twenty-first as future generations of women athletes seized the chance to play and compete. As sprinter Willye White put it in 1998, "Today's young women athletes don't have a clue they're where they are because of the courage of Billie Jean King." Or as basketball player Nancy Lieberman observed recently:

"Billie Jean King never played basketball, but her fingerprints are on the WNBA. Her fingerprints are on women's professional softball, soccer, golf, tennis, and just about any other sport you can think of. She risked her reputation and her career because she believed so strongly that women should have the right to play on and to be part of a team."[10]

Billie Jean King has always had an incredibly strong sense of history and an almost messianic belief in its relevance for future generations. She understands how difficult it is for a sports figure to create a lasting legacy, to leave something concrete for those who follow. "Performing is very fleeting, it's very intangible, it's very momentary," she says. "And it's wonderful. But it's not lasting, and if you can do things that last, that each generation can build on, then that's when you're cooking."[11] Using her tennis celebrity to open doors not just for women in sports but in society as a whole, Billie Jean King's life confirms the proposition that sport truly does matter.

Notes

Source Abbreviations

BJK, *Billie Jean* (1974)	Billie Jean King with Kim Chapin, *Billie Jean: An Autobiography* (New York: Harper and Row, 1974)
BJK, *Billie Jean* (1982)	Billie Jean King with Frank Deford, *Billie Jean* (New York: Viking Press, 1982)
Dunkle	Margaret Dunkle Papers
NOW	National Organization for Women Records
PEER	Project on Equal Education Rights Records
PSEW	Project on the Status and Education of Women (Association of American Colleges) Records
Sandler	Bernice Resnick Sandler Papers
SL	The Arthur and Elizabeth Schlesinger Library on the History of Women in America, Radcliffe Institute for Advanced Study, Harvard University
WEAL	Women's Equity Action League Records
WSF Archives	Women's Sports Foundation Archives, East Meadow, N.Y.

Prologue

1 For a general introduction to the match, see Selena Roberts, *A Necessary Spectacle: Billie Jean King, Bobby Riggs, and the Tennis Match That Leveled the Game* (New York: Crown Publishers, 2005).

2 "The Troubles, and Triumph, of Billie Jean King," *New York Times*, May 6, 1981, A30; Bruce Lowitt, "25 years ago, she was King of a cause," *St. Petersburg Times*, September 20, 1998, 1C; Jere Longman, "Soccer's Move: Grass Roots to Grand Stage," *New York Times*, July 10, 1999, D1.

3 Billie Jean King, "I Just Had to Win," *Tennis*, August 1998, 30; Barbara Huebner, "When King Reigned," *Boston Globe*, November 18, 1998, C7; BJK, *Billie Jean* (1974), 170; "The Hustler Outhustled," *Newsweek*, October 1, 1973, 63. See also Lucinda Hahn, "The shots heard 'round the World," *Tennis*, August 1998, 22.

4 Dan Wakefield, "My Love Affair with Billie Jean King," *Esquire*, October 1974, 138.

5 George Solomon, "Queen Ready for King," *Washington Post*, February 5, 1973, D4; Hahn, "The shots heard 'round the World," 25.

6 Joel Drucker, "The Battles of the Sexist," *Tennis*, August 1998, 33; Nora Ephron, "Bobby Riggs, The Lady-Killer," *New York Magazine*, September 10, 1973, 53. See also Tom LeCompte, *The Last Sure Thing: The Life and Times of Bobby Riggs* (Easthampton, Mass.: Skunkworks Publishing, 2003).

7 Joe Jares, "Riggs to Riches—Take Two," *Sports Illustrated*, September 10, 1973, 24–25. Chapter 1 of Roberts, *A Necessary Spectacle*, describes the match.

8 See, for example, Pete Axthelm, "The Battle of the Sexes," *Newsweek*, September 24, 1973, 82–85; and "How Bobby Runs and Talks, Talks, Talks," *Time*, September 10, 1973, 54–60.

9 Jares, "Riggs to Riches," 25; LeCompte, *The Last Sure Thing*, 298; Ephron, "Bobby Riggs, The Lady-Killer," 53.

10 Axthelm, "The Battle of the Sexes," 85.

11 Wakefield, "My Love Affair with Billie Jean King," 138; John Leonard, "When She Was King," *New York Magazine*, May 1, 2006, 118. The quote appeared in the HBO documentary that Leonard was reviewing, *Billie Jean King: Portrait of a Pioneer*, which first aired on April 26, 2006.

12 William Gildea, "Tennis Match Just Last Act," *Washington Post*, September 20, 1973, D1; Michael Murray, "Media," *Commonweal*, October 19, 1973, 63; "One Vote for Billie Jean," *Wall Street Journal*, September 18, 1973, 20. The editorial reasoned that she was the better player but couldn't resist adding, "And never let it be said we never stuck out our necks on behalf of women's liberation."

13 Axthelm, "The Battle of the Sexes," 85; Grace Lichtenstein, "Mrs. King Calls Victory 'Culmination' of Career," *New York Times*, September 21, 1973, 31. Lichtenstein also wrote a book about her year following the women's tour, which prominently mentioned the role Marilyn Barnett played in Billie Jean King's life. See Grace Lichtenstein, *A Long Way, Baby: The Inside Story of the Women in Pro Tennis* (New York: William Morrow, 1974).

14 Murray, "Media," 63; Barry Tarshis, "A Lot Preceded the Ms.-Match," *New York Times*, September 23, 1973, 215. Originally Jack Kramer had been scheduled to be a

commentator on ABC, but King threatened to pull out of the match entirely if he was onscreen because he had been so antagonistic to women's tennis. See chapter 1.

15 Erik Brady, "King-Riggs match took a giant step for equality," *USA Today*, September 18, 1998, 9C; King, "I Just Had to Win," 26.

16 King, "I Just Had to Win," 28. This was such a favorite phrase that she chose it for the title of a recent book: Billie Jean King, *Pressure Is a Privilege: Lessons I've Learned from Life and the Battle of the Sexes* (New York: LifeTime Media, 2008).

17 William Gildea, "Ms. King Puts Mr. Riggs in His Place," *Washington Post*, September 21, 1973, A1; "How King Rained on Riggs' Parade," *Time*, October 1, 1973, 111.

18 For a synopsis of the match, see "The Texas Showdown: Key Moments in the Match," *Tennis*, August 1998, 29. For her recollections, see King, *Pressure Is a Privilege*, passim.

19 Curry Kirkpatrick, "There She Is, Ms. America," *Sports Illustrated*, October 1, 1973, 32; King, "I Just Had to Win," 29. LeCompte, *The Last Sure Thing*, 367–72, settles the case of whether Riggs threw the match definitively.

20 Roberts, *A Necessary Spectacle*, 131; Christine Brennan, *Best Seat in the House: A Father, A Daughter, A Journey through Sports* (New York: Scribner, 2006), 83.

21 For a good introduction to Title IX, see Linda Jean Carpenter and R. Vivian Acosta, *Title IX* (Champaign, Ill.: Human Kinetics, 2005). See also chapter 2.

22 The term "second-wave feminism," while not without its detractors, serves as a useful shorthand designation for the period of feminist activism in the 1960s, 1970s, and 1980s. I use it interchangeably with "modern feminism." The term was originally coined to distinguish it from the woman suffrage movement (the so-called first wave). Younger feminists in the 1990s adopted the designation "third-wave" to describe their unique generational take on the movement.

23 For general histories of second-wave feminism, see Ruth Rosen, *The World Split Open: How the Modern Women's Movement Changed America* (New York: Viking, 2000); Sara M. Evans, *Tidal Wave: How Women Changed America at Century's End* (New York: Free Press, 2003); Estelle Freedman, *No Turning Back: The History of Feminism and the Future of Women* (New York: Ballantine, 2002); and Gail Collins, *When Everything Changed: The Amazing Journey of American Women from 1960 to the Present* (New York: Little, Brown and Company, 2009).

24 "How Bobby Runs and Talks, Talks, Talks," 60. The article was quite prescient when it pointed out that "five years ago these superheated matches could not have happened, and five years from now they would not mean anything."

25 Lichtenstein, *A Long Way, Baby*, 150; Roberts, *A Necessary Spectacle*, 2.

26 Joel Drucker, "Billie Jean King: Leveling the Playing Field," *Biography*, September 1998, 102; Billie Jean King, Publisher's Letter, *womenSports*, October 1976, 4.

27 Carol Slezak, "Ahead of Her Time; King focuses on a vision of sports that is equitable . . . and fun," *Chicago Sun-Times*, March 16, 1997, 15.

28 Grace Lichtenstein, "Billie Jean King, the Brooklyn Dodgers, and Me," *Redbook*, November 1974, 104–5.

29 In addition to Carpenter and Acosta, *Title IX*, see Welch Suggs, *A Place on the Team: The Triumph and Tragedy of Title IX* (Princeton, N.J.: Princeton University Press,

2005); and Susan Ware, *Title IX: A Brief History with Documents* (Boston: Bedford/ St. Martin's, 2007).

30 Eleanor Roosevelt quoted in Ruby A. Black, "Is Mrs. Roosevelt a Feminist?" *Equal Rights*, July 27, 1935, 163. Sometimes liberal feminism is referred to as "me-too feminism" or "piece of the pie" feminism. For a fuller discussion of its importance to twentieth-century women's history, see Susan Ware, *Still Missing: Amelia Earhart and the Search for Modern Feminism* (New York: W. W. Norton, 1993).

31 See Alison M. Jaggar, *Feminist Politics and Human Nature* (Totowa, N.J.: Rowman and Allanheld Publishers, 1983); and Zillah Eisenstein, *The Radical Future of Liberal Feminism* (New York: Longman, 1981).

32 See, for example, the opening epigraph to her 1982 autobiography: "I have always disliked the labels that were arbitrarily placed on me, whether in feminist, heroic, or less flattering terms. This book may serve to remove some of those misconceptions. At times I may be tough and at other times extremely sensitive. I'm an individual. Those closest to me have always recognized this, and have allowed me to be my own person." BJK, *Billie Jean* (1982).

Chapter One

1 BJK, *Billie Jean* (1982), 18; Carol Slezak, "Ahead of Her Time; King focuses on a vision of sports that is equitable . . . and fun," *Chicago Sun-Times*, March 16, 1997, 15.

2 James Stewart-Gordon, "Billie Jean King—Queen of the Rackets," *Reader's Digest*, June 1974, 155; Robert Lipsyte, "Softening Sports' Culture Shock," *New York Times*, May 6, 1994, B16; Sally Jenkins, "Racket Science," *Sports Illustrated*, April 29, 1991, 69. King was one of four athletes; the others were Babe Ruth, Muhammad Ali, and Jackie Robinson.

3 Deborah Larned, "The Bodacious Billie Jean King," *womenSports*, May 1977, 60.

4 BJK, *Billie Jean* (1982), 47.

5 BJK, *Billie Jean* (1974), 29–30; Selena Roberts, *A Necessary Spectacle: Billie Jean King, Bobby Riggs, and the Tennis Match That Leveled the Game* (New York: Crown Publishers, 2005), 50. In addition to his work as a firefighter, Moffitt later served as a scout for the Milwaukee Brewers. He retired from the Long Beach Fire Department in 1977, and he and Betty retired to Prescott, Arizona. Obituaries of Bill Moffitt appeared in the *Los Angeles Times*, June 18, 2006, and the *Globe and Mail* (Canada), June 20, 2006.

6 John Leonard, "When She Was King," *New York Magazine*, May 1, 2006, 118. He used similar language in "Billie Jean King: An Existential Success," *New York Times*, June 30, 1982, B9.

7 Lisa McGirr, *Suburban Warriors: The Origins of the New American Right* (Princeton, N.J.: Princeton University Press, 2001), chapter 1; Eric Anderson, *In the Game: Gay Athletes and the Cult of Masculinity* (Albany: State University of New York Press, 2005), 1. Anderson should know: in 1993 he came out as the first openly gay track coach at a southern California high school.

8   BJK, *Billie Jean* (1974), 30; Frank Deford, "Mrs. Billie Jean King," *Sports Illustrated*, May 19, 1975, 74.

9   BJK, *Billie Jean* (1974), 30, 48; Betty Moffitt, "My Daughter, Billie Jean by her Mother," *Ladies' Home Journal*, April 1974, 141; BJK, *Billie Jean* (1982), 11.

10 BJK, *Billie Jean* (1982), 181; Anne Taylor Fleming and Annie Leibovitz, "The battles of Billie Jean King," *Women's Sports & Fitness*, September/October 1998, 130.

11 "When I was a little girl, I took piano lessons, sang in the glee club, and dreamed of Ricky Nelson; I also climbed trees, shot baskets, and threw spirals. That, I was told, made me a tomboy. . . . My mother wanted me to be a lady; my father wanted me to be an athlete or better yet, an athletic lady." Billie Jean King, Publisher's Letter, *womenSports*, August 1977, 4.

12 Susan Ware, *Letter to the World: Seven Women Who Shaped the American Century* (New York: W. W. Norton, 1998), 169.

13 Billie Jean King, Publisher's Letter, *womenSports*, June 1974, 4; Jim Murray quoted in Johnette Howard, *The Rivals: Chris Evert vs. Martina Navratilova: Their Epic Duels and Extraordinary Friendship* (New York: Broadway Books, 2005), 46–47.

14 "Billie Jean King," in Lynn Gilbert and Gaylen Moore, eds., *Particular Passions: Talks with Women Who Have Shaped Our Times* (New York: Clarkson N. Potter, 1981), 173–74.

15 BJK, *Billie Jean* (1974), 27. There are multiple versions of this story; another involves a conversation while drying the dishes.

16 Moffitt, "My daughter, Billie Jean," 141; Roberts, *A Necessary Spectacle*, 67.

17 Moffitt, "My daughter, Billie Jean," 142.

18 Roberts, *A Necessary Spectacle*, 54; U.S. Senate, Committee on Labor and Public Welfare, Subcommittee on Education, *Hearings on the Women's Educational Equity Act, October 17 and November 9, 1973*, 93rd Cong., 1st sess. (Washington, D.C.: Government Printing Office, 1973), 83.

19 BJK, *Billie Jean* (1982), 51; Robert Lipsyte, "If I Were King," *New York Times*, March 28, 1968, 63.

20 For stories from that world of tennis, see Bud Collins, *My Life with the Pros* (New York: Dutton, 1989); and Ted Tinling with Rod Humphries, *Love and Faults: Personalities Who Have Changed the History of Tennis in My Lifetime* (New York: Crown Publishers, 1979).

21 Here is King on Perry Jones: "In those days, before open tennis, the amateur poohbahs, like Mr. Jones (everybody always called him Mr., and I can't stop myself from doing it even now, no matter how much I disliked the man), could make or break you. Mr. Jones had even more power because, at least until about this time, Southern California produced a preponderance of the best players in the country. He was a fussy old bachelor who hated girls. The boys got all the breaks in the Association. Of course, it helped to have money, too. If you did, the parents could donate some and get a tax write-off, and then Mr. Jones would use the money to send the rich parents' kid off to the tournament. It was a public-service laundering." BJK, *Billie Jean* (1982), 53.

22 For a general history of tennis, see Billie Jean King with Cynthia Starr, *We Have Come a Long Way: The Story of Women's Tennis* (New York: McGraw-Hill, 1988). Also of interest are the memoirs by the leading players of the day, such as Helen Wills, *Fifteen-Thirty* (New York: C. Scribner's, 1937); Althea Gibson, *I Always Wanted to Be Somebody* (New York: Harper and Brothers, 1958); Alice Marble, *The Road to Wimbledon* (New York: Charles Scribner's Sons, 1946); and Helen Hull Jacobs, *Beyond the Game* (Philadelphia: J. B. Lippincott, 1936).

23 King and Starr, *We Have Come a Long Way*, 76–78.

24 BJK, *Billie Jean* (1982), 53.

25 John Jeansonne, "Tennis' Serve to Billie Jean," *Newsday*, August 29, 2006, A04. See also the epilogue.

26 See Marble's posthumously published autobiography: Alice Marble with Dale Leatherman, *Courting Danger: My Adventures in World-Class Tennis, Golden-Age Hollywood, and High-Stakes Spying* (New York: St. Martin's Press, 1991). Her *New York Times* obituary on December 24, 1990, quoted her as having only two regrets about her tennis career: "I did not get to see myself on television and I did not get to play the tie breaker."

27 BJK, *Billie Jean* (1982), 81.

28 BJK, *Billie Jean* (1974), 37; Marble, *Courting Danger*, 245–46; BJK, *Billie Jean* (1974), 38. King claims she later learned that Connolly was just trying to use reverse psychology to goad her to higher performance.

29 Grace Lichtenstein, "Straight Talk from Billie Jean King," *Seventeen*, May 1974, 38, 43; Molly Haskell, "Hers," *New York Times*, March 4, 1982, C2.

30 Faces in the Crowd, July 17, 1961, included in *Sports Illustrated* special issue, December 15, 2006, 36; BJK, *Billie Jean* (1982), 115, 219.

31 John Lovesey, "Better than Fancy Pants," *Sports Illustrated*, July 15, 1963, 12–15.

32 Picture caption, *Washington Post*, July 3, 1963, A23; Lovesey, "Better than Fancy Pants," 14; "Little Miss Moffitt," *Time*, July 6, 1962, 50; Fred Tupper, "Billie Jean Moffitt's Bon Mots Create Army of Fans in Gallery," *New York Times*, July 1, 1963, 44.

33 BJK, *Billie Jean* (1974), 190; Jenkins, "Racket Science," 71; Parton Keese, "Billie Jean King: An Attitude, Instinct and Sense of Urgency," *New York Times*, January 14, 1976, 45.

34 BJK, *Billie Jean* (1974), 50–53.

35 Roberts, *A Necessary Spectacle*, 60–64.

36 BJK, *Billie Jean* (1982), 56.

37 BJK, *Billie Jean* (1974), 54–55.

38 King always credited her husband, Larry, with initially pushing her toward a feminist standpoint: "My interest in Women's Lib comes from my husband Larry. He got me thinking about it in sports a long, long time ago. You know, the men are really behind us. It's the women who keep us down." Quoted in Judy Klemesrud, "Billie Jean King Scores an Ace at a Fund-raising Rally," *New York Times*, October 21, 1972, 24.

39 BJK, *Billie Jean* (1982), 59; Larry King, "My Wife, Billie Jean by her Husband," *Ladies' Home Journal*, April 1974, 144; Mary Kates, "Tennis Tycoon: Billie Jean King

Finds Sport Profitable Even When She Isn't Playing," *Wall Street Journal*, September 19, 1973, 1.

40 Roberts, *A Necessary Spectacle*, 143; Fleming and Leibovitz, "The battles of Billie Jean King," 130.

41 Corri Planck, "Portrait of a Legend," *Lesbian News*, April 1999, 18. In this interview King talks about how hard it was for her and her parents, although they are "great now . . . they've come a long way. It was very difficult for them. Being raised in a homophobic family, you just keep trying to face your fears and step by step do the best you can and get more comfortable in your own skin. That is not always easy if you haven't been brought up that way."

42 Roberts, *A Necessary Spectacle*, 169, 146–47, 180. See Robert Lipsyte and Peter Levine, *Idols of the Game: A Sporting History of the American Century* (Atlanta: Turner Publishing, 1995), for many examples of how male sports figures led boisterous and unconventional lives off the field but their exploits were rarely reported in print. This is why Grace Lichtenstein's book, *A Long Way, Baby: The Inside Story of the Women in Pro Tennis* (New York: William Morrow, 1974) is so interesting—it doesn't keep quiet about Billie Jean King's carrying on, to her consternation.

43 King, "My Wife, Billie Jean," 149; Lichtenstein, *A Long Way, Baby*, 178.

44 Lichtenstein, *A Long Way, Baby*, 179; "Playboy Interview: Billie Jean King," *Playboy*, March 1975, 60. See also chapter 6.

45 Roberts, *A Necessary Spectacle*, 143.

46 "Larry and Billie Jean King Work to Renew Their Marriage—and Put Her Affair Behind Them," *People Magazine*, May 25, 1981, 77; "Mrs. King Will Swap Racket for Recipes," *Washington Post*, August 28, 1966, C5.

47 Dave Kindred, "King and Wimbledon: a Long Road to Greatness," *Washington Post*, June 25, 1982, D1; Gilbert and Moore, *Particular Passions*, 174–75; BJK, *Billie Jean* (1982), 62.

48 Robin Herman, "Billie Jean King's Lifestyle: Innovate and Take a Chance," *New York Times*, June 15, 1975, S1; Deford, "Mrs. Billie Jean King," 73. Larry King echoed the same sentiments: "Over there she's considered the third best known American athlete, behind Muhammad Ali and Jim Ryun. Over there they don't know who Mickey Mantle is. But here, they don't know Billie Jean. . . . LBJ could care less about Billie Jean winning Wimbledon—twice." Dave Anderson, "Billie Jean: Tennis Queen Who Obeys Her King," *New York Times*, September 10, 1967, 226. Note how sexist the headline is.

49 John Lovesey, "Manolo's King, but a King is Queen," *Sports Illustrated*, July 11, 1966, 50; Michele Kort, "Ms. Conversation: Billie Jean King and Martina Navratilova," *Ms.*, February 1988, 58; "Mrs. King Sweeps at Wimbledon," *Washington Post*, July 9, 1967, C6; Robert Lipsyte, "Billie Jean," *New York Times*, August 27, 1970, 59.

50 "Mrs. King To Shoot for 'Grand Slam,'" *New York Times*, August 27, 1967, 148. Or as she put it another time, "For too long our image was Gussie Moran's 1951 lace panties." "Women Lobbers," *Newsweek*, May 3, 1971, 90.

51 BJK, *Billie Jean* (1974), 82–83; Bud Collins, "Billie Jean King Evens the Score," *Ms.*,

July 1973, 101; Bill Bruns, "World's Top Woman Tennis Players Says 'U.S. Men Are Losers,'" *Life*, September 22, 1967, 109.

52 BJK, *Billie Jean* (1974), 82; Kim Chapin, "Goodbye Billie Jean, with love from Nancy," *Sports Illustrated*, April 8, 1968, 85.

53 Lipsyte and Levine, *Idols of the Game*, 284; BJK, *Billie Jean* (1974), 85.

54 Figures about the 1968 purses are drawn from the official Wimbledon website: ⟨http://www.wimbledon.org⟩

55 BJK, *Billie Jean* (1974), 91; "Playboy Interview: Billie Jean King," 60. Larry avoided the draft by serving in the Army Reserve ("My Wife, Billie Jean King by her Husband"). See also Mark Asher, "Across the Net," *Washington Post*, September 10, 1967, B7, for fears he might be drafted after law school.

56 Roberts, *A Necessary Spectacle*, 68.

57 Chapter 6 of Mary Jo Festle, *Playing Nice: Politics and Apologies in Women's Sports* (New York: Columbia University Press, 1996), provides an overview of the rise of women's professional tennis; pp. 144–46 discuss the founding.

58 Jane Leavy, "Whatever Happened to Peaches Bartkowicz?" *womenSports*, January 1978, 20–24, 46–48, 52; King and Starr, *We Have Come a Long Way*, 127. See also Nancy E. Spencer, "Once Upon a Subculture: Professional Women's Tennis and the Meaning of Style, 1970–1974," *Journal of Sport and Social Issues* 21 (November 1997): 363–78; and Spencer, "Reading Between the Lines: A Discursive Analysis of the Billie Jean King vs. Bobby Riggs 'Battle of the Sexes,'" *Sociology of Sport Journal* 17 (2000): 386–402.

59 Jane Leavy, "Daring Decade: How Women Served and Won," *womenSports*, January 1978, 23. See chapter 3 for more on how Larry King's business dealings often overlapped with his wife's, causing potential conflicts of interest.

60 Parton Keese, "Women Set Up Tennis Tour," *New York Times*, October 8, 1970, 66; Dan Wakefield, "My Love Affair with Billie Jean King," *Esquire*, October 1974, 386.

61 Gilbert and Moore, *Particular Passions*, 171; Chris Evert, "Happy Birthday, TENNIS," *Tennis*, May 2005, 16.

62 BJK, *Billie Jean* (1974), 112. When the final was delayed by rain, King sent this telegram to Evert: "When you left New York, the skies opened up and it poured rain. The heavens weren't happy you were gone." Recalled Evert to a reporter years later, "You know, Billie didn't have to do that." Howard, *The Rivals*, 51.

63 King and Starr, *We Have Come a Long Way*, 142; Festle, *Playing Nice*, 149; King and Starr, *We Have Come a Long Way*, 120. See also Spencer, "Once Upon a Subculture."

64 Burling Lowrey, "Women's Tennis: A Call for a Realistic Appraisal," *New York Times*, August 31, 1975, 152; Mark Asher, "Women's Lob Championed by Top Lady," *Washington Post*, September 5, 1971, 162. For a general discussion of the issue, see John L. Crompton, "Sponsorship of Sport by Tobacco and Alcohol Companies: A Review of the Issues," *Journal of Sport and Social Issues* 17 (December 1993): 148–67.

65 Marty Bell, "Is She Paying Off?" *womenSports*, December 1976, 61; Gregory M. Lamb, "Virginia Slims Tennis Tournament—linking smoking and sports?" *Christian Science Monitor*, February 11, 1983, 10.

66 Collins, "Billie Jean King Evens the Score," 40; Curry Kirkpatrick, "The Ball in

Two Different Courts," *Sports Illustrated*, December 25, 1972, 33. Robert Lipsyte, for example, was so outspoken in a November 20, 1992, piece in the *New York Times* ("Amid All the Smoke, the Ethics are Indistinct") that Billie Jean King accused him of crossing the line "from acceptable advocacy to unacceptable insult" in a letter to the editor on December 20, 1992, S9. In 1993 Ira Berkow compared her to an ostrich with her head in the sand by claiming that not smoking meant not endorsing cigarette consumption. "A Match for Smoking, Not Tennis," *New York Times*, December 7, 1993, B15.

67 Kirkpatrick, "The Ball in Two Different Courts," 32–33; "Playboy Interview: Billie Jean King," 70; King and Starr, *We Have Come a Long Way*, 120; BJK, *Billie Jean* (1982), 146. Billie Jean King's was an equal-opportunity sexism: "I like to see guys' legs and their bahoolas." "Playboy Interview: Billie Jean King," 67.

68 Stephan Wilkinson, "The Visionary of Tennis," *Working Woman*, September 1988, 86–87; U.S. Senate, *Hearings on the Women's Educational Equity Act, 1973*, 83.

69 Robin Herman, "Court Queen and Women's Lib Symbol," *New York Times*, September 10, 1974, 47; "Billie Jean King goes for the Net Profits," *Life*, November 1971, 109; Lichtenstein, *A Long Way, Baby*, 154. Even some feminists, King complained, were hypercritical of her emphasis on money, causing her to dismiss them as "liberal Democrats who couldn't stand to see anyone make a profit." BJK, *Billie Jean* (1982), 160.

70 Jenkins, "Racket Science," 77; BJK, *Billie Jean* (1974), 124; Evert, "Happy Birthday, TENNIS," 16. To those who envied the supposedly glamorous life of a touring pro, she would retort that they'd never seen her washing her tennis dresses and socks in a motel sink. Stewart-Gordon, "Billie Jean King—Queen of the Rackets," 155.

71 BJK, *Billie Jean* (1974), 130; BJK, *Billie Jean* (1982), 20–21.

72 Mark Asher, "Abortion Made Possible Mrs. King's Top Year," *Washington Post*, February 22, 1972, D1; "Playboy Interview: Billie Jean King," 64. She felt "it was absolutely the wrong time for me to bring a child into the world," a direct reference to her marriage, not because of concern about how a pregnancy would affect her tennis career. BJK, *Billie Jean* (1974), 156–57. See also BJK, *Billie Jean* (1982), 22–23.

73 "We have had abortions," *Ms.*, Spring 1972, 34–35; Asher, "Abortion Made Possible Mrs. King's Top Year." See "Playboy Interview: Billie Jean King," 64, on not having the "guts" to tell her mother herself.

74 "Two Pros," *Time*, March 20, 1972, 103; BJK, *Billie Jean* (1974), 157; BJK, *Billie Jean* (1982), 22–23; Roberts, *A Necessary Spectacle*, 87. In her defense, note the double standard at work: few male sports figures would ever have to field such personal questions. "They ask me about my abortion. Do they ask a football player if he's had a vasectomy?" Collins, "Billie Jean Evens the Score," 40.

75 BJK, *Billie Jean* (1974), 147.

76 See epilogue.

77 Collins, "Billie Jean King Evens the Score," 43; Billie Jean King, Publisher's Letter, *womenSports*, March 1975, 4. Of all her activism, King always said that this moment meant the most to her. Bud Collins, "Starry Tribute was Fit for King," *Boston Globe*, November 10, 2003, D7.

78 Lichtenstein, *A Long Way, Baby*, 244.

79 Larned, "The Bodacious Billie Jean King," 60; Robert Lipsyte, "Helping Others Before Helping Herself," *New York Times*, July 12, 1998, SP11.

80 This section owes a debt to Lipsyte and Levine, *Idols of the Game*; the "Godded up" quote is on p. 82. See also Dave Zirin, *What's My Name, Fool? Sports and Resistance in the United States* (Chicago: Haymarket Books, 2005); and *A People's History of Sports in the United States* (New York: New Press, 2008).

81 For general histories of women and sport, see Susan K. Cahn, *Coming on Strong: Gender and Sexuality in Twentieth-Century Women's Sport* (New York: Free Press, 1994); and Lissa Smith, ed., *Nike Is a Goddess: The History of Women in Sports* (New York: Atlantic Monthly Press, 1998). See also chapter 4.

82 Lipsyte and Levine, *Idols of the Game*, chapter 7.

83 Roger Kahn quoted in Lipsyte and Levine, *Idols of the Game*, 164–65. See also Zirin, *What's My Name, Fool?* on Jackie Robinson's significance.

84 Robert Lipsyte, "Instant Legends and Super Heroes," *Washington Post*, March 30, 1978, DC7.

85 Deford, "Mrs. Billie Jean King," 72.

86 Dave Anderson, "Now I Can Have Beer and Ice Cream," *New York Times*, July 5, 1975, 21.

87 Tony Kornheiser, "Smile, Even Though You're Aching," *New York Times*, November 22, 1977, 59; Larry Eldridge, "King still volleys with abandon, but what comes after tennis?" *Christian Science Monitor*, March 15, 1983, 18; Jane Gross, "Billie Jean King Is Up to Her Old Tricks," *New York Times*, March 17, 1980, C1. Navratilova, in turn, totally challenged the timeframe of an athletic career by competing successfully until her fiftieth birthday loomed. She too was on a quest for Wimbledon titles, eventually tying King for the record with a total of twenty. See Howard, *The Rivals*.

88 BJK, *Billie Jean* (1974), 201; Pete Axthelm, "The Battle of the Sexes," *Newsweek*, September 24, 1973, 84; Joel Drucker, "The Once and Future King," *Women's Sports and Fitness*, November/December 1992, 78; Donna Carter, "Title IX Turns 25: A Struggle from Entitlement to Empowerment," *Denver Post*, June 10, 1997, D10.

Chapter Two

1 Selena Roberts, *A Necessary Spectacle: Billie Jean King, Bobby Riggs, and the Tennis Match That Leveled the Game* (New York: Crown Publishers, 2005), 93; Mark Starr, "The Battle of the Sexes," *Newsweek*, September 21, 1998, 90; Billie Jean King, *Pressure Is a Privilege: Lessons I've Learned from Life and the Battle of the Sexes* (New York: LifeTime Media, 2008), 22. Here is the full quote: "In the early 1970s, I was playing regularly while also working to get the women's professional tennis tour (then known as the Virginia Slims Series) started and helping to get Title IX—the groundbreaking legislation that would require all high schools, colleges, and universities receiving federal funds for education to spend those funds equally on boys and girls—passed in Congress. (It was eventually passed on June 23, 1972, about a year before the Battle of the Sexes.)"

2 She added: "It's not just sports. Women or men should not be discriminated against."

Sara Glassman, "Still in the Battle; Tennis Champion Billie Jean King changed women's sports, and if she has her way, she's not done yet. Not even close," *Minneapolis Star-Tribune*, February 26, 2006, 1E.

3 U.S. House of Representatives, *Hearings before the Special Subcommittee on Education of the Committee on Education and Labor*, 92nd Cong., 1st sess., March 1971 (Washington, D.C.: Government Printing Office, 1971), 580. See also Jane Sims, "Sex Bias Ban for Colleges Urged on Hill," *Washington Post*, August 31, 1971, A2, where Green says the antidiscrimination provision "would be the most revolutionary cause of the 1970s for women." Cynthia Harrison, *On Account of Sex: The Politics of Women's Issues, 1945–1968* (Berkeley: University of California Press, 1988) provides general background on the passage of the legislation. See also Jo Freeman, "How 'Sex' Got Into Title VII: Persistent Opportunism as a Maker of Public Policy," *Law and Inequality* 9 (1990–1991): 163–84.

4 Bernice R. Sandler, "'Too Strong for a Woman'—The Five Words that Created Title IX," in National Association for Women in Education newsletter, *About Women on Campus* (Spring 1977): 2.

5 Ibid., 1. The "godmother" quote was originally from the *New York Times*. See ⟨http://bernicesandler.com⟩.

6 Sandler, "'Too Strong for a Woman,'" 3–4. See also Bernice Resnick Sandler, "Title IX: How We Got It and What a Difference it Made," *Cleveland State Law Review* 55 (2007): 473. See also the oral history of Bunny Sandler conducted by Jill Reid, December 9, 1985, part of a series of oral histories the Equality Center in Washington, D.C., undertook in the mid-1980s for a manuscript on the early history of Title IX. This manuscript was never published, but drafts are found in Dunkle, SL. Unless otherwise noted, all subsequent references to oral histories are ones done in conjunction with this project.

7 For background on the passage of the law, see Karen Blumenthal, *Let Me Play: The Story of Title IX: The Law that Changed the Future of Girls in America* (New York: Atheneum, 2005); and Welch Suggs, *A Place on the Team: The Triumph and Tragedy of Title IX* (Princeton, N.J.: Princeton University Press, 2005). The quote from Sandler is from "'Too Strong for a Woman,'" 4.

8 A detailed legislative history is found in Rep. Patsy Mink's remarks, "In Celebration of the 30th Anniversary of the Education Amendments of 1972," *Congressional Record*, July 17, 2002, H4860–4863.

9 Sandler, "'Too Strong for a Woman,'" 5. See, for example, Albert A. Logan Jr., "Universities Told They Must Grant Equal Opportunity for Women," July 6, 1970, 5; Cheryl M. Fields, "House Bill's Sex-Discrimination Ban Worries Newly Co-Ed Institutions," October 18, 1971, 1, 2; Fields, "There's Still a Long Road to Travel Before Colleges Get U.S. Aid," November 15, 1971, 1, 3; Fields, "Senate Approves College Aid Bill; Forbids Sex Bias," March 6, 1972, 1, 2, all from the *Chronicle of Higher Education*. In general, the *Chronicle* gave fairly extensive coverage to how the emerging feminist movement was challenging business as usual in higher education, providing stories starting in the late 1960s and continuing throughout the 1970s on the beginnings of Women's Studies, the WEAL class action case, and the general struggle for academic

women to find a stronger niche in the male bastion of higher education at the time. Bunny Sandler had a regular column called "The Academic Woman" on gender issues in education in 1973.

10 "Sex Balance by Edict," *New York Times*, August 15, 1971, E14. See also the editorial "Women's Rights and the Colleges," *Washington Post*, September 16, 1971, A18, which was more supportive of the pending legislation. Both the *New York Times* and the *Washington Post* discussed the sex discrimination provision in passing, but not as fully as did the *Chronicle*.

11 If Congress had intended to exclude athletics, it could have amended the original language the way it did for admissions, the service academies, and certain religious schools. See Charles Percy to Caspar Weinberger, May 1, 1974, Dunkle, SL.

12 *Congressional Record*, August 6, 1971, S13554; *Congressional Record*, July 17, 2002, H4861–4862. In October 2002 Title IX was renamed the Patsy Takemoto Mink Equal Opportunity in Education Act in honor of the legislator who had died the previous month.

13 Cheryl M. Fields, "$19-Billion Higher Education Bill Wins Passage, Nixon's signature," *Chronicle of Higher Education*, July 3, 1972, 1; "How Supporters and Opponents View the Higher Education Bill," *Chronicle of Higher Education*, June 5, 1972, 1. The Pell Grants were named for Senator Claiborne Pell, the chair of the Senate Education Committee, who was their main proponent. In later years Edith Green, who grew increasingly conservative politically in the 1970s (she left Congress in 1975), spoke out against Title IX, claiming the regulations went far beyond her original intent in areas such as athletics and physical education. See Edith Green, "The Road Is Paved with Good Intentions: Title IX and What it is Not," *Vital Speeches of the Day* 43 (March 1, 1977): 300–303. See also Edith Green to Patricia Harris, November 17, 1979, Dunkle, SL.

14 Suggs, *A Place on the Team*, contains the full text of Title IX in Appendix A. The rest of Title IX concerns the exemptions of admissions, single-sex colleges, religious organizations, and the military academies, as well as language describing federal administrative enforcement, judicial review, and amendments to other laws.

15 "Sex Discrimination and Intercollegiate Athletics: Putting Some Muscle on Title IX," *Yale Law Journal* 88 (May 1979): 1264.

16 Sandler, "'Too Strong for a Woman,'" 7–8. Sandler also paid tribute to Rep. Green's skill as a politician, and her connections. "She was able to get the men on that committee to support the bill primarily because it was *her* bill! They owed her one or more or whatever. So she got their support."

17 Quoted in Amy Erdman Farrell, *Yours in Sisterhood: Ms. Magazine and the Promise of Popular Feminism* (Chapel Hill: University of North Carolina Press, 1998), 18.

18 Gwen Gregory oral history, Dunkle, SL; Stanley Kutler, *The Wars of Watergate* (New York: Knopf, 1990), 361.

19 For example, a group of Michigan activists filed a fifty-eight-page complaint with twenty-four exhibits charging "Gross Discrimination in Athletics Against Women at the University of Michigan" on August 19, 1973. The effort was spearheaded by local NOW activist Marcia Federbush, along with six other complainants, including

one undergraduate, Barb Stellard, who at one point played Little League "until she doffed her hat after hitting a home run." Two years later nothing had happened in the case. See Federbush to Caspar Weinberger, August 19, 1973, and Federbush to Peter Holmes, August 1, 1975, PEER, SL. There is also additional documentation in NOW, SL.

20 J. Stanley Pottinger to Bernice Sandler, July 27, 1972, Dunkle, SL; Dunkle notes, August 4, 1972, Dunkle, SL; Dunkle to Bertrand [sic] Taylor, August 9, 1972, PEER, SL.

21 Unedited transcript of oral history of Bernice Sandler conducted by Julia Lamber and Jean Robinson, June 28–29, 2004, 50, found in Sandler, SL. This oral history was separate from the Bernice Sandler oral history done by the Equality Center. She made a similar point when I interviewed her in February 2008. See also Sandler, "Title IX," 473.

22 Gwen Gregory to J. Stanley Pottinger, "Sex Discrimination in Athletics," October 4, 1972, Dunkle, SL. This memo is the closest thing to a smoking gun that I found: the first sustained attention to the issue.

23 Deborah Brake, "The Struggle for Sex Equality in Sport and the Theory Behind Title IX," *University of Michigan Journal of Law Reform* 34 (Fall 2000/Winter 2001): 25; Gregory to Pottinger, "Sex Discrimination in Athletics."

24 Gregory to Pottinger, "Sex Discrimination in Athletics," and Pottinger response, October 20, 1972, Dunkle, SL.

25 Ann Scott, "It's Time for Equal Education," *Ms.*, October 1973, 122–25. She also discusses the recently passed Equal Rights Amendment, which had already been ratified by twenty states. Another early reference appeared in the newsletter *On Campus with Women*, November 1972, which made a brief parenthetical reference that the regulations being drafted for Title IX were expected to cover sex discrimination in sports.

26 Handwritten note on letter from Grant to Pottinger, January 28, 1973, Dunkle, SL; Bunny Sandler to Ruth Bader Ginsburg, February 8, 1973, PSEW, SL. Professor Ginsburg, who had recently left Rutgers for Columbia, was very much on top of all these developments.

27 Memo, Margaret Dunkle to "Bunny," April 11 [1973], Dunkle, SL; Margaret Dunkle, "Equal Opportunity for Women in Sports," April 13, 1973, Dunkle, SL.

28 Bil Gilbert, "Thank Heaven for . . .", *Sports Illustrated*, November 27, 1967, 72–74; Bil Gilbert and Nancy Williamson, "Sport is Unfair to Women," *Sports Illustrated*, May 28, 1973, 88, 90. See also personal communication from Bil Gilbert to Susan Ware, October 24, 2005.

29 Parts two and three of the series were Bil Gilbert and Nancy Williamson, "Are You Being Two-Faced?" *Sports Illustrated*, June 4, 1973, 44–50, 53–54; and Gilbert and Williamson, "Programmed to Be Losers," *Sports Illustrated*, June 11, 1973, 60–62, 65–66, 68, 73.

30 "Guidelines on Equality of Sexes Due from Government in January," *Chronicle of Higher Education*, November 5, 1973, 4. There is some confusion about when the NCAA learned that sports would be included. The "historical note" that accom-

panies the NCAA memo, February 21, 1974, presents this detailed chronology: "Although the educational community has been aware of the general implications of Title IX since its passage in 1972, its application to intercollegiate athletics came as a surprise. We understand athletics was not covered in the initial draft of the regulations in February, 1973. First public knowledge of the application to athletics came at an early November, 1973 meeting of the Association for Intercollegiate Athletics for Women. Immediate inquiry to HEW brought a response that the regulations were not final and it was not until mid-December that a copy was made available to the NCAA." [Dunkle, SL] It is extremely unlikely, however, that the NCAA didn't have some inkling before then. For example, presumably they subscribed to *Sports Illustrated* and would have read the series on women in sports in May and June 1973. Perhaps it is best to rephrase the question as, when did it really sink in that Title IX could be a threat warranting NCAA action? That awareness was certainly rising by the summer of 1973.

31 Elizabeth M. Bolton, "Legislating Equity: The History of Title IX" (M.A. thesis, American University, 2008), 51; U.S. Senate, Committee on Labor and Public Welfare, Subcommittee on Education, *Hearings on the Women's Educational Equity Act, October 17 and November 9, 1973*, 93rd Cong., 1st sess. (Washington, D.C.: Government Printing Office, 1973), 83. See also "Billie Jean King Tells Senators of Bias in School Sports," *Chronicle of Higher Education*, November 19, 1973, 5.

32 U.S. Senate, *Hearings on the Women's Educational Equity Act, 1973*, 77, 81, 82. At the request of Senator Mondale's office, King had help preparing her testimony from Bunny Sandler (and probably Margaret Dunkle, too) at the Project on the Status and Education of Women. See Sandler to Billie Jean King, October 26, 1973, PSEW, SL. For more on the scope and history of the WEEA, see Andrew Fishel and Janice Pottker, *National Politics and Sex Discrimination in Education* (Lexington, Mass.: D.C. Heath, 1977), chapter 4; and Irene Tinker, ed., *Women in Washington: Advocates for Public Policy* (Beverly Hills, Calif.: Sage Publications, 1983).

33 For background on the NCAA, see Ying Wushanley, *Playing Nice and Losing: The Struggle for Control of Women's Intercollegiate Athletics, 1960–2000* (Syracuse, N.Y.: Syracuse University Press, 2004); Brian L. Porto, *A New Season: Using Title IX to Reform College Sports* (Westport, Conn.: Praeger, 2003); and Suggs, *A Place on the Team*.

34 William A. Sievert, "NCAA Concerned About Legality of its Exclusion of Women," *Chronicle of Higher Education*, January 17, 1972, 1, 4. See also Ying Wu, "Early NCAA Attempts at the Governance of Women's Intercollegiate Athletics, 1968–1973," *Journal of Sport History* 26 (Fall 1999): 585–601.

35 Margot Polivy oral history, Dunkle, SL. This incident took place in 1979; the skeptic was Duke president Terry Sanford, who was spearheading a public relations effort against Title IX at the time.

36 For a general overview, see Michael Oriard, *King Football: Sport and Spectacle in the Golden Age of Radio and Newsreels, Movies and Magazines, the Weekly and the Daily Press* (Chapel Hill: University of North Carolina Press, 2001).

37 Candace Lyle Hogan, "Football is Hardly Sugar Daddy," *New York Times*, December 10, 1978, 52.

38 "Give 'Em a Break, Ma'am," *Washington Post*, February 10, 1974, C7; *Sports Illustrated* Scorecard, January 28, 1974; "Rules Due to Aid Women in Sports," *New York Times*, February 9, 1974, 21. See also Ellen Weber, "The Long March," *womenSports*, September 1974, 34–46; Margaret Dunkle, "College Athletics: Tug-of-War for the Purse Strings," *Ms.*, September 1974, 114, 117; and Dunkle, "What Constitutes Equality for Women in Sport? Federal Law Puts Women in the Running" (Washington, D.C.: Project on the Status and Education of Women, Association of American Colleges, 1974).

39 "Memorandum to Chief Executive Officers of NCAA Member Institutions," February 21, 1974, Dunkle, SL; Cheryl M. Fields, "Fear of Effect on Athletics Delays Sex-Bias Guidelines," *Chronicle of Higher Education*, March 18, 1974, 5. The article quotes from the NCAA memo of February, but also quotes Gwen Gregory complaining that they are misstating what the regulations would do, including "one of the most persistent and untrue reports" that HEW would require equal funding of men's and women's sports, despite an explicit statement that this was not true.

40 "Sports May be Excluded from Equality Guidelines," *Chronicle of Higher Education*, April 22, 1974, 4.

41 Gwen Gregory recalled that HEW had at first tried to avoid publicity, but quickly learned how useful it could be: "in fact it turned out to be our greatest ally. . . . I think the publicity really did help a lot, because they say that a law that is not accepted by the public at large is a useless law. Before all the publicity, we did not have the grass roots support for Title IX and the concept of equality in the schools." Gregory oral history, Dunkle, SL.

42 For more on the Tower Amendment, see Fishel and Pottker, *National Politics and Sex Discrimination*, 82–83; and Blumenthal, *Let Me Play*, 66–68.

43 Billie Jean King form letter, June 7, 1974, Dunkle, SL. A subsequent amendment, sponsored by Senator Jacob Javits of New York in July and included in the Education Amendments of 1974 enacted in August, clarified that Title IX regulations must take into account the nature of particular sports, in effect saying that spending $1,000 to outfit a male football player and only $100 on a female swimmer would not automatically count as discrimination. The Javits Amendment finally put to rest the NCAA contention that athletics were not covered by Title IX. Blumenthal, *Let Me Play*, 68, says the Javits Amendment was drafted by Margot Polivy, the attorney for the Association for Intercollegiate Athletics for Women, a view seconded by Margaret Dunkle. Memorandum by Dunkle to "Jill," February 26, 1986, Dunkle, SL.

44 Robert Perrin, "Making Everyone Into a Minority," *Washington Post*, February 10, 1975, A21. One area that was left out of the regulations was a provision prohibiting discrimination in textbooks and other curricular materials. Even though HEW recognized that sex stereotyping was a serious problem, it concluded that regulating textbook content would raise insurmountable First Amendment issues.

45 "Guidelines Under Fire," *Chronicle of Higher Education*, July 8, 1974, 8; *Federal Register* 39 (June 20, 1974): 22236, reprinted in Suggs, *A Place on the Team*, 208–9; Gwen Gregory oral history, Dunkle, SL. HEW wouldn't have had the authority to require equal aggregate expenditures anyway because it was only charged with addressing

discrimination against individuals. See also Martin Gerry oral history, Dunkle, SL, on extension.

46 According to Terry H. Anderson, *The Pursuit of Fairness: A History of Affirmative Action* (New York: Oxford University Press, 2004), the zenith of affirmative action was the late 1960s and early 1970s. The divided Supreme Court decision in *Regents of the University of California v. Allan Bakke* (1978) signaled the onset of a backlash.

47 Welch Suggs, "Title IX Has Done Little for Minority Female Athletes—Because of Socioeconomic and Cultural Factors, and Indifference," *Chronicle of Higher Education*, November 30, 2001, 35. See also Yevonne Smith, "Sociohistorical Influences on African American Elite Sportswomen," in Dana Brooks and Ronald Althouse, eds., *Racism in College Athletics: The African American Athlete's Experience* (Morgantown, W. Va.: Fitness Information Technology, 2000), 173–98; and Women's Sports Foundation, "Title IX and Race in Intercollegiate Sport" (East Meadow, N.Y., 2003).

48 "HEW Head Says Title IX Won't 'Bankrupt' Schools," *New York Times*, June 27, 1975, 15.

49 See Hon. Bella Abzug, *Congressional Record*, July 18, 1974, 24222–24228 for WEAL's perspective. (Abzug's remarks were actually written by Bunny Sandler and Margaret Dunkle. See Margaret Dunkle to "Jill," February 26, 1986, Dunkle, SL.) For NOW's critique, see chapter 5.

50 NCAA to Weinberger, October 15, 1974, PEER, SL. The comments run thirty-one pages, single-spaced, and read like a legal brief, complete with case citations.

51 Martin Gerry put it more bluntly, calling the process a "political shell game": "The regulations had to be changed in the final version to show responsiveness." Gerry oral history, Dunkle, SL. One solution was to craft concessions to the male sports establishment that focused more on process than substance.

52 "Anti-Sex-Bias Rules: White House Reviewing Proposals," *Chronicle of Higher Education*, March 10, 1975, 10; Cheryl M. Fields, "H.E.W. Softens Bias Stand," *Chronicle of Higher Education*, April 7, 1975, 1, 11; Michael Scott quoted in Gerald Eskenazi, "Title IX Rules Issued for Equality in Sports," *New York Times*, June 4, 1975, 29. In turn, Weinberger often voiced exasperation with the NCAA. In testimony before Congress on June 26, 1975 (Dunkle, SL), to a list of things that Title IX did not require (like equal expenditures, coed showers, or requiring women to play football with men), he added a seventh: "It does NOT mean the National Collegiate Athletic Association (NCAA) will be dissolved and will have to fire all of its highly vocal staff."

53 Cheryl M. Fields, "H.E.W. Softens Bias Stand," 1, 11. Senator Birch Bayh's decision in December 1974 to support an amendment that exempted sororities and fraternities stemmed from a similar inclination: exempt a small but highly emotional element in order to forestall other efforts to weaken the whole law. The contact sports exclusion was not the last word, however. Girls have successfully sued to play contact sports under the equal protection clause of the Fourteenth Amendment. See Sarah K. Fields, *Female Gladiators: Gender, Law, and Contact Sport in America* (Urbana: University of Illinois Press, 2005). See also chapter 5.

54 *Federal Register* 40 (June 4, 1975): 24142–43. See also Dunkle, "What Constitutes Equality."

55 This account draws heavily on Therese Pasquale and Margaret Dunkle, "An Upset Victory for Women: The blow-by-blow story of the battle for equal rights in education," *Women's Agenda*, June 1976. See also Margaret Dunkle, "Title IX: New Rules for an Old Game," *Capitol Hill Forum*, July 28, 1975.

56 Bunny Sandler oral history, Dunkle, SL. Fishel and Pottker, *National Politics and Sex Discrimination*, make the link between activism for the WEEA and Title IX on p. 91.

57 Pasquale and Dunkle, "An Upset Victory for Women." One of those buttons, courtesy of Margaret Dunkle, hangs above my desk as I write.

58 Pasquale and Dunkle, "An Upset Victory for Women."

59 Blumenthal, *Let Me Play*, 74. For the original quote, see Eric Wentworth, "Ban on Sex Integration is Rejected," *Washington Post*, July 19, 1975, A1. For more on women's influence, see Tinker, *Women in Washington*; and Joyce Gelb and Marian Lief Palley, *Women and Public Policies: Reassessing Gender Politics* (Charlottesville: University Press of Virginia, 1996).

60 Sandler oral history, Dunkle, SL.

61 For more on the episode, including a copy of the letter of protest, see Susan Ware, *Title IX: A Brief History with Documents* (Boston: Bedford/St. Martin's, 2007). See also the documentary film by Mary Mazzio, *A Hero for Daisy* (1999).

62 See Susan Hartmann, "Feminism, Public Policy, and the Carter Administration," in Gary M. Fink and Hugh Davis Graham, eds., *The Carter Presidency: Policy Choices in the Post-New Deal Era* (Lawrence: University Press of Kansas, 1998); and Marjorie J. Spruill, "Gender and America's Right Turn: The 1977 IWY Conferences and the Polarization of American Politics," in Bruce Schulman and Julian Zelizer, eds., *Rightward Bound: Making America Conservative in the 1970s* (Cambridge: Harvard University Press, 2008).

63 Candace Lyle Hogan, "Shedding Light on Title IX," *womenSports*, February 1976, 45; Cheryl M. Fields, "HEW Policy on Sports Bias Raises New Questions," *Chronicle of Higher Education*, December 11, 1978, 9.

64 Project on Equal Education Rights, *Stalled at the Start: Government Action on Sex Bias in the Schools* (Washington: NOW Legal Defense and Education Fund, 1978), 17. HEW's record was the most deficient in the third category: only twelve independent investigations were launched, with few tangible results.

65 In November 1974 WEAL, along with the National Education Association, the National Organization for Women, the National Student Association, the Federation of Organizations for Professional Women, and the Association for Women in Science, filed suit in U.S. District Court for the District of Columbia, charging HEW with failure to fulfill its responsibility to enforce Title IX (*WEAL v. Califano*). As a result of the suit, HEW was ordered in December 1977 to move forward according to a timetable, and to close all complaints by September 1979. HEW also decided to initiate its own compliance reviews, rather than relying just on complaints that had been filed. See United States Commission on Civil Rights, *More Hurdles to Clear: Women and Girls in Competitive Athletics*, Clearinghouse Publication no. 63 (Washington, D.C.: United States Commission on Civil Rights, July 1980), 33.

66 PEER, *Stalled at the Start*, 5, 13. See also the extensive PEER records at the Schlesinger Library.

67 PEER, *Stalled at the Start*, 19, 33–34.

68 Ibid., 22, 30.

69 See the September 1975 Sports Memorandum found in United States Commission on Civil Rights, *More Hurdles to Clear*, 4. This memo on the subject of "Elimination of Sex Discrimination in Athletic Programs" was an attempt to diffuse some of the fears raised by the July regulations, but it was more of a public relations effort and broke no new ground in terms of coverage and compliance.

70 Hogan, "Shedding Light on Title IX," 44.

71 Mary Jo Festle, *Playing Nice: Politics and Apologies in Women's Sports* (New York: Columbia University Press, 1996), 127; Nancy Scannell, "Title 9 Crackdown Nears," *Washington Post*, July 20, 1978, F1. See also Cheryl M. Fields, "July 31: Title IX Deadline," *Chronicle of Higher Education*, November 14, 1977, 9–11.

72 Cheryl M. Fields, "Spend About the Same on Women Athletes As on Men, Government Will Tell Colleges," *Chronicle of Higher Education*, November 20, 1978, 1, 7; "Sex-Bias Rules Would Protect Bigtime Football," *Chronicle of Higher Education*, December 11, 1978, 13; Fields, "HEW Policy on Sports Bias Raises New Questions," *Chronicle of Higher Education*, December 18, 1978, 9.

73 "As Criticism Continues, U.S. Prepares Final Policy on Sex-Bias in Sports," *Chronicle of Higher Education*, March 19, 1979, 4; Joan Ryan, "Crisis Time for Equality," *Washington Post*, April 20, 1979, D1; Cheryl M. Fields, "Women's Sports Groups Campaign to Preserve Proposed Anti-Bias Rules," *Chronicle of Higher Education*, April 23, 1979, 19. The NCAA was appealing its case challenging the inclusion of athletics at this point.

74 Nancy Scannell, "Proposals on Title 9 Criticized," *Washington Post*, March 14, 1979, D1, D4.

75 Sandler, "Title IX," 483; U.S. Department of Education, Secretary's Commission for Opportunity in Athletics, *Open to All: Title IX at Thirty* (Washington, D.C.: Government Printing Office, 2003), 2. See also Donna Lopiano to Howard McKeon, May 15, 1995, in U.S. House of Representatives, Subcommittee on Postsecondary Education, Training and Life-Long Learning of the Committee on Economic and Educational Opportunities, *Hearing on Title IX of the Education Amendments of 1972*, 104th Cong., 1st sess., May 9, 1995 (Washington, D.C.: Government Printing Office, 1995).

76 Quoted in Jessica Gavora, *Tilting the Playing Field: Schools, Sports, Sex, and Title IX* (San Francisco: Encounter Books, 2002), 73. This became known as the "Field of Dreams" rationale, following the 1989 movie of that name.

77 Ware, *Title IX*, 75–76.

78 Polivy oral history, Dunkle, SL. The NCAA wasn't just interested in women's sports: it was also engaged in a turf war with the Amateur Athletic Union (AAU). For more, see Wushanley, *Playing Nice and Losing*.

79 Nancy Scannell, "Détente's Gone Awry in Wake of NCAA, AIAW Conventions," *Washington Post*, January 13, 1980, N9. Tongue-in-cheek, Candace Lyle Hogan com-

pared the NCAA's interest to the contemporary energy crisis: oil has been discovered in the AIAW, and it is valuable. Hogan, "NCAA Discovers Women Athlete: A Valuable Resource," *New York Times*, March 30, 1980, S2.

80 Affidavit of Donna A. Lopiano, October 9, 1981, *Association for Intercollegiate Athletics for Women v. National Collegiate Athletic Association*, U.S. District Court for the District of Columbia, 157, 119. A similar process occurred in the South after *Brown v. Board of Education*, where black educational leaders lost their positions and power when schools were consolidated.

81 "Strides," *Women's Sports*, May 1980, 61–62. At the New Agenda Conference in November 1983, Donna de Varona noted: "We've always had warning signals. The shift came when the NCAA changed and embraced women's sports and we had to start to define ourselves through the establishment." Jane Leavy, "Women's Sports Seeks Visibility," *Washington Post*, November 4, 1983, C1.

82 Bart Barnes, "Lack of Money Halts Boom in Women's Sports," *Washington Post*, July 5, 1981, D4. A good summary is United States Commission on Civil Rights, *More Hurdles to Clear: Women and Girls in Competitive Athletics*.

83 Kathryn Jay, *More Than Just a Game: Sports in American Life Since 1945* (New York: Columbia University Press, 2004), 162.

84 A prime example is Gavora, *Tilting the Playing Field*.

85 Quoted in George Vecsey, "Help on Way for Title IX," *New York Times*, April 22, 1984, 53.

86 Diane Heckman, "The Glass Sneaker: Thirty Years of Victories and Defeats involving Title IX and Sex Discrimination in Athletics," *Fordham Intellectual Property, Media and Entertainment Law Journal* 13 (Winter 2003): 551–614. She first used the phrase in Heckman, "Women and Athletics: A Twenty Year Retrospective on Title IX," *University of Miami Entertainment and Sports Law Review* 9 (1992). The Women's Sports Foundation based its conclusion on figures provided by the National Federation of State High School Associations for 2006–7. Press release posted on WSF website ⟨http://womenssportsfoundation.org⟩ (October 22, 2007).

87 Barnes, "Lack of Money," D4.

88 In this case, it actually peaked in 1976–77.

89 Candace Lyle Hogan anticipated this conclusion in "From Here to Equality: Title IX," *womenSports*, September 1977, 16. These conclusions are based on my analysis of participation figures from the National Federation of State High School Associations from 1970 to 2005; and "Comparative Analysis—Increase in Membership and Women's Sports," in the National Collegiate Athletic Association, *The Sports and Recreation Programs of the Nation's Universities and Colleges*, Report #7 (1985), 23–27.

90 Hogan, "Football is Hardly Sugar Daddy," 52.

91 Hogan, "From Here to Equality," 17, 18. For another early warning about the decline in women coaches and administrators, see Linda Jean Carpenter, "The Impact of Title IX on Women's Intercollegiate Sports," in Arthur T. Johnson and James H. Frey, eds., *Government and Sport: The Public Policy Issues* (Totawa, N.J.: Rowman and Allanheld, 1985), 67–69.

92 Barnes, "Lack of Money," D4.

Chapter Three

1 Billie Jean King, Publisher's Letter, *womenSports*, January 1976, 4. Of that list, the one business venture that went nowhere was Billie Jean's broadcasting career. With great fanfare she was signed by ABC to a multiyear contract in January 1975 for a reported $200,000, but then became, in *Sports Illustrated*'s apt phrase, "TV's version of a missing person." King claimed she wanted to do more shows, but she had not really cut back on her tennis at that point and didn't seem to have the time or the inclination to retool herself for a career in broadcasting, as had other female sports figures such as Donna de Varona and, later, Mary Carillo. Melissa Ludtke, "King Does Not Reign on ABC," *Sports Illustrated*, March 8, 1976, 48. See also "People in Sports," *New York Times*, December 19, 1974, 97.

2 Christine Terp, "A Whole New Ball Game," *Christian Science Monitor*, May 22, 1981, 12; "King Explains Abilities Gap," *Washington Post*, September 3, 1974, D1.

3 Mary Kates, "Tennis Tycoon: Billie Jean King Finds Sport Profitable Even When She Isn't Playing," *Wall Street Journal*, September 19, 1973, 1; William Wong, "Tennis, No One? Billie Jean King Faces Financial Setback Because of Her Teaching Firm's Trouble," *Wall Street Journal*, February 10, 1975, 26; Robin Herman, "Court Queen and Women's Lib Symbol," *New York Times*, September 10, 1974, 47.

4 Elizabeth Wheeler, "The Men Behind the Women: Five Men Who Have Helped Shape Women's Sports," *Women's Sports*, December 1980, 23–24. Larry also was president of Future, Inc., which served as the business agent for Billie Jean King and twenty-three other athletes, including her brother Randy and golfer Jane Blalock. Larry King, "My Wife, Billie Jean King by her Husband," *Ladies' Home Journal*, April 1974, 146; Kates, "Tennis Tycoon."

5 Frank Deford, "Mrs. Billie Jean King," *Sports Illustrated*, May 19, 1975, 81. According to Grace Lichtenstein, Larry King was known on the tour as an "over-zealous 'pusher.'" Grace Lichtenstein, *A Long Way, Baby: The Inside Story of the Women in Pro Tennis* (New York: William Morrow, 1974), 178.

6 Kates, "Tennis Tycoon." Ironically TennisAmerica, a company founded in 1969 by the Kings and fellow player Dennis Van der Meer to teach tennis, was one company that failed to fly. The Kings probably lost several hundred thousand dollars when the company went bankrupt in 1975. See Kates, "Tennis Tycoon," for a fuller description of the Kings' role in this enterprise, which was not insubstantial. The final bankruptcy was reported in "TennisAmerica Attorneys File for Bankruptcy," *Washington Post*, February 16, 1975, 53. See also Wong, "Tennis, No One?"

7 See chapter 4.

8 Billie Jean King, Publisher's Letter, *womenSports*, November 1975, 4; Robin Herman, "Billie Jean King's Lifestyle: Innovate and Take a Chance," *New York Times*, June 15, 1975, 51. For example, *Newsweek* noted that Billie Jean King "has sometimes been criticized for launching projects like the women's organization, grabbing public attention and then abandoning them to the stewardship of outsiders or her traveling secretary Marilyn Barnett." "Sportswomanlike Conduct," *Newsweek*, June 3, 1974, 52.

9 Billie Jean King, Publisher's Letter, *womenSports*, June 1974, 4; Billie Jean King, Publisher's Letter, *womenSports*, July 1974, 4.

10 Jay Searcy, "Magazine Venture is a Risky Game for Mrs. King," *New York Times*, September 8, 1974, 248; Billie Jean King, Publisher's Letter, *womenSports*, January 1978, 4. In her initial publisher's letter in June 1974, King prominently mentions the financial risk involved ("I'm willing to risk my earnings"), but never gives a figure of how much she and Larry actually invested. Searcy, "Magazine Venture," said melodramatically (and inaccurately, it seems), "If the magazine fails, it could wipe her out financially." There never is any mention again of major money lost, so presumably this investment was fairly negligible and involved the goodwill of King's name and time as much as cash.

11 Stephanie Wilkinson, "The Visionary of Tennis," *Working Woman*, September 1988, 86–87. Diamond concluded: "The magazine has become a relative success, but not under Billie's guidance, which is unfortunate."

12 Joan Ryan, "Something-for-Everyone Theory Gluts Magazine Market," *Washington Post*, June 13, 1976, 38; Jill Gerston, "New Magazine Says Right Things About Women," *New York Times*, September 16, 1973, 232. The *Sportswoman* got circulation up to 12,000 but suspended publication in 1976 when it was sold to Allen Hanson, the publisher of *Bicycling*. A May 1976 issue of the *Sportswoman* found at the Schlesinger Library at Radcliffe pitches it as the "only magazine that covers the national amateur and collegiate championships in every major sport."

13 Kates, "Tennis Tycoon." The article referred to it as forthcoming for November, but it didn't hit the newsstands until the following May, with a June 1974 date.

14 Billie Jean King, Publisher's Letter, June 1974. On Pat Carbine: "I think she's a tremendous human being; she has a lot of humor. She helped Larry a lot with getting our magazine started." "Playboy Interview: Billie Jean King," *Playboy*, March 1975, 60.

15 This account of *Ms.* magazine draws heavily on Amy Erdman Farrell, *Yours in Sisterhood: Ms. Magazine and the Promise of Popular Feminism* (Chapel Hill: University of North Carolina Press, 1998). See also Amy Farrell, "Attentive to Difference: *Ms.* Magazine, Coalition Building, and Sisterhood," in Stephanie Gilmore, ed., *Feminist Coalitions: Historical Perspectives on Second-Wave Feminism in the United States* (Urbana: University of Illinois Press, 2008).

16 Kates, "Tennis Tycoon"; Billie Jean King, Publisher's Letter, June 1974. The magazine received an especially warm welcome at the offices of the Project on the Status and Education of Women in Washington, D.C., which was delighted to receive a copy of the inaugural issue autographed by Billie Jean King. Bernice Sandler to Eva Atkin, July 1, 1974, PSEW, SL.

17 For Larry's role, see Searcy, "Magazine Venture." See Billie Jean King, Publisher's Letter, *womenSports*, July 1975, 4, about the potential conflict between wearing two hats as publisher and athlete, and Rosalie Wright's determination to get the best stories and different points of view, even if King might disagree. Wright was recruited for the job from her position as managing editor of *Philadelphia* magazine. Another staff member (secretary at first, soon assistant editor) was former junior tennis champion Anne Lamott, later a successful writer.

18 Joan F. Healey, Harrison, N.J., to editors, and editors' response, *womenSports*, Sep-

tember 1974, 7. "I was a little embarrassed by the number of advertisements in the first issue of *womenSports* that were for products I endorse. Because I have a close relationship with those companies, they were willing to help support the launching of *womenSports*." Billie Jean King, Publisher's Letter, July 1974.

19 Le Anne Schreiber, Publisher's Letter, *womenSports*, May 1977, 4; Deborah Larned, "The Bodacious Billie Jean King," *womenSports*, May 1977, 26. King made suggestions for the article but asked for no changes. As editor Le Anne Schreiber put it, "She didn't mind being characterized as a woman who held grudges, for instance; she just wanted to make sure that we got her grudges straight." Schreiber, Publisher's Letter, May 1977.

20 Billie Jean King, Publisher's Letter, *womenSports*, December 1974, 4. They received 1,000 responses, but only analyzed the first 500.

21 Billie Jean King, Publisher's Letter, *womenSports*, October 1974, 4.

22 Farrell, *Yours in Sisterhood*, 6. The sentence is about *Ms.*, but every word of it applies to *womenSports*.

23 Ellen Weber, "The Title IX Controversy," *womenSports*, June 1974, 74–77; Billie Jean King, Publisher's Letter, *womenSports*, January 1975, 4; "Here Come the Carpetbaggers," *womenSports*, September 1974, 49–52; Dori Niccolls, "Update: Power Grab in the Locker Room," *womenSports*, June 1975, 18; Candace Lyle Hogan, "NCAA and AIAW: Will the Men Score on Women's Athletics?" *womenSports*, January 1977, 46; Hogan, "The Rumormongers," *womenSports*, November 1977, 60; Elizabeth Wheeler, "NCAA v. AIAW: The Battle for Control of Women's Collegiate Athletics Heats Up," *Women's Sports*, June 1980, 20–23; and "Strides," *Women's Sports*, January 1981, 60.

24 In July 1976, *womenSports* joined thirty women's magazines to discuss the Equal Rights Amendment as part of the bicentennial; its November 1976 insert—an eight-page essay on Ford and Carter by Doris Kearns Goodwin—was done jointly with *Ladies' Home Journal*, *Redbook*, and *American Home*.

25 Jane Leavy, "Sports Chic," *womenSports*, March 1977, 53–57. Examples include Bud Collins, "Billie Jean King Evens the Score," *Ms.*, July 1973, 39–43, 101–102; Brenda Feigen Fasteau, "Giving Women a Sporting Chance," *Ms.*, July 1973, 56–58; Ann Crittenden Scott, "Closing the Muscle Gap: New Facts about Strength, Endurance—and Gender," *Ms.*, September 1974, 49–52; and Carolyn Kane, "Why Can't a Woman Throw More Like a Man?" *Ms.*, April 1976, 88–89. See also chapter 5.

26 Collins, "King Evens the Score"; Billie Jean King, "How to Win," *womenSports*, June 1974, 34–38.

27 Billie Jean King, Publisher's Letter, *womenSports*, November 1975, 4.

28 See *womenSports*, August 1974, November 1974, and May 1977, respectively.

29 "The Third Annual *womenSports* Scholarship Guide," *womenSports*, September 1977, 31. The product was Sheer Energy pantyhose.

30 Andy Meiser, "Nobody Stops womanSport of the Year Linda Jefferson," *womenSports*, June 1975, 28–30. Alas, Jefferson's planned trip to New York to receive the award personally from Billie Jean King was cancelled at the last minute due to a scheduling conflict. And to maintain her AAU eligibility (she only received expense

money when she played football), Jefferson had to turn down the new automobile that went with the prize. Lena Williams, "Award Brings Only Publicity for Half-back," *New York Times*, June 8, 1975, 221.

31 See the ballot in *womenSports*, January 1977, 61, which describes the procedures and gives the earlier winners. From then on, the choices were fairly obvious: well-known Olympic athletes and personalities who had the highest name recognition in a fairly narrow palette of sports.

32 Farrell, *Yours in Sisterhood*, chapter 4; Billie Jean King, Publisher's Letter, July 1974.

33 Denise Douchette, Sarasota, Fla., to editors, *womenSports*, July 1975, 6.

34 Martha Rockwell, West Lebanon, N.H., to editors, *womenSports*, October 1974, 8; Lynn Vera and Elaine Esty, Milton, Vt., to editors, *womenSports*, September 1977, 6. Rockwell was identified as America's top female cross-country skier.

35 Lois Vuono Mullarkey, Summit N.J., to editors, *womenSports*, June 1975, 6; Billie Jean King, Publisher's Letter, July 1975.

36 Shelly Gardner, Minneapolis, Minn., to editors, *womenSports*, September 1974, 8; Billie Jean King, Publisher's Letter, December 1974.

37 Farrell, *Yours in Sisterhood*, 86.

38 Catherine Vrdolyak, Chicago, Ill., to editors, *womenSports*, April 1975, 6; Joanne Dyke [*sic*], Shushan, N.Y., to editors, *womenSports*, November 1974, 13. See Farrell, *Yours in Sisterhood*, 34, 73–74, 78–79, and 166–69 for how *Ms.* covered lesbian issues. Sometimes it had nothing to do with the articles. The September 1974 *Ms.* cover featuring two bicyclists was known informally as the "Dykes on Bikes" cover, according to Leavy, "Sporting Chic."

39 March Schultz, Sacramento, Calif., to editors., *womenSports*, January 1975, 11; Miriam Stern, Athens, Ga., to editors, and editors' response, *womenSports*, May 1975, 6.

40 Diane P. Kertkhoff, Kettering, Ohio, to editors, *womenSports*, July 1975, 6; Debbie Davis, Pittsville, Md., to editors, *womenSports*, October 1975, 7; Chrissie Maclay, Big Cedar Lake, Wis., to editors, *womenSports*, August 1975, 7.

41 "How to Pick up Men and Throw Them against the Wall," *womenSports*, August 1974; Ad found in *womenSports*, July 1974; Editorial, *Women's Sports*, November 1982, 4; Jan Cunningham memorandum, February 21, 1975, NOW, SL. She suggests subscribing to the *Sportswoman* (published in Culver City, Calif.) instead.

42 Wright quickly found another job as a contributing sports editor at the *San Francisco Chronicle*. She publicly aired her feelings when she sent a congratulatory letter to the *Sportswoman*, which they ran in May 1976: "It is lively, well-written and probably just the kind of magazine *womenSports* should have been had not the advertising department insisted on diluting the hard sports aspects we originally hoped to cover. We wanted to get the nonathletic woman involved in sports as well as appealing to the active competitor, but I think you're right in keeping your scope focused instead of trying to be all things to all people." Soon after the *Sportswoman* ceased publication. To understand the *Cosmopolitan* reference, see Jennifer Scanlon, *Bad Girls Go Everywhere: The Life of Helen Gurley Brown* (New York: Oxford University Press, 2009).

43 Susan Cheever Cowley, "Kings and the Court," *Newsweek*, June 9, 1975, 86; Philip H. Dougherty, "Time Magazine's Audience Study," *New York Times*, September 18, 1975,

67. Charter owned 81 percent of the magazine, which suggests the Kings' financial liability was more limited than they let on. Philip H. Dougherty, "Setting New Goals for *womenSports*," *New York Times*, October 18, 1977, 65.

44 Dougherty, "Setting New Goals for *womenSports*"; Barry Lorge, "Set for Final Fling at Wimbledon, King Continues Crusade," *Washington Post*, June 27, 1976, 42.

45 Billie Jean King, Publisher's Letter, January 1978.

46 "Sports Fanfare," *Washington Post*, January 4, 1978, D7.

47 Douglas Latimer, Publisher's Letter, *Women's Sports*, January 1979, 9.

48 See Virginia M. Leath and Angela Lumpkin, "An Analysis of Sportswomen on the Covers and in the Feature Articles of *Women's Sports and Fitness* Magazine, 1975–1989," *Journal of Sport and Social Issues* 16 (December 1992): 121–26.

49 Farrell, *Yours in Sisterhood*, 190, 194–95; Keith J. Kelly, "Conde Nast Takes Over Competition," *New York Daily News*, January 13, 1998, 47; John Moore, "S + F Demise No Victory for Women," *Denver Post*, February 10, 1998, D12. *Sports Illustrated for Women* folded with its December–January 2002–2003 issue.

50 Billie Jean King, Publisher's Letter, *womenSports*, September 1976, 4; Rachel Shuster and Julie Ward, "King: Advocate, activist, champion 'Battle of the Sexes' victory helped women, girls build their self-esteem," *USA Today*, September 20, 1999, 1C. See also Donna Lopiano: "The function of the Women's Sports Foundation is to be the impatient, intolerant voice of women's sports. . . . I wish in my lifetime I could see no need for the Women's Sports Foundation." Quoted in Jennifer Lawler, *Punch! Why Women Participate in Violent Sports* (Terre Haute, Ind.: Wish Publishing, 2002), 6.

51 Donna de Varona, foreword, in Cynthia Lee A. Pemberton, *More Than A Game: One Woman's Fight for Gender Equity in Sport* (Boston: Northeastern University Press, 2002), xvi. See also Judy Klemesrud, "Suzy Chaffee—Somersaults and Serious Thoughts," *New York Times*, May 12, 1978, A16.

52 Billie Jean King says it was while lobbying for Title IX, but I think her testimony in support of the Women's Educational Equity Act in November 1973 is the more likely occasion. See chapter 2.

53 This reconstruction draws heavily on "History of the Beginnings and Leadership of the Women's Sports Foundation" (c. 2000–2001), found in the WSF archives. See also the ad for the Women's Sports Foundation in the *Sportswoman* (March–April 1976), that lists those purposes in a slightly different wording. Billie Jean King's check came from the Bob Hope Gillette Cavalcade Awards tournament.

54 *Frontiers: The Women's Sports Foundation Newsletter*, April–May 1976, found in WEAL, SL; Don Sabo and Janie Victoria Ward, "Wherefore Art Thou Feminisms? Feminist Activism, Academic Feminisms, and Women's Sports Advocacy," *Scholar and Feminist Online*, 4.3 (Summer 2006), n 17.

55 Billie Jean King, Publisher's Letter, September 1976; Billie Jean King remarks in "All Star Salute to Women's Sports," Las Vegas, February 17–19, 1978, WSF archives.

56 Margaret Roach, "A Women's Sports Unit Seeks an Increased Role," *New York Times*, November 21, 1976, 185; *Frontiers: The Women's Sports Foundation Newsletter*, June 1978. By 1978 local women's sports associations were being formed in Atlanta;

Boston; Bridgeport, Conn.; Chicago; Delaware; New Jersey; New York City and Westchester County; Oklahoma; the San Francisco Bay area; Seattle; St. Louis; Stamford, Conn.; and Washington, D.C. These groups investigated sports development opportunities and arranged some competitive events but were disbanded between 1982 and 1984. See "Women's Sports Foundation Timeline," at ⟨http://womenssportsfoundation.org⟩ (accessed May 1, 2004).

57 "Women's Sports Scrapbook," *Women's Sports and Fitness*, October 1997.

58 See Jon Carroll, "Twenty-three of America's greatest athletes battled it out at the Houston Astrodome," *womenSports*, April 1975, 37–42; Curry Kirkpatrick, "There Is Nothing Like a Dame," *Sports Illustrated*, January 6, 1975, 22–24; and Molly Tyson, "Women's Superstars, The Great Bright Hope?" *womenSports*, December 1975, 37–39, 57. The special aired on ABC in February 1975. Billie Jean King's publisher's letter (April 1975) made the point about athletes not knowing each other. Even she knew only four of the twenty-three competitors before Houston.

The Superstars competition demonstrates once again the complicated financial dealings of Billie Jean and Larry King. Inspired by the original men's Superstars format, the Kings wanted to stage a similar event for women. Encouraged by a vice president at the Houston Astrodome who promised $150,000 in prize money, Larry and Jim Jorgensen, the president of *womenSports* magazine, started signing up athletes. Not surprisingly, the promoters of the men's event threatened to sue. In the end, *womenSports* had to withdraw as a sponsor of the event, and Larry King dropped out, too. Billie Jean King, Publisher's Letter, *womenSports*, April 1975, 4.

59 "Dinah's Place: An Interview with television's most famous amateur golfer," *womenSports*, April 1975, 29–30.

60 "History of the Beginnings and Leadership of the WSF" lists Schulz as a trustee starting in July 1979. *Peanuts* illustrations are featured in Deborah Larned, "An Interview with Peppermint Patty," *womenSports*, August 1977, 57–58. Another example is the United States Commission on Civil Rights, *More Hurdles to Clear: Women and Girls in Competitive Athletics* (Washington, D.C.: Government Printing Office, 1980). For more on the cartoonist, see David Michaelis, *Schulz and Peanuts: A Biography* (New York: Harper, 2007).

61 "History of the Beginnings and Leadership of the WSF."

62 This goal was finally achieved in 2008, as part of the Sports Museum of America in lower Manhattan. Unfortunately this for-profit undertaking failed to draw visitors and closed down in February 2009, orphaning the Women's Sports Hall of Fame. See Richard Sandomir, "Financial Problems Shut Down Museum," *New York Times*, February 22, 2009, 3; and Sandomir, "Sports Museum Files Petition in Court," *New York Times*, March 14, 2009.

63 Advertisement for the Women's Sports Foundation found in the *Sportswoman*, March–April 1976; Eva Auchincloss to Mary Dockry, July 21, 1976, WEAL, SL. Perhaps linked to the difficulties that amateur female athletes had in finding support for their training, a fairly strong initial thrust of the WSF seems to have been giving actual cash grants for such things as camps and travel to competition. Perhaps they hoped that they could be a major funder here, but of course the needs

of so many individual sportswomen would have swamped all but the wealthiest of foundations.

64 Eva Auchincloss, "A Certain Perspective: Reflections of the founding executive director (1974–1986)," cited in "History of the Beginnings and Leadership of the WSF."

65 "All Star Salute to Women's Sports," WSF archives; "Miss Blazejowski Gets Award as Top Player," *New York Times*, April 25, 1978, 34. See also Byron Rosen, "King Bounces Back in Magazine Field," *Washington Post*, January 10, 1978, D5.

66 "Strides," *Women's Sports*, October 1980, 68–69. The Women's Sports Foundation claimed this coalition represented some 15 million people.

67 Nancy Scannell, "Carter Meets With Women on Title 9," *Washington Post*, September 14, 1979, E7.

68 The Women's Sports Foundation Annual Report, June 1982, found in WEAL, SL, discusses the relationship, which had tax implications. The Women's Sports Foundation was still associated with the magazine in its last issue (April 1998), although it no longer had a column. There is no mention of the foundation in the debut issue of *Women's Sports & Fitness* (more confusion for librarians and archivists with the ampersand!) in June 1998.

69 Minutes from 1981 advisory board meeting, found in WEAL, SL; "History of the Beginnings and Leadership of the WSF."

70 Pat Griffin, "Changing the Game: Homophobia, Sexism, and Lesbians in Sport," in Jean O'Reilly and Susan K. Cahn, eds., *Women and Sports in the United States: A Documentary Reader* (Boston: Northeastern University Press, 2007), 220–21.

71 Press Release, August 7, 1975, WEAL, SL; Sports Kit, Summer 1978, WEAL, SL.

72 "In the Running," February 1982, found in WEAL, SL.

73 "Strides," *Women's Sports*, February 1981, 60; "History of the Beginnings and Leadership of the WSF."

74 "History of the Beginnings and Leadership of the WSF." In 2000 de Varona was not pleased to have been demoted (in her view) from her role as one of the founders of the Women's Sports Foundation as part of the organization's attempt to write its early history. It is a technicality, but only three people signed the original incorporation papers—Billie Jean and Larry King and their business manager—so the Women's Sports Foundation now only refers to Billie Jean King as the founder. De Varona told Donna Lopiano that she found it disturbing that the Women's Sports Foundation was directing people to drop a reference that has been used for many years [de Varona to Lopiano, October 20, 2000, WSF archives]. Trying to soothe her ruffled feelings, Lopiano acknowledged de Varona's enormous contributions to the Women's Sports Foundation over the years but still stuck to her guns about the founders. Lopiano to de Varona, October 20, 2000, WSF Archives.

75 Billie Jean King, Publisher's Letter, *womenSports*, October 1976, 4.

76 For the debate about the relation between women's sports, feminism, and consumption, see Cheryl L. Cole and Amy Hribar, "Celebrity Feminism: Nike Style; Post-Fordism, Transcendence, and Consumer Power," *Sociology of Sport Journal* 12 (1995): 347–69. See also Leslie Heywood and Shari L. Dworkin, *Built to Win: The Female Athlete as Cultural Icon* (Minneapolis: University of Minnesota Press, 2003).

77 A prime example of the inhibiting effect of such reliance on corporate support occurred at the New Agenda Conference in November 1983, when the Women's Sports
Foundation planners removed references to lesbianism from promotional material
for fear of offending corporate sponsors. See chapter 6.

78 Lopiano made the point about King in a presentation at the Humanities Center at
Harvard on November 17, 2008. For her earlier thoughts on how radical and mod-
erate feminist positions play off each other in the struggle for social change, see
Donna A. Lopiano, "Political Analysis: Gender Equity Strategies for the Future," in
Greta L. Cohen, ed., *Women in Sport: Issues and Controversies* (Newbury Park, Calif.:
Sage Publications,1993), 104–16. On the limits of the WSF's liberal feminist agenda,
see Michael Messner, *Taking the Field: Women, Men, and Sports* (Minneapolis: University of Minnesota Press, 2002), 146–50; M. Ann Hall, *Feminism and Sporting Bodies: Essays on Theory and Practice* (Champaign, Ill.: Human Kinetics, 1996), 96–99;
and Griffin, "Changing the Game."

79 Don Sabo, who has conducted major research projects for the organization, made
this point in Messner, *Taking the Field*, 191.

80 James Martin, "The World According to Billie Jean King," *Tennis*, June 2002, 18;
Everett Groseclose, "New Team-Tennis Circuit Opens for Business Tonight, Chal-
lenging the Sport's Traditions," *Wall Street Journal*, May 6, 1974, 32. General tennis
histories treat team tennis only in passing. See Bud Collins, *My Life With the Pros*
(New York: Dutton, 1989); Peter Bodo, *The Courts of Babylon: Tales of Greed and
Glory in the Harsh New World of Professional Tennis* (New York: Scribner, 1995); and
Billie Jean King with Cynthia Starr, *We Have Come a Long Way: The Story of Women's
Tennis* (New York: McGraw-Hill, 1988).

81 George Solomon, "Team Tennis Seeks Identity," *Washington Post*, August 15, 1973,
D8; Paul Attner, "Team Tennis Debuts Monday," *Washington Post*, May 5, 1974, D1.
As Billie Jean King put it optimistically: "Some day team tennis will be all over the
world. That's why we put the 'World' in the league's name. That vision was the idea
from the beginning, even though not many people were sharp enough to notice it."
John S. Radosta, "Apples Set Tonight for Call of 'Linesmen Ready? Play!'" *New York
Times*, April 28, 1977, 99.

82 Joel Drucker, "The Once and Future King," *Women's Sports and Fitness*, November/
December 1992, 78–79; Wheeler, "The Men Behind the Women," 23–24; Bud Collins, "The Sex-Free Zone," *Tennis*, August 1998, 36.

83 Groseclose, "New Team Tennis Circuit Opens."

84 "Playboy Interview: Billie Jean King," 196; "People in Sports," *New York Times*, June
7, 1974, 28.

85 Tony Kornheiser, "Footing Is Firmer as W.T.T. Slips Into Its Third Season," *New York
Times*, May 2, 1976, S1.

86 "Quotation of the Day," *New York Times*, February 6, 1975, 71; "What They Are Saying," *New York Times*, July 20, 1975, 59; Herman, "Billie Jean King's Lifestyle."

87 Kornheiser, "Footing Is Firmer." Laver was the highest-paid player, guaranteed
a salary of $165,000, followed by Evonne Goolagong ($150,000) and Chris Evert
($140,000).

88 Radosta, "Apples Set Tonight"; Gerald Eskenazi, "Conflict-of-Interest Questions Confront Sports," *New York Times*, January 8, 1977, 12. See also Kornheiser, "Footing is Firmer"; "Buchholz is Named Commissioner of W.T.T.," *New York Times*, September 17, 1976, 91; and "People in Sports," *New York Times*, October 8, 1976, 25. When Team Tennis was reincarnated in a much smaller version in the 1980s, this same pattern continued, according to Frederick C. Klein, "Will Larry King's Team Tennis Net a Profit?" *Wall Street Journal*, July 6, 1983, 24: "Mr. King's approach to leadership in Team Tennis couldn't be simpler: He's it. He owns it, signs the players, controls the purses, and sells franchises for a fee like McDonald's does." Larry and Billie Jean also owned the Chicago team. Larry admitted that this could be a conflict of interest "if we were important enough for that."

89 Greg Hoffman provides a full discussion and detailed chronology in "Sudden Death: Why Did World Team Tennis Fail? Let Us Count the Ways," *Women's Sports*, August 1979, 34–38, 52–53; the quote from Larry King is on p. 36. See also Gerald Eskenazi, "How W.T.T. Became World team-less Tennis," *New York Times*, November 20, 1978, C9; and Barry Lorge, "WTT Plans Signings, Then Draft of Players," *Washington Post*, March 30, 1977, D5.

90 Eskenazi, "How W.T.T. Became World team-less Tennis."

Chapter Four

1 Jere Longman, *The Girls of Summer: The U.S. Women's Soccer Team and How It Changed the World* (New York: Harper Collins, 2000) offers a well-paced narrative. See also Brandi Chastain and Gloria Averbuch, *It's Not About the Bra* (New York: Harper Collins, 2004).

2 Elliott Almond, "Kick Start: Groundwork in Place for Women's Team Sports to Make Move," *Pittsburgh Post-Gazette*, July 11, 1999, D1.

3 See Jessica Gavora's complaints about how the media uncritically linked the soccer success with Title IX, such as *Time* calling the team the "daughters of Title IX." Jessica Gavora, *Tilting the Playing Field: Schools, Sports, Sex and Title IX* (San Francisco: Encounter Books, 2002), 5. For more on the media's coverage, see Neil Christopherson, Michelle Janning, and Eileen Diaz McConnell, "Two Kicks Forward, One Kick Back: A Content Analysis of Media Discourses on the 1999 Women's World Cup Soccer Championship," *Sociology of Sport Journal* 19 (2002): 170–88; and C. L. Cole, "The Year That Girls Ruled," *Journal of Sport and Social Issues* 24 (February 2000): 3–7.

4 Stephanie Twin, *Out of the Bleachers: Writings on Women and Sport* (Old Westbury, N.Y.: Feminist Press, 1979), 93.

5 Betty Spears, "The Emergence of Women in Sport," in Barbara J. Hoepner, ed., *Women's Athletics: Coping with Controversy* (Washington, D.C.: Division for Girls and Women's Sports of the American Association for Health, Physical Education, and Recreation, 1974), 26–42. For a general history of women's higher education, see Barbara Miller Solomon, *In the Company of Educated Women* (New Haven: Yale University Press, 1987).

6 For a lively discussion of the intersection of fashion and sports history, see Patricia Campbell Warner, *When the Girls Came Out to Play: The Birth of American Sportswear* (Amherst: University of Massachusetts Press, 2006). For general histories of men's sports, see Benjamin G. Rader, *American Sports: From the Age of Folk Games to the Age of Televised Sports,* 4th ed. (Upper Saddle River, N.J.: Prentice-Hall, 1999); Michael Oriard, *King Football* (Chapel Hill: University of North Carolina Press, 2001); S. W. Pope, ed., *The New American Sport History: Recent Approaches and Perspectives* (Urbana: University of Illinois Press, 1997); and Randy Roberts and James Olson, *Winning Is the Only Thing: Sports in America since 1945* (Baltimore: Johns Hopkins University Press, 1989).

7 Chapter 4 of Warner, *When the Girls Came Out to Play,* covers the history of bathing costumes. Of course, as James Laver remarked, "the only sensible costume for bathing in is no costume at all" (ibid., 61), which was precisely the practice for men before the activity became coed.

8 Quoted in Susan Ware, "Gertrude Ederle: 'America's Best Girl,'" in Ware, ed., *Forgotten Heroes: Inspiring Portraits from Our Leading Historians* (New York: Free Press, 1998), 311. On the WSA, see Linda J. Borish, "'The Cradle of American Champions, Women Champions . . . Swim Champions': Charlotte Epstein, Gender and Jewish Identity, and the Physical Emancipation of Women in Aquatic Sports," *International Journal of the History of Sport* 21 (March 2004): 197–235. For a general history of the sport, see Karen Karbo, "Swimming: From Gold Spangles to Gold Medals," in Lissa Smith, ed., *Nike Is a Goddess: The History of Women in Sports* (New York: Atlantic Monthly Press, 1998).

9 At Beijing in 2008, women represented 42 percent of athletes (4,746 out of 11,196). For general introductions to the history of women and the Olympics, see Paula Welch and D. Margaret Costa, "A Century of Olympic Competition," in D. Margaret Costa and Sharon R. Guthrie, eds., *Women and Sport: Interdisciplinary Perspectives* (Champaign, Ill.: Human Kinetics, 1994); Jennifer Hargreaves, "Olympic Women: A Struggle for Recognition," in Jean O'Reilly and Susan K. Cahn, eds., *Women and Sports in the United States: A Documentary Reader* (Boston: Northeastern University Press, 2007); and Helen Jefferson Lenskyj, *The Best Olympics Ever? Social Impacts of Sydney 2000* (Albany: State University of New York Press, 2002).

10 Anita L. DeFrantz, "The Olympic Games: Our Birthright to Sports," in Greta L. Cohen, ed., *Women in Sport: Issues and Controversies* (Newbury Park, Calif.: Sage, 1993).

11 Ellen W. Gerber, "Chronicle of Participation," in Ellen W. Gerber, Jan Felshin, Pearl Berlin, and Waneen Wyrick, eds., *The American Woman in Sport* (Reading, Mass.: Addison-Wesley, 1974), 72; Richard Swanson, "From Glide to Stride: Significant Events in a Century of American Women's Sport," in Hoepner, *Women's Athletics,* 49. See also Nancy Theriot, "Toward a New Sporting Ideal: The Women's Division of the National Amateur Athletics Federation," *Frontiers* 3 (1978): 1–7; and Nancy Theberge, "Women's Athletics and the Myth of Female Frailty," in Jo Freeman, ed., *Women: A Feminist Perspective,* 4th ed. (Mountain View, Calif.: Mayfield Publishing Company, 1989).

12 Gerber, "A Chronicle of Participation," 64–68.

13 Susan K. Cahn, *Coming on Strong: Gender and Sexuality in Twentieth-Century Women's Sport* (New York: Free Press, 1994), 98. This quote from sport historian Joan Hult actually came from the 1940s or 1950s, inspired by the disconnect between her teachers telling her not to engage in high-level competition and those same women all turning out for a field hockey tournament on the weekend.

14 Celeste Ullrich makes this observation in Mary Jo Festle, *Playing Nice: Politics and Apologies in Women's Sports* (New York: Columbia University Press, 1996), 134. In 2005, field hockey was offered as a varsity high school sport for boys at only 5 schools, compared to 1,684 schools offering participation opportunities to 62,980 girls. National Federation of State High School Associations, *Sports Participation Survey* (2005), ⟨http://www.nfhs.org⟩.

15 For background on industrial teams, see Cahn, *Coming on Strong*, chapter 3; and Robert W. Ikard, *Just for Fun: The Story of AAU Women's Basketball* (Fayetteville: University of Arkansas Press, 2005).

16 See Amy Bass, ed., *In the Game: Race, Identity, and Sports in the Twentieth Century* (New York: Palgrave Macmillan, 2005); Dana Brooks and Ronald Althouse, eds., *Racism in College Athletics: The African American Athlete's Experience*, 2nd ed. (Morgantown, W. Va.: Fitness Information Technology, 2000); and Cahn, *Coming on Strong*, chapter 5.

17 Karen H. Weiller and Catriona T. Higgs, "The All American Girls Professional Baseball League, 1943–1954: Gender Conflict in Sport?" *Sociology of Sport Journal* 11 (1994): 289–97. See also Cahn, *Coming on Strong*; and Barbara Gregorich, *Women at Play: The Story of Women in Baseball* (San Diego: Harcourt Brace Jovanovich, 1993).

18 Festle, *Playing Nice*, 17; Bil Gilbert and Nancy Williamson, "Programmed To Be Losers," *Sports Illustrated*, June 11, 1973, 73.

19 The best example is Meg Christian's song "Ode to a Gym Teacher" found on her album *I Know You Know* (Olivia Records, 1974). See also many of the essays in Susan Fox Rogers, ed., *Sportsdykes: Stories from On and Off the Field* (New York: St. Martin's Press, 1994).

20 See Carol A. Maccini, "Present in the Fifties," *womenSports*, October 1975, 52; and Anne Beatts, "How High School Sports Made My Life a Living Hell," *womenSports*, June 1975, 12–14. I was one of those gym-dreading, bloomer-clad girls. My transcript from New Trier High School in Winnetka, Ill., showed practically straight As in academic subjects—and a C in "girls PE" my senior year. I bet my gym teachers would be amazed at my adult interest in sports and sports history.

21 Cahn, *Coming on Strong*, and Festle, *Playing Nice*, both make this point about the changes already underway. The quotation is from Festle, *Playing Nice*, 20. See also Bonnie J. Hultstrand, "The Growth of Collegiate Women's Sports: the 1960s," *Journal of Physical Education, Recreation and Dance* 64 (March 1993): 41–43; and L. Leotus Morrison, "The AIAW: Governance by Women for Women," in Cohen, *Women in Sport*.

22 Festle, *Playing Nice*, 98–101. See also Ying Wushanley, *Playing Nice and Losing: The*

Struggle for Control of Women's Intercollegiate Athletics, 1960–2000 (Syracuse, N.Y.: Syracuse University Press, 2004).

23 "Here Come the Carpetbaggers," *womenSports*, September 1974, 52; AIAW Position Paper on Intercollegiate Athletics for Women, approved May 1974, found in Dunkle, SL; Festle, *Playing Nice*, 183–84.

24 Festle, *Playing Nice*, 92; Kathryn Jay, *More Than Just a Game: Sports in American Life* (New York: Columbia University Press, 2004), 57, 161. While later revelations suggested Eastern Bloc countries supplied their athletes with steroids and other performance-enhancing drugs, at first the difference between Soviet and American women athletes came down to the fact that the former embraced weight training and conditioning practices long before American women did.

25 Jennifer H. Lansbury, "'The Tuskegee Flash' and 'the Slender Harlem Stroker': Black Women Athletes on the Margin," *Journal of Sport History* 28 (Summer 2001): 233–52; Theberge, "Women's Athletics," 514; Doris Corbett and William Johnson, "The African American Female in Collegiate Sport: Sexism and Racism," in Brooks and Althouse, *Racism in College Athletics*, 199–225. See also Bass, *In the Game*.

26 Billie Jean King with Cynthia Starr, *We Have Come a Long Way: The Story of Women's Tennis* (New York: McGraw-Hill, 1988), 96. Jay, *More Than Just a Game*, 69–78, traces the growing racial integration in sports. See also Patricia Vertinksy and Gwendolyn Captain, "More Myth than History: American Culture and Representations of the Black Female's Athletic Ability," *Journal of Sport History* 25 (Fall 1998): 532–61. Gibson later played on the Ladies Professional Golf Association tour.

27 President's Conference on Fitness of American Youth, *A Report to the President of the United States on the Fort Ritchie Meeting* (Washington, D.C.: Government Printing Office, 1958), 1. President's Council on Physical Fitness, *4 Years for Fitness, 1961–1965: A Report to the President* (Washington, D.C.: Government Printing Office, 1965), 12, compares mean performances of boys and girls for 1958 and 1965, with dramatic improvement for both. By 1967, four out of five students now passed the standardized fitness tests, up from two out of three in 1961. See President's Council on Physical Fitness, *Youth Physical Fitness: Suggested Elements of a School-Centered Program* (Washington, D.C.: Government Printing Office, 1967), frontispiece.

28 Many of these developments are covered in Jan Felshin, "The Social Anomaly of Women in Sports," *Physical Educator* 30 (October 1973): 122–24. See also Smith, *Nike Is a Goddess*, 23–24, 49–50; Nora Ephron, "Women," *Esquire*, January 1973, 36, 40; Kenny Moore, "Case of the Ineligible Bachelorette," *Sports Illustrated*, April 17, 1972, 82–85; Curry Kirkpatrick, "In Stratford, Nobody Beats the Raybestos Brakettes," *Sports Illustrated*, September 11, 1967, 92–93; and Dorothy V. Harris, *DGWS Research Reports: Women in Sports* (Washington, D.C.: American Association for Health, Physical Education, and Recreation, 1971).

29 Candace Lyle Hogan, "From Here to Equality: Title IX," *womenSports*, September 1977, 16–26, 60; the quote appears on p. 16.

30 Candace Lyle Hogan, "Title IX: From Here to Equality," in D. Stanley Eitzen, ed., *Sport in Contemporary Society: An Anthology* (New York: St. Martin's Press, 1979), 417; Maury Z. Levy, "The Girls of Summer," *womenSports*, August 1974, 36–39, 64.

See also Susan E. Jennings, "'As American as Hot Dogs, Apple Pie and Chevrolet': The Desegregation of Little League Baseball," *Journal of American Culture* 4 (Winter 1981): 81–91.

31 Levy, "Girls of Summer." Boys were much more nonplussed. "You're okay with me," said one to Jenny Fuller of Mill Valley, California. "We needed a good first baseman."

32 Jennings, "As American as Hot Dogs"; Tom Tutko and Patsy Neal, quoted in Bonnie L. Parkhouse and Jackie Lapin, *Women Who Win: Exercising Your Rights in Sport* (Englewood Cliffs, N.J.: Prentice-Hall, 1980), 58–59.

33 Peg Burke, "Taking Title IX into Your Own Hands," *womenSports*, October 1976, 13.

34 Susan Birrell, "The Woman Athlete's College Experience: Knowns and Unknowns," *Journal of Sport and Social Issues* 11 (December 1987): Table 1. Jessica Gavora, *Tilting the Playing Field*, originally drew attention to how just leaping from the 1971 figure to later figures flattened out how much of the increase took place between 1971 and 1973, well before it could be attributed to Title IX.

35 Birrell, "The Woman Athlete's College Experience"; Participation figures from the yearly National Federation of State High School Associations, *Sports Participation Survey*; Susan Ware, *Title IX: A Brief History with Documents* (Boston: Bedford/St. Martin's, 2007), 21. See figure 4 in Ware, *Title IX*, 8, for the long range view from the 1970s to the present.

36 United States Commission on Civil Rights, *More Hurdles to Clear: Women and Girls in Competitive Athletics*, Clearinghouse Publication no. 63 (Washington, D.C.: United States Commission on Civil Rights, July 1980), 11, 22. See also National Collegiate Athletic Association, *The Sports and Recreation Programs of the Nation's Universities and Colleges*, Report no. 7 (1987), found in Dunkle, SL. According to the NCAA report, "From 1976–77 to 1981–82, it appeared that the growth of women's sports had reached a climax and was slowing down. However, the evidence presented here indicates that this may not be the case." It is true that the number of participants grew from 60,769 in 1981–82 to 74,429 in 1986–87, but that was still well below the 82,453 figure for 1976–77.

37 Paula D. Welch, *Silver Era, Golden Moments: A Celebration of Ivy League Women's Athletics* (Lanham, Md.: Madison Books, 1999), contains numerous examples of multisport athletes. James L. Shulman and William G. Bowen, *The Game of Life: College Sports and Educational Values* (Princeton, N.J.: Princeton University Press, 2001), 159, finds women athletes in the 1976 cohort were very much like female students in general. The gap will widen in later cohorts from the 1980s and 1990s.

38 Bil Gilbert and Nancy Williamson, "Women in Sport: A Progress Report," *Sports Illustrated*, July 29, 1974, 26–31; "Sportswomanlike Conduct," *Newsweek*, June 3, 1974, 50–55; *Seventeen* (1975) quoted in Jane Leavy, "Sports Chic," *womenSports*, March 1977, 53–57. For examples of the coverage in *Ms.*, see Lucinda Franks, "See Jane Run: Women in the 1972 Olympics," *Ms.*, January 1973, 98–100, 104; Brenda Feigen Fasteau, "Giving Women a Sporting Chance," *Ms.*, July 1973, 56–58, 103, as well as Bud Collins's cover story on Billie Jean King; Ann Crittenden Scott, "Closing the Muscle Gap," *Ms.*, September 1974, 49–50, 55, 89; and Anne Roiphe, "Playing the Field," *Ms.*,

September 1974, 67–69. The September 1974 issue also had a feature called "Found Women: Nine Sporting Lives," 96.

39 See Louis Harris and Associates, *Fitness in America—The Perrier Study: A National Research Report of Behavior, Knowledge and Opinions Concerning the Taking Up of Sports and Exercise* (New York: Garland Publishing, 1984). The original 1979 study was copyrighted under the title "The Perrier Study: Fitness in America."

40 It didn't last. By 1985 the number of tennis players had dropped precipitously to 16 million. In 2009 27 million Americans play the game, a 12 percent increase over 2003. Andrew Adam Newman, "Bringing the Human Factor Back to Pro Tennis," *New York Times*, July 21, 2009, B4. For the flavor of tennis in the 1970s, sample Bud Collins, *My Life With the Pros* (New York: Dutton, 1989).

41 Gilbert and Williamson, "Women in Sport," 29; "Comes the Revolution," *Time*, June 26, 1978, 54.

42 Donna Lopiano noted physical educators' disconnect from both politics and feminism: "We are not participants in politics. Most physical educators are labeled, and are indeed, very conservative to the extent that they don't participate in political groups. I was astounded yesterday when (the institute participants) were asked how many were members of women's political organizations, and I saw all of eight hands go up out of 150 or 200 women who are in the forefront of one of the most visible women's issues in the United States." Quoted in Cheryl M. Fields, "Women in Sports Scout Power Politics," *Chronicle of Higher Education*, January 12, 1976, 12.

43 This quote from a physical education leader may be a bit too harsh but does capture a certain resistance to change: "A good many of these people still are afraid of what competition will do for girls. I think they also are afraid of what competition will do to them. For years they have had easy jobs. They bring in the girls for a class, let them spend 15 minutes putting on their gym suits, then spend 15 minutes with some ladylike archery or volleyball, and the last 15 minutes of the period are devoted to taking a shower. Marks are given out on the basis of how often a girl remembers to bring her gym suit and how well she showers." Gilbert and Williamson, "Programmed To Be Losers," 66.

44 Festle, *Playing Nice*, 98–99.

45 Ted Green, "Basketball Goes Big Time at UCLA," *womenSports*, March 1977, 28. This quote from Judith Holland, women's athletic director at UCLA, is from later in the decade, but it captures the philosophical divide well.

46 Wushanley, *Playing Nice and Losing*, chapter 6. See also memo and supporting material from Mary E. Rekstad to AIAW Active Institutions, March 5, 1973, found in PSEW, SL.

47 Cheryl M. Fields, "Rules Violations Grow in Women's Sports" *Chronicle of Higher Education*, May 17, 1976, 7; Grace Lichtenstein, "The Wooing of Women Athletes," *New York Times Magazine*, February 8, 1981, 27; Cheryl M. Fields, "Demands of Women Athletes Rivaling Those of Men," *Chronicle of Higher Education*, May 24, 1976, 7; Fields, "Women's Athletic Group Votes to Bar Payments to Coaches for Recruiting," *Chronicle of Higher Education*, January 10, 1977, 9; Fields, "Striking a Balance in Women's Sports," *Chronicle of Higher Education*, January 23, 1978, 5; Nancy

Scannell, "Colleges Bewildered by Women's Recruiting Rules," *Washington Post*, September 2, 1979, D4.

48 Neil Amdur, "As AIAW Grows, So Do Its Problems," *New York Times*, April 8, 1979, 57; Fields, "Demands of Women Athletes."

49 Kent Hannon, "Too Far, Too Fast," *Sports Illustrated*, March 20, 1978, 36. See also Linda Jean Carpenter in Arthur T. Johnson and James H. Frey, eds., *Government and Sport: The Public Policy Issues* (Totawa, N.J.: Rowman and Allanheld, 1985), 66.

50 Hannon, "Too Far, Too Fast," 36; William A. Sievert, "'We Have 30 Teams—All of Them Major,'" *Chronicle of Higher Education*, June 20, 1977, 9.

51 For an overview, see Pamela Grundy and Susan Shackelford, *Shattering the Glass: The Remarkable History of Women's Basketball* (New York: New Press, 2005). See also the chapter on basketball, "Not Quite the Game Intended," by Shelley Smith in Smith, *Nike Is a Goddess*.

52 Caryl Rivers, "God and the Free Throw," *womenSports*, March, 1977, 64.

53 Rita Liberti, "'We Were Ladies, We just Played Basketball Like Boys': African American Womanhood and Competitive Basketball at Bennett College, 1928–1942," *Journal of Sport History* 26 (Fall 1999): 575; Grundy and Shackleford, *Shattering the Glass*, 163.

54 Ikard, *Just for Fun*, 13.

55 Elva Bishop and Katherine Fulton, "Shooting Stars: The Heyday of Industrial Women's Basketball," *Southern Exposure* 7 (Fall 1979). See Ikard, *Just for Fun*, for more on Nashville Business College.

56 Shackleford and Grundy, *Shattering the Glass*, 110; Ikard, *Just for Fun*, 104–115.

57 Festle, *Playing Nice*, 249; Kay, *More Than Just a Game*, 169.

58 Janice A. Beran, *From Six-on-Six to Full Court Press: A Century of Iowa Girls' Basketball* (Ames: Iowa State University Press, 1993), 148. Here is Heywood Hale Broun's full quote: "When I went out to Iowa, I went as an Eastern media snob. I was prepared to be snobby. I was prepared to make fun of the rubes in bloomers. But I couldn't, not when I sensed the intensity all around me. I have never felt at any sport event such excitement as being inside this storage battery.... The important thing is all the girls the next day, winners and losers alike, were winners. They had all had a vivid sporting experience. It was sport at its best; full of joy and zest and excitement and a kind of nobility, because they didn't cheat; it was done on a very high level."

59 Ikard, *Just for Fun*, 99. Statewide, girls made up 50.6 percent of all high school athletes that year. Even today the high school percentage nationwide is stuck in the low 40s.

60 For a superb combination of religious, feminist, and sport history, see Julie Byrne, *O God of Players: The Story of the Immaculata Mighty Macs* (New York: Columbia University Press, 2003); the story of the championships is on 173–75. Examples of general media attention to the team include Jane Gross, "She's the Center of Attention," *Sports Illustrated*, April 9, 1973, 30–31; Joe Marshall, "On and Up with the Mighty Macs," *Sports Illustrated*, February 3, 1975, 50; and Mike Mallowe, "The Game Gets Tougher for the Mighty Macs," *womenSports*, July 1975, 36–39, 50–52.

61 Pete Axthelm, "Women Who Win," *Newsweek*, September 8, 1975, 51; Grundy and

Shackleford, *Shattering the Glass*, 162–66. See also Larry Van Dyne, "Women's Bas-ketball: Too Good to Put Down," *Chronicle of Higher Education*, March 31, 1975, 6–7; Sarah Pileggi, "New Era for Delta Dawns," *Sports Illustrated*, March 31, 1975, 67–68; and Pat Tashima, "Delta State Rebounds for Glory," *womenSports*, December 1975, 35–36, 50.

62 Byrne, *O God of Players*, 183; Green, "Basketball Goes Big-Time at UCLA," 26–30; Hannon, "Too Far, Too Fast," 34–35.

63 The following year the AIAW negotiated a television pact to show the champion-ships and special events, yet another example of how they were mimicking the NCAA. Beverly T. Watkins, "Pact Offered for Televising Women's Sports," *Chronicle of Higher Education*, January 26, 1976, 8.

64 Grundy and Shackleford, *Shattering the Glass*, 166; Cathy Rounds, "Basketball," *womenSports*, February 1975, 15; Ray Melnick, "Pat Summit Reaches the Salary Peak," *Birmingham (Ala.) News*, June 1, 2006, 1C.

65 Todd W. Crosset, *Outsiders in the Clubhouse: The World of Women's Professional Golf* (Albany: State University of New York Press, 1995), 126.

66 In addition to Pat Griffin, *Strong Women, Deep Closets: Lesbians and Homophobia in Sport* (Champaign, Ill.: Human Kinetics, 1998), see also chapter 7, "Beauty and the Butch: The 'Mannish' Athlete and the Lesbian Threat," in Cahn, *Coming on Strong*. When golfer Betty Hicks informally polled a range of women athletes in 1979, most said that they were athletes before they knew they were lesbians. Betty Hicks, "Les-bian Athletes," *Christopher Street*, October 1979, 46. For more on Billie Jean King's struggle with her sexuality, see chapter 6.

67 Griffin, *Strong Women, Deep Closets*, 26; Eric Anderson, *In The Game: Gay Athletes and the Cult of Masculinity* (Albany: State University of New York Press, 2005); Larry Gross, *Up from Invisibility: Lesbians, Gay Men, and the Media in America* (New York: Columbia University Press, 2001), 204. See also Michael A. Messner, *Taking The Field: Women, Men, and Sports* (Minneapolis: University of Minnesota Press, 2002). Anderson thinks it might be changing. If a gay man is an asset to the team, who cares if he's gay?

68 Jan Felshin, "The Triple Option . . . for Women in Sport," *Quest* 21 (1974): 36–40; Griffin, *Strong Women, Deep Closets*, ix–x.

69 Cahn *Coming on Strong*, 189. See also Rogers, *Sportsdykes*, for many examples.

70 Judy Van Handle, "Sports and the Closet of Public Relations," *Harvard Gay and Les-bian Review* 5 (Fall 1998): 49.

71 Griffin, *Strong Women, Deep Closets*, x, 46, 82. For more on Rene Muth Portland, see Byrne, *O God of Players*.

72 For their personal stories of sexual harassment by their coaches, see "My Coach Says He Loves Me" in Mariah Burton Nelson, *The Stronger Women Get, The More Men Love Football* (New York: Harcourt Brace, 1994); and Leslie Heywood, *Pretty Good for a Girl: An Athlete's Story* (Minneapolis: University of Minnesota Press, 1998). Peter Bodo, *The Courts of Babylon: Tales of Greed and Glory in the Harsh New World of Professional Tennis* (New York: Scribner, 1995), discusses the problem in tennis. See also Griffin, *Strong Women, Deep Closets*, 191, 200.

73 Griffin, *Strong Women, Deep Closets*, 71, quotes Martina Navratilova in the video *Out for a Change: Addressing Homophobia in Women's Sports* (1992): "We should make men coach in those things."

74 Festle, *Playing Nice*, 185–86, 267–68.

75 Lucy Jane Bledsoe, "Team Sports Brought Us Together," *Harvard Gay and Lesbian Review* 4 (Spring 1997): 18–20.

76 Gerald R. Gems, Linda J. Borish, and Gertrud Pfister, *Sports in American History: From Colonization to Globalization* (Champaign, Ill.: Human Kinetics, 2008).

77 Lynn Glatzer, "Women's Professional Basketball: Anatomy of a Failure," *women-Sports*, December 1977, 19–21; Grace Lichtenstein, "Women's Pro Basketball League: The New Million Dollar Baby," *Ms.*, March 1980, 70.

78 Thomas Boswell, "WBL Pioneers: A Cold-Gym Life; Low-rent Lives Between Jumpers and Drives," *Washington Post*, February 25, 1979, G1. See also Grundy and Shackelford, *Shattering the Glass*, 183–87.

79 Lichtenstein, "Women's Pro Basketball League," 72.

80 Billie Jean King, Publisher's Letter, *womenSports*, May 1976, 4; King, Publisher's Letter, *womenSports*, December 1977, 4; King, Publisher's Letter, *womenSports*, November, 1975, 4; Grace Lichtenstein, "Women on the Diamond," *New York Times Magazine*, August 4, 1974, 14–18; Jane Bosveld, "The Little-Known World of Big-time Softball," *Ms.*, June 1983, 63.

81 Christine Terp, "A Whole New Game?" *Christian Science Monitor*, May 22, 1981, 12.

82 Letty Cottin Pogrebin, "Working Women: Making It in Sports," *Ladies' Home Journal*, October 1974, 63–64.

83 For golf, see Crosset, *Outsiders in the Clubhouse*; and Melanie Hauser, "Selling Their Game," in Smith, *Nike Is a Goddess*. See also "Dinah's Space: An Interview with Television's Most Famous Amateur Golfer," *womenSports*, April 1975, 29–30.

84 Janet Guthrie, *Janet Guthrie: Life at Full Throttle* (Wilmington, Del.: Sport Media Publishing, 2005), 382; introduction by Billie Jean King in ibid., xii. Given the miniscule chance to make a living as a professional athlete, some women found alternative career paths in broadcasting and journalism, although they had to fight for acceptance in these male-dominated fields. Probably fewer than thirty women nationwide worked fulltime as sportswriters on major newspapers or magazines by the end of the 1970s, including Jane Gross at *Newsday*, Robin Herman at the *New York Times*, Lawrie Mifflin at the *New York Daily News*, Betty Cuniberti at the *Washington Post*, Sheila Moran at the *Los Angeles Times*, Stephanie Salter at the *San Francisco Examiner*, and Sheryl Flatow at UPI. Jane Gross, "Female Sportswriters Make Their Mark," *New York Times*, May 26, 1988, 23; Melissa Ludtke, "Women in Locker Rooms: It's no longer a laughing matter," *St. Petersburg Times*, October 14, 1990, 1D. In 1978 Melissa Ludtke of *Sports Illustrated* successfully sued to win women reporters access to locker rooms. Full documentation of the case is found in Melissa Ludtke's papers at the Schlesinger Library.

85 Kathrine Switzer, *Marathon Woman* (New York: Carroll and Graf, 2007), has a picture of the outfit.

86 "Function First," *Women's Sports and Fitness,* January/February 1988, 63. See also the ad for the JogBra in *Women's Sports,* February 1979.

87 "A Sporting Chance: Women gain equal footing in area of athletic apparel," *St. Louis Post-Dispatch,* December 27, 1990, 5. See also Candace Campbell, "Running a Clothes Biz," *Women's Sport,* March 1983, 46, on the company. Missy Park followed a similar pattern when she founded her company, Title 9, in Berkeley in 1987. See Beatrice Motamedi, "Sports Gear Just for Women: Mail Order Firm in Berkeley Carves Out a New Niche," *San Francisco Chronicle,* March 16, 1991, B1. Both companies are still going strong today, and mainstays of my running gear.

88 Quoted in Longman, *The Girls of Summer,* 281.

Chapter Five

1 Billie Jean King, Publisher's Letter, *womenSports,* November 1977, 4. For a historical overview of the Houston Conference, see Marjorie J. Spruill, "Gender and America's Right Turn: The 1977 IWY Conferences and the Polarization of American Politics," in Bruce Schulman and Julian Zelizer, eds., *Rightward Bound: Making America Conservative in the 1970s* (Cambridge: Harvard University Press, 2008). Archival material is found in the papers of the National Commission on the Observance of International Women's Year, SL. See also the PBS documentary *Sisters of '77* (2005); and Gloria Steinem, "Houston and History," *Outrageous Acts and Everyday Rebellions* (New York: Henry Holt, 1983).

2 See Lisa Tetrault, "The Memory of a Movement: Woman Suffrage and Reconstruction America, 1865–1890" (Ph.D. diss., University of Wisconsin, 2004), on why we can't call Seneca Falls the first women's rights convention, and certainly not the first in the world. See also Lisa Levenstein, "Rethinking the Origins of Woman's Rights: Gender and Nineteenth-Century Political Culture," *Reviews in American History* 34 (March 2006): 28–33.

3 National Commission on the Observance of International Women's Year, *The Spirit of Houston: The First National Women's Conference* (Washington, D.C.: Government Printing Office, 1978). This account is drawn from the section in the official report on the Torch Relay, 192–203.

4 Ibid., 200.

5 The picture is reproduced in ibid., 128. According to the official report, the photos were so striking that they appeared on the front pages of many newspapers that otherwise ignored the conference.

6 King, Publisher's Letter, November 1977; National Commission on the Observance of International Women's Year, *The Spirit of Houston,* 34. Sports activists had convened a caucus on women in sports and circulated various sports resolutions at the conference but failed to mobilize enough support or interest to press the issue. Carole Oglesby, who served as the IWY sports consultant, concluded ruefully, "When the torch run was completed, and the 'real conference' begun, the concerns of sports women and health/physical educators were deemed too trivial to be added

to the deliberation." Carole A. Oglesby, "Coping with Trauma: Staying the Course," in Pirkko Markula, ed., *Feminist Sport Studies: Sharing Experiences of Joy and Pain* (Albany: State University of New York Press, 2006), 106.

7   Measuring the role that sports played in second-wave feminism will have to wait until more local studies and oral histories explore whether this issue had a more broad-based resonance at the local level than with national leadership, but there are intriguing suggestions that sports-based activism was more likely to be undertaken at the local level, acting out of concern for specific issues or problems in their communities. For example, the New Jersey chapter of NOW supported Maria Pepe in her effort to play Little League baseball in 1973; in Dayton, Ohio, NOW activism on Title IX resulted in $3 million of funding being put in escrow between 1975 and 1977; WEAL members took the lead in filing Title IX complaints or other legal challenges in Texas, South Carolina, New Jersey, and Pennsylvania. For glimpses of how second-wave feminism played out at the grassroots level, see Judith Ezekiel, *Feminism in the Heartland* (Columbus: Ohio State University, 2002); and Anne Enke, *Finding the Movement: Sexuality, Contested Space, and Feminist Activism* (Durham, N.C.: Duke University Press, 2007).

8   Billie Jean King, Publisher's Letter, *womenSports*, August 1976, 4; Selena Roberts, *A Necessary Spectacle: Billie Jean King, Bobby Riggs and the Tennis Match That Leveled the Game* (New York: Crown Publishers, 2005), 63; Robert Lipsyte, "Billie Jean," *New York Times*, August 27, 1970, 59; Frank Deford, "Mrs. Billie Jean King," *Sports Illustrated*, May 19, 1975, 82.

9   Mark Asher, "Abortion Made Possible Mrs. King's Top Year," *Washington Post*, February 22, 1972, D1. The quote continues: "Rod Laver when he won the Grand Slam they wrote about him as a tennis player. The only way I get into things is because of my connection with Women's Lib. I run just as many laps as he does. I train just as hard. Women's Lib should be secondary." See also BJK, *Billie Jean* (1982), 126.

10 Billie Jean King, Publisher's Letter, *womenSports*, July 1976, 4; BJK, *Billie Jean* (1982), 16–17.

11 BJK, *Billie Jean* (1974), 142; "Playboy Interview: Billie Jean King," *Playboy*, March 1975, 58; Cori Planck, "Portrait of a Legend: Billie Jean King Talks About the Game She Loves and the World She Changed," *Lesbian News*, April 1999, 18–19. King is making a larger point about fighting for equality, regardless of race, gender, or sexual orientation: "We have to be fighting for equality for everyone. I always wonder if the world was in reverse. . . . I hope I would fight for the equality of men."

12 Billie Jean King, Publisher's Letter, *womenSports*, August, 1976, 4; Bud Collins, "Billie Jean King Evens the Score," *Ms.*, July 1973, 43; Grace Lichtenstein, "Straight Talk from Billie Jean King," *Seventeen*, May 1974, 38, 43. "My husband's the one who thinks women's lib is really great," she said in 1970. "He feels everybody should be equal" (Lipsyte, "Billie Jean," 59). See also Judy Klemesrud, "Billie Jean King Scores Ace at Fund-Raising Rally," *New York Times*, September 21, 1972, 24.

13 In Deford, "Mrs. Billie Jean King," 82, she went into a diatribe against NOW for requesting ten press passes to a tournament. In her 1982 autobiography, she even talked

about being a "cult figure"—"the Feminist Athletic Doll"—who was "lumped with Jane Fonda and Gloria Steinem and Betty Friedan and Bella Abzug" (BJK, *Billie Jean*, 161).

14 BJK, *Billie Jean* (1974), 138. Or as she said in Curry Kirkpatrick, "The Ball in Two Different Courts," *Sports Illustrated*, December 25, 1972, 33: "In my work for the Women's Political Caucus, I think of myself as a woman, not an athlete, and yet what makes me valuable is that I'm a tennis star. It's an athlete's privilege, like anybody else's, to speak out on issues."

15 Grace L. Lichtenstein, *A Long Way, Baby: The Inside Story of the Women in Pro Tennis* (New York: William Morrow, 1974), 150; Jane Leavy, "Whatever Happened to Peaches Bartkowicz?" *womenSports*, January 1978, 20–24, 46–47.

16 Grace Lichtenstein, "Billie Jean King, the Brooklyn Dodgers, and Me," *Redbook*, November 1974, 104–5; "Two Pros," *Time*, March 20, 1972, 103.

17 Hollis Elkins, "Time for a Change: Women's Athletics and the Women's Movement," *Frontiers* 3 (1978): 22–23. See also Mary Jo Festle, *Playing Nice: Politics and Apologies in Women's Sports* (New York: Columbia University Press, 1996); and Ying Wushanley, *Playing Nice and Losing: The Struggle for Control of Women's Intercollegiate Athletics, 1960–2000* (Syracuse, N.Y.: Syracuse University Press, 2004).

18 Lichtenstein, *A Long Way, Baby*, 150; Dan Wakefield, "My Love Affair with Billie Jean King," *Esquire*, October 1974, 386; Joel Drucker, "Billie Jean King: Leveling the Playing Field," *Biography*, September 1998, 102–7; BJK, *Billie Jean* (1982), 82; Karen Blumenthal, *Let Me Play: The Story of Title IX, the Law that Changed the Future of Girls in America* (Atheneum: New York, 2005), 51. Here is the full quote: "I'm sorry that the women's movement didn't include sports enough. We were so visible. We could have been a great conduit for social change. But while the women's movement was very friendly, we didn't connect like we could have. The discussion always went to legislation, to what Congress was doing. We were all so busy."

19 Lichtenstein, "King, the Brooklyn Dodgers, and Me," 104–5; Lopiano quoted in Roberts, *A Necessary Spectacle*, 159. Lopiano was making a broader point about how "the women's movement never embraced Title IX as an athletics position." As sports psychologist Jan Felshin noted in 1973, "The women's movement has seemed reluctant to confront the institution of sport directly. It has been dismissed as a 'fascist' domain by some, and the woman athlete has not been embraced as a sister in the struggle for liberation. Perhaps, as a symbolic sphere, sport does not seem a crucial testing ground for women's power, and, possibly, sport achievement is always singularly related to excellence and, therefore, of limited usefulness as a source of expanding opportunities for women." Elkins, "Time for Change," 24.

20 Valerie Miner and Helen E. Longino, eds., *Competition: A Feminist Taboo?* (Old Westbury, N.Y.: Feminist Press, 1987); Boston Women's Health Book Collective, *Our Bodies, Ourselves: A Book By and For Women* (New York: Simon and Schuster, 1973), 86–87. This is the first mass-market paperback edition; the original New England Free Press version, *Women and Their Bodies: A Course by the Women's Health Collective* (1970), did not say anything about physical activity and sports.

21 Pat Griffin, "Diamonds, Dykes, and Double Plays," in Susan Fox Rogers, ed., *Sports-dykes: Stories from On and Off the Field* (New York: St. Martin's Press, 1994), 191–201. See also Enke, *Finding the Movement*.

22 Elkins, "Time for a Change," 24; Donna Lopiano, "A Political Analysis of the Possibility of Impact Alternatives for the Accomplishment of Feminist Objectives Within American Intercollegiate Sport," in Richard E. Lapchick, ed., *Fractured Focus: Sport as a Reflection of Society* (Lexington, Mass.: D. C. Heath, 1986), 168. The essay originally dates to 1982.

23 M. Ann Hall, "The Significance of the Body," *Feminism and Sporting Bodies: Essays on Theory and Practice* (Champaign, Ill.: Human Kinetics, 1996), 50. *Ms.* devoted its entire August 1977 issue to sports, including a Tomboy Hall of Fame. Not surprisingly, many of the unconventional women who embraced feminism had also been unconventional as young girls, often earning them the tag of tomboy. But rarely did their tomboy days translate into a lifelong interest in sports.

24 The voluminous National Organization for Women papers are at the Schlesinger Library, and I have sampled them selectively. The majority of material on sports is found in boxes 31 and 49.

25 Judy Wenning to NOW National Board of Directors, July 3, 1973, NOW, SL; Goals of the NOW National Task Force on Sports, 1973–1974, no date [probably summer 1973], NOW, SL. For example, the national office forwarded all mail and inquiries on sports topics to the task force, which then only had $50 allotted for postage for correspondence; due to financial and time constraints, the task force was unable to answer all letters personally.

26 Anne Grant and Judy Wenning to NOW task forces, March 8, 1974, NOW, SL; Char Mollison to Anne Perry, December 28, 1977, WEAL, SL; Mary Jean Collins letter, April 16, 1985, NOW, SL. WEAL was just setting up its clearinghouse and hoped to work in cooperation with NOW.

27 Ann Scott and Mary Ellen Verheyden-Hilliard to State Legislative Coordinators, n.d. [summer 1974], NOW, SL. This firm stand by the national leadership may or may not have been shared by activists at the grassroots level. For example, a memo from Jan Cunningham to the Women in Sports Task Force People dated February 21, 1975 [NOW, SL] took note of what she called the "separatists vs. integrationists controversy": "The integrationist argument that we've had separate but equal in the past and it hasn't worked is valid. On the other hand, the separatist argument that women are not physically capable of competing with men (in some sports) or aren't ready to compete with men, is also valid. Obviously, the answer lies somewhere in between and we should begin re-evaluating our individual positions on this question in an attempt to find a workable compromise." It didn't seem to occur to her that there might not be a compromise between those two positions.

28 For background on protective legislation, see Alice Kessler-Harris, *Out to Work: A History of Wage-Earning Women in the United States* (New York: Oxford University Press, 1982); and *In Pursuit of Equity: Women, Men, and the Quest for Economic Citizenship in 20th-Century America* (New York: Oxford University Press, 2001). See also

Nancy Woloch, *Muller v. Oregon: A Brief History with Documents* (Boston: Bedford/ St. Martin's, 1996).

29 In addition to Kessler-Harris, *In Pursuit of Equity*, see Cynthia Harrison, *On Account of Sex: The Politics of Women's Issues, 1945–1968* (Berkeley: University of California Press, 1988); and Dorothy Sue Cobble, *The Other Women's Movement: Workplace Justice and Social Rights in Modern America* (Princeton, N.J.: Princeton University Press, 2004).

30 Ellie Smeal to NOW Chapter President, Convenor, Sports or Education Chair-One, November 14, 1973, NOW, SL.

31 Holly Knox to NOW Legal Defense and Education Fund Board members, October 31, 1974, PEER, SL. Unless otherwise indicated, quotes are drawn from the document that was submitted to HEW. The Center for National Policy Review was located at the School of Law, the Catholic University of America in Washington. See also their background legal memorandum: "Validity of the 'Separate but Equal' Policy of the Title IX Regulation on Athletics" [1974], PEER, SL.

32 Anne Grant to J. Stanley Pottinger, January 28, 1973, Dunkle, SL.

33 NOW-LDEF comments to HEW, October 31, 1974, PEER, SL.

34 Grant to Pottinger, January 28, 1973, Dunkle, SL.

35 "A Proposal for a New Pennsylvania NOW Sports Position in Light of the Commonwealth Court Decision Against the PIAA," n.d. [c. 1974–1975], NOW, SL. "Because girls and boys will be separated many will be encouraged to argue they should be separated. . . . There is also the real possibility that girls sports themselves will instill in girls the illusion that they cannot compete with boys." For more on affirmative action, see note 40.

36 Billie Jean King used this formulation when I interviewed her in Boston on November 27, 2007. Over the years she has often used the phrase when discussing her frustrations with how second-wave feminists failed to understand the importance of sports and physical activity.

37 Interview with Gwen Gregory, May 9, 1986, transcript found in Dunkle, SL.

38 Bernice Resnick Sandler, "Title IX: How We Got It and What a Difference It Made," *Cleveland State Law Review* 55 (2008): 482; Nancy F. Cott, *The Grounding of Modern Feminism* (New Haven: Yale University Press, 1987), especially chapter 7.

39 Mary Jo Kane, "Resistance/Transformation of the Oppositional Binary: Exposing Sport as a Continuum," *Journal of Sport and Social Issues* 19 (May 1995): 191–218. See also the final section of this chapter.

40 The attempt to increase opportunities for women in sports unfolded independently of the contentious debates on affirmative action in the 1970s. In some ways this is surprising, since there are many similarities between affirmative action's attempt to remedy or overcome the effects of past conditions that have limited inclusion or advancement, especially in employment, and the corresponding desire to win women spots in the male hierarchy of sports. Title IX does not require affirmative action, but it can be imposed after a finding of discrimination by HEW; like the empty threat to withhold federal money from offending institutions, HEW never pursued

this remedy. In general, in the 1970s the sports debate was never framed around giving women preference or setting quotas; the assumption was that men's and women's interests could both be accommodated without undue sacrifice in separate but equal programs. Not until the 1990s do issues of "reverse discrimination" (the key issue of the 1978 *Bakke* case) become prominent as men's teams cut by their universities blame Title IX for their losses. For a general history of affirmative action, see Terry H. Anderson, *The Pursuit of Fairness: A History of Affirmative Action* (New York: Oxford University Press, 2004). See also N. Peggy Burke, "Remedial and Affirmative Action," in Patricia L. Geadelmann, Christine Grant, Yvonne Slatton, and N. Peggy Burke, eds., *Equality in Sport for Women* (Washington, D.C.: American Alliance for Health, Physical Education, and Recreation, 1977).

41 For a summary of Title IX in the courts, see chapters 6 and 7 in Linda Jean Carpenter and R. Vivian Acosta, *Title IX* (Champaign, Ill.: Human Kinetics, 2005).

42 Susan Ware, *Title IX: A Brief History with Documents* (Boston: Bedford/St. Martin's, 2007), 9; Sarah K. Fields, *Female Gladiators: Gender, Law, and Contact Sport in America* (Urbana: University of Illinois Press, 2005), 70–71.

43 Patricia Geadelmann, "Court Precedents," in Geadelmann, *Equality in Sport for Women*, 71; Eileen McDonagh and Laura Pappano, *Playing with the Boys: Why Separate Is Not Equal in Sports* (New York: Oxford University Press, 2008), 125. Most of the decisions that did not take that stand came from the very early period (c. 1972–73), before the implications of cases such as *Reed v. Reed* were widely known.

44 Geadelmann, "Court Precedents," 75; Fields, *Female Gladiators*, 41. For the activism of Pennsylvania NOW, see "A Proposal for a New Pennsylvania Sports Position in Light of the Commonwealth Court Decision against the PIAA"; Smeal to NOW chapter president, November 14, 1973; and "Pennsylvania NOW Supports State Board of Education—Opposes PIAA," May 11, 1974, NOW, SL. In a similar case the Massachusetts Supreme Judicial Court rejected a law that would have excluded girls from football and wrestling teams because it violated the state's equal rights amendment.

45 PIAA decision quoted in Gaedelmann, "Court Precedents," 81.

46 *Reed v. Nebraska School Activities Association* (1972), cited in "Note: Sex Discrimination in High School Athletics," *Minnesota Law Review* 57 (December 1972): 359.

47 Deborah Brake, "The Struggle for Sex Equality in Sport and the Theory Behind Title IX," *University of Michigan Journal of Law Reform* 34 (Fall 2000/Winter 2001): 25.

48 Fields, *Female Gladiators*, xi.

49 *Sweatt v. Painter*, 339 U.S. 629 (1950).

50 An excellent introduction is Linda K. Kerber, *No Constitutional Right to Be Ladies: Women and the Obligations of Citizenship* (New York: Hill and Wang, 1998); the quotation from *Hoyt v. Florida* is on p. 181.

51 "Note: Sex Discrimination in High School Athletics," 344–45.

52 Kerber, *No Constitutional Right to Be Ladies*, 199–203; Katherine Ann Austin, "Recent Development: Constitutional Law—Equal Protection—Sex Discrimination in Secondary School Athletics," *Tennessee Law Review* 222 (Fall 1978): 225–27. In an earlier case (*Weeks v. Southern Bell Telephone Company* [1969]), the Fifth Circuit had

overturned one of the last vestiges of protective legislation by ruling that a limit on women lifting no more than thirty pounds on the job was discriminatory. The Weeks case has some interesting parallels to sports, offering a potential precedent that if an activity requires a physical attribute, the determination of qualifications for the job should be made on an individual basis, not based on an entire sex.

53 For example, it employed this standard in *Craig v. Boren* (1976) to declare unconstitutional an Oklahoma law that prohibited the sale of 3.2 percent beer to males under the age of twenty-one while setting the age for females at eighteen. Jody Feder, "Sex Discrimination and the United States Supreme Court: Developments in the Law," *Congressional Research Service* (updated August 25, 2006), 2.

54 When draft registration was revived in the late 1970s during the Iranian and Afghanistan crises, President Jimmy Carter initially supported registering women for the draft, but many people did not and Congress limited the registration to men only. The Supreme Court upheld this male-only draft in *Rostker v. Goldberg* (1981), ruling that the decision to register and/or draft women was up to Congress. Kerber, *No Constitutional Right to Be Ladies*, 288–99. Consistent with its reasoning about sports, the amicus brief in the draft case submitted by NOW-LDEF argued that excluding women from military service perniciously reinforced prevailing stereotypes: either there should be no draft, or both men and women should be drafted. Cited in Jane J. Mansbridge, *Why We Lost the ERA* (Chicago: University of Chicago Press, 1986), 75.

55 For general treatments of second-wave feminism and the ERA, see Ruth Rosen, *The World Split Open: How the Modern Women's Movement Changed America* (New York: Viking, 2000), and Sara M. Evans, *Tidal Wave: How Women Changed America at Century's End* (New York: Free Press, 2003). See also Mansbridge, *Why We Lost the ERA*; and Donald G. Mathews and Jane Sherron DeHart, *Sex, Gender, and the Politics of ERA: A State and the Nation* (New York: Oxford University Press, 1990).

56 United States Commission on Civil Rights, *Sex Bias in the U.S. Code: A Report of the U.S. Commission on Civil Rights* (Washington, D.C.: Government Printing Office, 1977), 5–6. The report was researched and written by Ruth Bader Ginsburg and Brenda Feigen Fasteau.

57 Evans, *Tidal Wave*, 64–65; Marcia Cohen, *The Sisterhood: The True Story of the Women Who Changed the World* (New York: Simon and Schuster, 1988), chapter 10. A paper by Barbara Brown and Ann Freedman of the Women's Law Project in Philadelphia dated May 6, 1975 [Dunkle, SL], looked at the application of the ERA to two cases of classifications based on sex which were purportedly justified by physical differences: athletics and life insurance. They concluded that the ERA would prohibit such classifications and that sex-blind systems would be "both fair and feasible."

58 Christine Brennan, "Comparing Men, Women is Foolish," *USA Today*, August 31, 2000, 3C. She adds parenthetically, "The more popular a woman's sport becomes, the louder the cacophony gets."

59 Billie Jean King, "Why I believe that women must enter the crucible of sports competition with men," *Glamour*, April 1984, 100; Cynthia Reader, "'I'm a Special Kind of Woman; I'm a Transsexual,'" *womenSports*, December 1976, 37; "Playboy Inter-

view: Billie Jean King," 67; Jane Bosveld, "Billie Jean Talks Team-Tennis," *Women's Sports and Fitness,* July 1985, 16.

60 King, "Why I believe," 100.

61 Barbara Gregorich, *Women at Play: The Story of Women in Baseball* (San Diego: Harcourt Brace, 1993), 206; McDonagh and Pappano, *Playing with the Boys,* 221. See also Jennifer Ring, *Stolen Bases: Why American Girls Don't Play Baseball* (Urbana: University of Illinois Press, 2009). As Laura Robinson put it in *She Shoots, She Scores: Canadian Perspectives on Women in Sport* (Toronto: Thompson Educational Publishing, 1997), 9–10, "The sports section exists, I would maintain, because it is one sure-bet place where MEN ALWAYS WIN. Even if it's not your team that won last night, teams of men won something."

62 Ellen J. Staurowsky, "Examining the Roots of a Gendered Division of Labor in Intercollegiate Athletics: Insights into the Gender Equity Debate," *Journal of Sport and Social Issues* 19 (February 1995): 36; Catharine R. Stimpson, "The Atalanta Syndrome: Women, Sports and Cultural Values," *Scholar and Feminist Online* 4.3 (2006).

63 Kane, "Exposing Sport as a Continuum," 192; Mariah Burton Nelson, *The Stronger Women Get, The More Men Love Football: Sexism and the American Culture of Sports* (New York: Harcourt Brace, 1994), 6–7; Jane English, "Sex Equality in Sports," *Philosophy & Public Affairs* 7 (1978): 276.

64 Simone de Beauvoir, *The Second Sex* (New York: Alfred A. Knopf, 1953), 373. Another group that challenges the current organization of sports is disabled athletes, who don't fit the categories but for different reasons: disabled athletes, male and female, can never compete on the same terms as physically able athletes; and yet with their dedication and skill they are clearly athletes, and they definitely compete, prodding us to think about what athletics means in new and different ways.

65 Michael A. Messner, *Taking the Field: Women, Men, and Sports* (Minneapolis: University of Minnesota Press, 2002), 144–45; Nelson, *The Stronger Women Get.* Catharine MacKinnon made a similar point: "Most athletics, particularly the most lucrative of them, have been internally designed to maximize attributes that are identical with what the male sex role values in men." Catharine MacKinnon, *Feminism Unmodified: Discourses on Life and Law* (Cambridge: Harvard University Press, 1987), 120.

66 Kane, "Exposing Sport as a Continuum," 193.

67 April Austin, "Superstar Emeritus of Women's Tennis Now on Business Side of Net," *Christian Science Monitor,* November 14, 1988, 24.

68 Ibid.

69 Bosveld, "Billie Jean Talks Team-Tennis," 16; Tom Cruze, "Ahead of Her Time; King focuses on a vision of sports that is equitable . . . and fun," *Chicago Sun-Times,* March 16, 1997, 15.

70 Cruze, "Ahead of Her Time," 15; Tom Weir, "King Triumph Monumental 20 Years Later," *USA Today,* September 20, 1993, 1C; Bosveld, "Billie Jean Talks Team-Tennis," 15–16.

71 King emphasized the importance of girls-only activity when I interviewed her in Boston on November 27, 2007. See Don Sabo, Kathleen E. Miller, Merrill J. Melnick, and Leslie Heywood, *Her Life Depends On It: Sport, Physical Activity, and the Health*

and *Well-Being of American Girls* (East Meadow, N.Y.: Women's Sports Foundation, 2004). See also Don Sabo and Phil Veliz, *Go Out and Play: Youth Sports in America* (East Meadow, N.Y.: Women's Sports Foundation, 2008). Two collections that capture the joys of women's sports especially well are Rogers, *Sportsdykes*, and Joli Sandoz and Joby Winans, eds., *Whatever It Takes: Women on Women's Sport* (New York: Farrar, Straus and Giroux, 1999). See also Cahn, *Coming On Strong*.

72 Estelle Freedman, "Female Institution Building and American Feminism, 1870–1930," *Feminist Studies* 5 (Fall 1979): 512–29. Fifty years after the *Brown* decision, with de facto school desegregation still firmly entrenched across the county, scholars and activists are rethinking some of the things lost, such as the leadership roles that black teachers in segregated schools had played in the African American community. See the special issue of the *Journal of American History* 91 (June 2004), especially Adam Fairclough, "The Costs of *Brown*: Black Teachers and School Integration," 43–55.

73 Fields, *Female Gladiators*, 70.

74 Ann Crittenden Scott, "Closing the Muscle Gap: New Facts about Strength, Endurance—and Gender," *Ms.*, September 1974, 89.

Chapter Six

1 Eliot Spitzer, John Edwards, Larry Craig, Jim McGreevy, Bill Clinton—what a list. At least Jenny Sanford, the wife of South Carolina governor Mark Sanford, refused the honor. See Lisa Belkin, "Public Displays of Disaffection," *New York Times Magazine*, July 12, 2009, 9–10.

2 BJK, *Billie Jean* (1982), 10.

3 Mariah Burton Nelson, *Are We Winning Yet? How Women Are Changing Sports and Sports Are Changing Women* (New York: Random House, 1991), 132-54; Neil Amdur, "Homosexuality Sets off Tremors," *New York Times*, May 12, 1981, B11. See also Eric Anderson, *In The Game: Gay Athletes and the Cult of Masculinity* (Albany: State University of New York Press, 2005); and Michael A. Messner, *Taking the Field: Women, Men, and Sports* (Minneapolis: University of Minnesota Press, 2002).

4 Michelangelo Signorile, "I, ayatollah," *Outweek*, May 29, 1991, 46–47, 78. Billie Jean King was not the first female public figure to be outed, although the only previous case that I can think of is feminist Kate Millett, the author of *Sexual Politics* (1970). Millett was married to an artist named Fumio Yoshimura but had a long history of involvements with women. When she was confronted about her sexuality at a Columbia forum in the fall of 1970, she admitted that she was a lesbian. *Time* magazine then used that admission to discredit the women's movement in general. Ironically, *Time* did not identify her as a lesbian, choosing instead to call her bisexual ("Women's Lib: A Second Look," *Time*, December 14, 1970). The end result was the same: "I had 'come out,'" Millett ruefully concluded, "in ninety-seven languages." For background on Millett, see Marcia Cohen, *The Sisterhood: The True Story of the Women Who Changed the World* (New York: Simon and Schuster, 1988); the quote is on p. 247.

5 "A Disputed Love Match," *Time*, May 11, 1981, 77. For a general overview of media

culture, see Larry P. Gross, *Up from Invisibility: Lesbians, Gay Men, and the Media in America* (New York: Columbia University Press, 2001).

6 Pat Griffin, *Strong Women, Deep Closets: Lesbians and Homophobia in Sport* (Champaign, Ill.: Human Kinetics, 1998), 180; "President Obama Names Medal of Freedom Recipients: 16 Agents of Change to Receive Top Civilian Honor." ⟨http://www.whitehouse.gov/the_press_office/president-obama-names-medal-of-freedom-recipients/⟩, accessed August 2, 2009. The ceremony was held on August 12, 2009. There is a certain irony here. The citation credits King with coming out in 1981, which makes it seem like her leadership in gay rights has been continuous since then. As this chapter demonstrates, it was only in the late 1990s that she publicly embraced the mantle of gay rights activist.

7 BJK, *Billie Jean* (1982), 20–21; "Larry and Billie Jean King Work to Renew Their Marriage—And Put Her Affair Behind Them," *People*, May 25, 1981, 76. See also Grace Lichtenstein, *A Long Way, Baby: The Inside Story of the Women in Pro Tennis* (New York: William Morrow, 1974), 175.

8 BJK, *Billie Jean* (1982), 26. The phrases are from the HBO documentary *Billie Jean King: Portrait of a Pioneer*, which first aired on April 26, 2006.

9 Selena Roberts, *A Necessary Spectacle: Billie Jean King, Bobby Riggs, and the Tennis Match That Leveled the Game* (New York: Crown Publishers, 2005), 142, 143, 149. King insisted that Barnett work for her, not just be a companion, stating, "I hate freeloaders." BJK, *Billie Jean* (1982), 31. See also Kenneth Denlinger, "King has Interference," *Washington Post*, January 31, 1974, D5.

10 Pete Axthelm, "The Battle of the Sexes," *Newsweek*, September 24, 1973, 85. See also Curry Kirkpatrick, "There She Is, Ms. America," *Sports Illustrated*, October 1, 1973, 32.

11 Lichtenstein, *A Long Way, Baby*, 118, 166–67; Stephen Banker, "Who's Afraid of Virginia Wade?" *Washington Post*, July 8, 1976, E8. Here is Larry Gross on the plot of *The Killing of Sister George*: "The real message of the film was that being out of the closet was dangerous to your health." Gross, *Up from Invisibility*, 62.

12 "Playboy Interview: Billie Jean King," *Playboy*, March 1975, 60; Frank Deford, "Mrs. Billie Jean King," *Sports Illustrated*, May 19, 1975, 80; Gross, *Up from Invisibility*, 110, 132. This certainly included Deford. When interviewed for the 2006 HBO documentary about King, he recounted being asked by senior editors at *Sports Illustrated* whether King was a lesbian when she was being considered for Sportswoman of the Year in 1972, to which he replied flippantly that they said that about all women athletes and left it at that. The clear implication was that he knew better.

13 "Playboy Interview: Billie Jean King," 196; "Larry and Billie Jean King Work to Renew Their Marriage," 74.

14 Marvin Kitman, "Dirty Linen," *New Leader*, June 15, 1981, 20. See also BJK, *Billie Jean* (1982), which contains some excerpts of testimony from the trial describing the chronology.

15 Anne Taylor Fleming and Annie Leibovitz, "The Battles of Billie Jean King," *Women's Sports & Fitness*, September/October 1998, 130; "Billie Jean's Odd Match," *Newsweek*, May 11, 1981, 36; "A Disputed Love Match," 77. Larry King opened the media event

by referring to her as the woman "he has loved dearly for 19 years." "Mrs. King Says She Had Lesbian Affair," *New York Times*, May 2, 1981, 9.

16 Mark Shields, "If at First You Don't Succeed, Confess," *Washington Post*, May 5, 1981, A19. Richard Cohen, "Billie Jean Apologizes — But Not Really," *Washington Post*, May 26, 1981, C1, notes that having run "the media gauntlet . . . she has now been restored to a state of grace," but at the cost of turning her back on her lover and her lifestyle. "There is a cheating quality to what King and the others have done. They do something, sometimes for quite a long time, and then duck the consequences when they get caught." Calling it a mistake, "it becomes something you do when your husband is terribly busy — not a life style or a sexual preference you yourself have opted for."

17 Kitman, "Dirty Linen," 19; "Larry and Billie Jean King Work to Renew Their Marriage," 73–77. The *People* interviewer was their friend Cheryl McCall, who had previously worked at *womenSports* magazine. See Cheryl McCall, "The Billie Jean King Case: A Friend's Outrage," *Ms.*, July 1981, 100. The Barbara Walters special aired on May 7, 1981.

18 Roberts, *A Necessary Spectacle*, 180; Jonathan Yardley, "Court and Sparkless," *Washington Post*, August 18, 1982, B1. The review gets worse: "From first page to last, *Billie Jean* is an exercise in special pleading." He calls her portrayal of herself "pushy, self-absorbed and self-deluded." I have to agree that this book is not her finest moment.

19 "Mrs. King Offers to Quit as W.T.A. Head, So Not to Hurt Players," *New York Times*, May 3, 1981, S5. "In many ways, my father is still in shock. My poor mother has been even slower to come around." BJK, *Billie Jean* (1982), 215. Not until the 1990s did they get this all sorted out. Probably this story is not all that different from many other coming out stories. The difference is that King had to play hers out in public, long before she was ready.

20 "Larry and Billie Jean King Work to Renew Their Marriage," 76; Deford, "Mrs. Billie Jean King," 81.

21 "Mrs. King Offers to Quit as W.T.A. Head," S5; "Larry and Billie Jean King Work to Renew Their Marriage," 75; BJK, *Billie Jean* (1982), 27, 26.

22 For example, skater Peggy Fleming (Jenkins) wrote a letter in support: "Billie Jean King should be measured by her tremendous contributions to women's sports, and particularly tennis. One's personal life should remain private unless you choose for it to be otherwise. Billie Jean has been a leader in the development of women's sports and I hope she will continue to be one in the years to come." *Women's Sports*, August 1981, 64. For Randy's reaction, see BJK, *Billie Jean* (1982), 216–17.

23 Richard Cohen, "Billie Jean King Pays for America's Fantasy," *Washington Post*, May 7, 1981, C1; "Sequel," *People*, December 28, 1981/January 4, 1982, 111. This fan reaction seems fairly typical: "Billie Jean, I don't care if you are gay, straight, bisexual, asexual, or neuter. To me and every woman who has been able to admit her love of sports without fear of chastisement you are a saint." Susan Caust, Flushing, N.Y., to editors, *Women's Sports*, July 1981, 59.

24 Shelley Roberts, "Bad Form, Billie Jean," *Newsweek*, May 25, 1981, 19. Cohen, "Billie Jean Apologizes — But Not Really" basically calls her actions reprehensible, not ad-

mirable. See also Dr. Roberta Bennett quoted in Betty Hicks, "The Billie Jean King Affair," *Christopher Street*, July 1981, 16: "It was scarcely a one-night stand. There must have been something there."

25 Helen Dude, Nashville, Ill., to editors, *Women's Sports*, January 1983, 6.

26 "A Disputed Love Match," 77.

27 *Facts on File*, April 20, 1979.

28 *Facts on File*, April 20, 1979. The Supreme Court decision is *Marvin v. Marvin*, 18 Cal.3d 660 (December 27, 1976). Thanks to Karen Simonson for tracking it down.

29 *Facts on File*, April 20, 1979. See also Judy Mann, "What Michelle Won and What Was Lost," *Washington Post*, April 20, 1979, C1. In the end Lee Marvin's victory was total, since Triola's award was overturned on appeal. See Nancy F. Cott, *Public Vows: A History of Marriage and the Nation* (Cambridge: Harvard University Press, 2000), 207–8. See also Stuart Auerbach, "Sealing It With a Contract; Lawyers Eye Written Agreements for Nonmarried Couples," *Washington Post*, August 11, 1977, A8; Richard Cohen, "Living in Sin Becomes Just Too Complicated," *Washington Post*, March 5, 1978, B1; and LaBarbara Bowman, "From Altar to Palimony?" *Washington Post*, July 3, 1979, B1, on the legal and social implications.

30 "Oh, Billy Jean," *National Review*, May 29, 1981, 600.

31 "A Disputed Love Match," 77; "Billie Jean's Odd Match," 36–37.

32 "Court Bars Publication of Letters from Billie Jean King to Woman," *New York Times*, May 6, 1981, A26; "Style," *Washington Post*, June 10, 1981, B2; "Mrs. King Loses Bid to Dismiss Lawsuit Brought by Ex-lover," *New York Times*, July 9, 1981, B5.

33 "Newsmakers," *Newsweek*, December 21, 1981, 59; "Style," *Washington Post*, December 12, 1981, C3; "Billie Jean King Upheld; Judge Hints at Extortion," *New York Times*, December 12, 1981, 10. In May, 1982, Larry King sued Barnett and her lawyers for a whopping $57.5 million, alleging malicious prosecution in the case over the Malibu house. He asked for damages based on the income he lost as a result of the adverse publicity. Presumably nothing ever came of this suit. *Washington Post*, May 22, 1982, C2.

34 "Judge Dismisses Suit Against Billie Jean King," *New York Times*, November 20, 1982, 10; Judith Cummings, "2 in Los Angeles Die Fighting Storm," *New York Times*, March 3, 1983, 16.

35 Nancy Cott, *Public Vows*, shows how much has changed in our understanding of marriage since the 1960s, but still its resilience as a legal, political, and cultural ideal.

36 Amdur, "Homosexuality Sets Off Tremors," B11; Roberts, *A Necessary Spectacle*, 181; Fleming and Leibovitz, "The Battles of Billie Jean King." Based on full access to King, Roberts concluded, "Billie had twisted the truth about the breadth of her lesbian experiences, in part to protect Ilana." A turning point in publicly acknowledging their relationship finally came around 2003–2004 when both King and Kloss agreed to cooperate with the HBO documentary which aired in 2006. See Richard Sandomir, "TV Sports," *New York Times*, April 25, 2006, 7.

37 Fleming and Leibovitz, "The Battles of Billie Jean King"; Michele Kort, "Finally,

after 17 years of dodging the subject in print, Billie Jean King comes all the way out," *Advocate*, August 18, 1998, 40–42.

38 Hicks, "The Billie Jean King Affair," 17.

39 Martina Navratilova with George Vecsey, *Martina* (New York: Alfred A. Knopf, 1985), 137. "If Chris and I do the same thing," Martina complained to Nora Ephron in 1985, "I'll be criticized and she'll come off smelling like a rose." Nora Ephron, "Martina's Unfairness Doctrine," *New York Times Magazine*, March 31, 1985, 52.

40 Kort, "King Comes All the Way Out."

41 Johnette Howard, *The Rivals: Chris Evert vs. Martina Navratilova: Their Epic Duels and Extraordinary Friendship* (New York: Broadway Books, 2005), 107. See also Nancy E. Spencer, "'America's Sweetheart' and 'Czech-Mate': A Discursive Analysis of the Evert-Navratilova Rivalry," *Journal of Sport and Social Issues* 27 (February 2003): 18–37.

42 Robert Lipsyte, "Connors the Killer Is Really Just a Child," *New York Times*, September 6, 1991, 36; Navratilova, *Martina*, 136.

43 The characterization is Jennifer Baumgardner's in *Look Both Ways: Bisexual Politics* (New York: Farrar, Straus and Giroux, 2007), 91.

44 Stephanie Mansfield, "Rita Mae Brown, Martina Navratilova and The End of the Affair; the Love Match; the Love Match Gone Sour," *Washington Post*, August 13, 1981, C1. See also Rita Mae Brown, *Sudden Death* (New York: Bantam Books, 1983).

45 "Playboy interview: Billie Jean King," 60. Grace Lichtenstein included the story in *A Long Way, Baby*.

46 Howard, *The Rivals*, 179–80; Jane Leavy, "Women's Tennis Makes the Grade in a Testing Year," *Washington Post*, January 3, 1982, L15.

47 Howard, *The Rivals*, 227–28. Lieberman's heterosexual charade didn't last. In 2000 while the head coach of the Detroit Shock in the WNBA, she faced accusations that she and WNBA rookie Anna DeForge were having a sexual relationship. At the end of the season, Lieberman was told she would not be offered a new contract. In 2001, she filed for divorce from her husband of thirteen years, Tim Cline. Grant Wahl, L. Jon Wertheim, and George Dohrman, "Passion Plays," *Sports Illustrated*, September 10, 2001.

48 Peter Bodo, *The Courts of Babylon: Tales of Greed and Glory in the Harsh New World of Professional Tennis* (New York: Scribner, 1995), 181; Mary Jo Festle, *Playing Nice: Politics and Apologies in Women's Sports* (New York: Columbia University Press, 1996), chapter 6. See also Grace Lichtenstein, *A Long Way, Baby*.

49 Bodo, *The Courts of Babylon*, 210; Lichtenstein, *A Long Way, Baby*, 85; Festle, *Playing Nice*, 243. See also Mary G. McDonald, "The Marketing of the Women's National Basketball Association and the Making of Postfeminism," *International Review for the Sociology of Sport* 35 (2000): 35–47; and Nancy E. Spencer, "Once Upon a Subculture: Professional Women's Tennis and the Meaning of Style, 1970–1974," *Journal of Sport and Social Issues* 21 (November 1997): 363–78.

50 Barry Lorge, "The Aftermath; Verbal Vultures Descend on Women's Tour; King Affair Puts Women's Sports on Trial," *Washington Post*, May 7, 1981, D1; Howard, *The*

Rivals, 81–83. See also Bodo, *The Courts of Babylon*. I use the term transsexual here because that is how Richards was described at the time. Now she would be called transgendered.

51 Joan Ryan, "Richards Pushes on For Friends," *Washington Post*, August 22, 1976, 37; Howard, *The Rivals*, 181–82. See also Renee Richards with John Ames, *Second Serve: The Renee Richards Story* (New York: Stein and Day, 1986), which was made into a TV movie starring Vanessa Redgrave.

52 Joan Ryan, "Richards Defended by Tourney Director," *Washington Post*, August 21, 1976, B1; Cynthia Reader, "'I'm a Special Kind of Woman; I'm a Transsexual,'" *womenSports*, December 1976, 37; Neil Amdur, "Miss Stoll, 16, Topples Dr. Richards in Semifinal," *New York Times*, April 17, 1977, S11. See also Marcia Seligson, "Transsexual Chic: The Packaging of Renee Richards," *Ms.*, January 1977, 74–76.

53 "King Cites Richards' 'Tremendous Advantage,'" *Washington Post*, August 31, 1976, C5.

54 BJK, *Billie Jean* (1982), 137. A subplot here: King was angry that she hadn't been given a wild-card entry to the Virginia Slims championship, so she decided to play in an unsanctioned tournament. Given her longstanding organizing on behalf of the women's tour, this stand angered the WTA and its elected leaders, including Chris Evert. See Neil Amdur, "Rebuff to Mrs. King Causes a Split in Women's Tennis," *New York Times*, March 23, 1977, 31.

55 Navratilova, *Martina*, 223.

56 One factor that swayed the judge was an affidavit from Billie Jean King: "From my observation of Dr. Richards and experience with her on the court, as well as my total knowledge of the sport of tennis, she does not enjoy physical superiority or strength so as to have an advantage over women competitors in the sport of tennis." Quoted in Neil Amdur, "Dr. Richards Gets Support of Mrs. King," *New York Times*, August 11, 1977, 76. Since Richard Raskind had reached the finals of the men's over-35 championship at the U.S. Open in 1972, her appearance in 1979 would make her the only person to have reached the finals in the same event as both a man and a woman.

57 Navratilova, *Martina*, 228.

58 Christine Jorgensen in the 1950s was the first transsexual to receive widespread publicity; British writer Jan Morris and Renee Richards were the best-known male-to-female transsexuals in the 1970s. For a general history, see Joanne Meyerowitz, *How Sex Changed: A History of Transsexuality in the United States* (Cambridge: Harvard University Press, 2002).

59 Gross, *Up from Invisibility*, 203. Other out athletes include tennis players Gigi Fernandez and Amelie Mauresmo and golfers Muffin Spencer-Devlin and Patty Sheehan. See ⟨http://outsports.com⟩.

60 Gross, *Up from Invisibility*, 204; Robert Lipsyte, "A Major League Player's Life of Isolation and Secret Fear," *New York Times*, September 6, 1999, A1; Mike Wilson, "Wanted: Gay Sports Hero," *St. Petersburg Times*, February 7, 1999, 1F.

61 BJK, *Billie Jean* (1982), 213; Roberts, *A Necessary Spectacle*, 178–79. In 1984 King upped the total to more than $2 million, presumably to include the business opportunities that Larry lost as well. "Sports Fanfare," *Washington Post*, January 6, 1984, C2.

62 Roberts, *A Necessary Spectacle*, 176; BJK, *Billie Jean* (1982), 188.

63 "Mrs. King May Retire," *New York Times*, February 4, 1982, D25; George Vecsey, "Billie Jean King Reaches 100," *New York Times*, June 25, 1982, A21; Neil Amdur, "Mrs. King Gains The Round of 16," *New York Times*, June 27, 1982, 170; Amdur, "Mrs. Lloyd Her Foe in Semifinals," *New York Times*, July 1, 1982, B9; Amdur, "Faces Miss Navratilova in Final," *New York Times*, July 3, 1982, 15; Amdur, "Mrs. King Ousted by Miss Mascarin, 18," *New York Times*, September 1, 1982, B7.

64 George Vecsey, "Mrs. King in a Familiar Spot," *New York Times*, June 28, 1983, A25; Neil Amdur, "Mrs. King Gains Semifinals," *New York Times*, June 29, 1983, B7; Amdur, "Miss Jaeger Trounces Mrs. King," *New York Times*, July 1, 1983, A13.

65 Women's Sports Foundation, *The New Agenda: A Blueprint for the Future of Women's Sports: A Summary* (1984), 2, copy found at WSF Archives; Jane Leavy, "Women's Sports Seek Visibility," *Washington Post*, November 4, 1983, C1. Grove City College in Pennsylvania deliberately avoided all federal aid to maintain its independence from federal interference, which it argued exempted it from Title IX's coverage. In a decision announced in March 1984 the Supreme Court ruled that certain financial grants to students did in fact trigger coverage. But then the justices significantly narrowed the coverage of the law from what Congress had seemingly intended—that it cover the entire institution, not just a specific program receiving aid—by ruling that if Grove City ever were found guilty of discrimination in a program not receiving federal aid, Title IX sanctions would not apply. Since no athletic departments received federal funds, suddenly they were not covered. Not until Congress passed the Civil Rights Restoration Act of 1988 over President Reagan's veto was Title IX's broad coverage restored. See Linda Jean Carpenter and R. Vivian Acosta, *Title IX* (Champaign, Ill.: Human Kinetics, 2005), 121, 179.

66 Leavy, "Women's Sports Seek Visibility"; Women's Sports Foundation, *The New Agenda*, 3.

67 In other versions, it is actual corporate threats that cause the panic, but I think Griffin has it right (*Strong Women, Deep Closets*, 7–10, 73) and that it was the Women's Sports Foundation folks who panicked first, fearful of what might happen, and then worked hard to keep the word out of the official proceedings. For a competing version, see Mariah Burton Nelson, *Are We Winning Yet?* 138: "In 1983, a major corporate sponsor of 'The New Agenda'—a national women's sports conference—threatened to pull out at the last minute if the word 'lesbian' were used in conference materials." As per its modus operandi, the Women's Sports Foundation had lined up support from ATT, American Express, Adidas, Virginia Slims, Anheuser-Busch, Coca-Cola, Nautilus, and Milky Way. In all, the WSF raised $130,000 to put on the conference. Women's Sports Foundation, *The New Agenda*, 2.

68 The final resolutions, which ran to almost ten pages, mentioned homophobia in two places. Under research, they called for "investigation of homophobia and women's sports, including the effectiveness of educational programs in homophobia awareness training." In the section of resolutions on implementing the New Agenda, it was resolved that future efforts include "a task force to explore homophobia in women's sports, with the purpose of counteracting myths about women in sports." Women's

Sports Foundation, *The New Agenda*, 15, 23. For an interesting perspective on the conference, see Don Sabo and Janie Victoria Ward, "Wherefore Art Thou Feminisms? Feminist Activism, Academic Feminisms, and Women's Sports Advocacy," *Scholar and Feminist Online* 4.3 (Summer 2006).

69 April Austin, "Superstar Emeritus of Women's Tennis Now on Business Side of Net," *Christian Science Monitor*, November 14, 1988, 24; Russ Atkin, "Billie Jean King Spearheads Revival of Team Tennis League from Top," *Christian Science Monitor*, July 8, 1985, 20; Paul Harber, "King Still Reigns in World of Women's Tennis," *Boston Globe*, October 20, 1988, 59.

70 Billie Jean King with Cynthia Starr, *We Have Come a Long Way: The Story of Women's Tennis* (New York: McGraw-Hill, 1988), chapter 8; Howard, *The Rivals*; BJK, *Billie Jean* (1982), 209.

71 "WTA Tour Seeks Answers," *New Orleans Times-Picayune*, May 15, 1994, C1; "Mrs. King Still Taking Bows," *New York Times*, March 22, 1983, B9; Peter Alfano, "Casals Laments Changes on Tour," *New York Times*, April 10, 1985, B12.

72 Michele Kort, "Ms. Conversation with Billie Jean King and Martina Navratilova," *Ms.*, February 1988, 60, 61.

73 Greg Wood, "Sport on TV: Outing for the Pioneering Spirit of a King," *London Independent*, July 17, 1999, 16; George Vecsey, "Billie Jean King and the Millionaire," *New York Times*, March 9, 1990, B7.

74 Nolan Zavoral, "Billie Jean King Tries to Slow Down a Bit; Tennis Great turns 50 in November," *Minneapolis Star Tribune*, May 12, 1993, 2C. Ashe likely contracted AIDS from a blood transfusion after open-heart surgery in 1983. An intensely private person, Ashe told few people about the diagnosis in order to protect his family, especially his young daughter. Yet a surprisingly large contingent of friends, including Billie Jean King, knew or guessed the truth and still kept the secret out of respect for Ashe's wishes. An anonymous tip to *USA Today* in 1992 forced his hand. King knew firsthand what it was like to be forced into the public eye before it was time: "I felt violated when it happened to me, I felt violated when I talked to Arthur before his news conference. I had total empathy with him." Ashe died in February 1993; King spoke at his memorial service. Joan Ryan, "Many friends guarded Ashe's secret," *St. Petersburg Times*, April 11, 1992, 2C; Christine Brennan and Christine Spolar, "Ashe Told Friends in '88; Stan Smith Says Media Forced Public Disclosure," *Washington Post*, April 9, 1992, D1; Bruce Lowitt, "King's Contributions to Tennis Increase as Team Tennis Grows," *St. Petersburg Times*, May 3, 1992, 2C.

75 Kort, "King Comes All the Way Out"; Roberts, *A Necessary Spectacle*, 181.

76 Billie Jean King, *Pressure Is a Privilege: Lessons I've Learned from Life and the Battle of the Sexes* (New York: LifeTime Media, 2008), 163; Corri Planck, "Portrait of a Legend," *Lesbian News*, April, 1999, 18; Sandomir, "A Complex Life Gets a Closer Look." This reconciliation would have been in 1994–1995.

77 Fleming and Leibovitz, "The Battles of Billie Jean King," 130.

78 Steven Seidman, *Beyond the Closet: The Transformation of Gay and Lesbian Life* (New York: Routledge, 2004), 123. See also Charles Kaiser, *The Gay Metropolis: The Landmark History of Gay Life in America* (New York: Grove Press, 2007), which starts

in the 1940s; and George Chauncey, *Gay New York: Gender, Urban Culture, and the Making of the Gay Male World, 1890–1940* (New York: Basic Books, 1994), which covers the earlier period.

79 Gross, *Up from Invisibility*, 50–51; Amy Hoffman, *An Army of Ex-Lovers: My Life at the Gay Community News* (Amherst: University of Massachusetts Press, 2007), 83, xv.

80 Marcia Gallo, *Different Daughters: A History of the Daughters of Bilitis and the Rights of the Lesbian Rights Movement* (New York: Carroll and Graf, 2006); Lillian Faderman, *Odd Girls and Twilight Lovers: A History of Lesbian Life in Twentieth-century America* (New York: Columbia University Press, 1991); and Leila J. Rupp, *A Desired Past: A Short History of Same-sex Love in America* (Chicago: University of Chicago Press, 1999).

81 Radicalesbians, *The Woman Identified Woman* (Pittsburgh: Know, 1970).

82 All the general sources on second-wave feminism cover the gay/straight split, but Cohen, *The Sisterhood*, does an especially good job of exploring the personalities involved.

83 She was aware of it, however, as the "Playboy Interview: Billie Jean King," 59, confirms. When asked if she ever felt pressure to try lesbianism as a way to demonstrate support for women's liberation (what a dumb question), she replied, "No. Gay women turn on to me sometimes, gay women's lib people. I get a lot of letters from them, but they're OK when I meet them. They don't make passes at all."

84 In addition to Gross and Seidman, general sources on gay history include John D'Emilio and Estelle Freedman, *Intimate Matters: A History of Sexuality in America*, 2nd ed. (Chicago: University of Chicago Press, 1997); Dudley Clendinen and Adam Nagourney, *Out for Good: The Struggle to Build a Gay Rights Movement in America* (New York: Simon and Schuster, 1999); and John D'Emilio, *The World Turned: Essays on Gay History, Politics and Culture* (Durham, N.C.: Duke University Press, 2002). On outing, see Signorile, "I, Ayatollah."

85 In a nice touch in the widely watched episode, Ellen's childhood bedroom was depicted as having a poster of Billie Jean King on the wall. A. J. Carson, "The Ellen Show," posted June 28, 2006, ⟨http://tvdvdreviews.com⟩.

86 Gross, *Up from Invisibility*, 195–201; Anderson, *In the Game*, 14. See also Baumgardner, *Look Both Ways*.

87 BJK, *Pressure Is a Privilege*, 155; Griffin, *Strong Women, Deep Closets*, 180; Kort, "King Comes All the Way Out"; Planck, "Portrait of a Legend."

88 Karen Ocamb, "Women's Night '99 filled with Surprises," *Lesbian News*, April 1999, 16; Sandomir, "A Complex Life."

Epilogue

1 John Jeansonne, "Tennis' Serve to Billie Jean," *Newsday*, August 29, 2006, A04; Jo Piazza, "King's Castle," *New York Daily News*, August 29, 2006, 9; Jeansonne, "Tennis' Serve to Billie Jean"; George Vecsey, "A Fitting Tribute for a Champion Who Didn't Always Fit In," *New York Times*, August 29, 2006, D1.

2 Richard Sandomir, "Tennis Center to be Named for King," *New York Times*, August 3, 2006, 1.

3 Bud Collins, "Naming Honor is fit for this King," *Boston Globe*, August 29, 2006, D2; "Quotation of the Day," *New York Times*, August 3, 2006, 2.

4 "People in Sports," *Houston Chronicle*, October 19, 1992, 12; Christine Brennan, "Prizing the Past in Taking the Prizes," *USA Today*, July 9, 2007. See also Billie Jean King, *Pressure Is a Privilege: Lessons I've Learned from Life and the Battle of the Sexes* (New York: LifeTime Media, 2008), 184.

5 John Jeansonne, "Call it the Billie Jean King National Tennis Center after tonight," *Newsday*, August 28, 2006, D03; Jon Carroll, "The Ballad of Billie Jean," *San Francisco Chronicle*, June 30, 1998, E10.

6 This is similar to the definition of third-wave feminism given by Leslie Heywood and Shari L. Dworkin: "Third wave feminism is a product of that contradiction between the continuation of sexism and an increasingly realizable feminist dream that today many women do have more opportunity." Leslie Heywood and Shari L. Dworkin, *Built to Win: The Female Athlete as Cultural Icon* (Minneapolis: University of Minnesota Press, 2003), 41.

7 Sheila Weller, *Just Like Us: Carole King, Joni Mitchell, Carly Simon—and the Journey of a Generation* (New York: Atria Books, 2008), makes this argument.

8 "Title IX question leaves Capriati without answer," *St. Petersburg Times*, August 30, 2002, 6C; Karen Blumenthal, *Let Me Play: The Story of Title IX, The Law that Changed the Future of Girls in America* (New York: Atheneum Books, 2005), 129.

9 Debra West, "Reschedule Girls' Soccer, 2 Schools Are Ordered," *New York Times*, June 5, 2004, B4. Leslie Heywood and Shari Dworkin refer to this as "stealth feminism." "Through their work on women's sports issues, every day feminists are advancing their causes in a kind of stealth feminism that draws attention to key feminist issues and goals without provoking the knee-jerk social stigmas attached to the word *feminist*, which has been so maligned and discredited in the popular imagination. At this historical moment, feminists need athletes to help advance agendas such as equal access to institutions, self-esteem for all women and girls, and an expanded possibility and fluidity within gender roles that embraces difference." Heywood and Dworkin, *Built to Win*, 51.

10 Mark Starr, "The Battle of the Sexes," *Newsweek*, September 21, 1998, 90; foreword by Nancy Lieberman-Cline in Marian Betancourt, *Playing Like a Girl: Transforming Our Lives Through Team Sports* (Chicago: Contemporary Books, 2001), ix.

11 Philip Reid, "A King Who Set Her People Free," *Irish Times*, June 26, 2000, 59.

Acknowledgments

Whenever I describe this project, the first question I am invariably asked is whether I interviewed Billie Jean King. The answer is yes, and I would like to thank her for taking time at a Women's Sports Foundation event in Boston in 2007 to talk to yet another in the long line of journalists and writers who have been wanting a piece of her since she burst onto the tennis scene in the 1960s. In addition to the insights she shared with me, including her observation that feminists often think "from the neck up," the occasion allowed me to experience firsthand her charismatic energy and passion for history, as well as watch her use her celebrity to work a room for a cause she believed in. I also benefitted from conversations with other major players in my story, including Donna Lopiano, Margaret Dunkle, and Bernice Sandler. In addition to serving as a commentator for a talk on Billie Jean King that I gave at the Harvard Humanities Center, Lopiano welcomed me to the Women's Sports Foundation while she was still its head and facilitated my use of its archives.

Once again my main scholarly home as I researched this book was the Schlesinger Library at the Radcliffe Institute for Advanced Study, Harvard University. The library contains a treasure trove of material on feminism in the 1970s, which I sampled extensively. For their help navigating this material and for always making me feel welcome when I turned up, I would like to thank the entire Public Services team: Ellen Shea, Sarah Hutcheon, Lynda Leahy, and Diana Carey. I would also like to recognize Johanna Carll and Jenny Gotwals, the archivists who processed the Margaret Dunkle and Bernice Sandler papers that were so central to my research. And special thanks to Kathy Jacob for a very special friendship forged over the past several years. I would also like to acknowledge the support I received from the Charles Warren Center at Harvard as a fellow in 2007–8. Arthur Patton-Hock and Larissa Kennedy keep the Warren Center running so smoothly I was free to interact with a wonderful group of fellows, including Albrecht Koschnik, Dorothy Sue Cobble, Françoise Hamlin, Tim McCarthy, Lisa Tetrault, Manisha Sinha, Dan Kryder, Lisa Materson, and Maartje Janse. Thanks also to Dan Carpenter and Lisa McGirr for their leadership of the Politics and Social Movements seminar where I presented my work.

At the University of North Carolina Press, I am tickled to be working again with Chuck Grench after a gap of more than twenty years. From his initial "absodarnlootly" response to the topic, he has been a steadfast supporter as the manuscript worked its way through the review process. Thanks, too, to Katy O'Brien, Ron Maner, and Liz Gray for making the process as easy and seamless as possible. The world of publishing, trade and academic, can be a scary place these days, and I am lucky to have landed at UNC Press.

On the friends and family front, Joyce Antler once again performed her now time-honored role as first reader, offering helpful comments and huge doses of encouragement as the book took shape. She was joined at an early stage by Claire Potter, whose sharp skills as a historian and critic are supplemented by her athlete's competitive sensibility, an excellent combination. I would also like to acknowledge the encouragement and support of Eileen McDonagh, whose work on Title IX pushed me to think more deeply about the separate-but-equal question as it applied to women's sports. On the home front, Don Ware gets credit for literally pushing me onto a tennis court when I was in college, something he perhaps regretted when I began to beat him regularly. It is a measure of the longevity of our relationship that we watched the Battle of the Sexes match together in 1973 and now celebrate the publication of a book inspired by that event almost forty years later.

This book is dedicated to Imogene Fish, an extraordinary competitive athlete and dear friend who has been my model of an engaged, athletic life for almost thirty-five years. Living proof that women excelled at sports long before Title IX, Imo still thinks of major birthdays divisible by ten as a chance to compete in a new age group! Raised in North Conway, New Hampshire, after her family fled Germany in 1940, Imogene Opton placed an amazing fifth in the slalom at the 1952 Winter Olympics in Oslo, Norway, when she was only nineteen. She later graduated from Mount Holyoke College, married attorney H. Kenneth Fish, and raised three talented daughters who found many more opportunities, athletic and otherwise, than had been open to their mother's generation. Imogene's lifelong passion for all things athletic, which she and Ken shared over years of cross-country skiing and hiking in the White Mountains, is truly inspirational. The dedication honors her pioneering role in the history of women's sports.